Caught in the Middle

Nonstandard Kids and a Killing Curriculum

Susan Ohanian

Foreword by Deborah Meier

HEINEMANN
PORTSMOUTH, NH

Heinemann
A division of Reed Elsevier Inc.
361 Hanover Street
Portsmouth, NH 03801-3912
www.heinemann.com

Offices and agents throughout the world

CIP data is on file with the Library of Congress.
ISBN: 0-325-00328-9

Editor: Lois Bridges
Production: Vicki Kasabian
Cover design: Catherine Hawkes/Cat and Mouse
Cover photograph: Joel Brown
Manufacturing: Louise Richardson

Printed in the United States of America on acid-free paper
04 03 02 01 00 DA 1 2 3 4 5

Contents

Foreword

It's hard to think about a book one loves, as I love everything Susan Ohanian writes, and try to imagine how others might see it. To me, Susan is the quintessential teacher in her passionate, quirky, thoughtful, and detailed look at life in schools with ordinary—which means extraordinary—kids and colleagues. You can recognize in her stories the kids and teachers you've known as well as those familiar situations that defied your sanity. And you recognize also that we take on a certain madness when we enter schools, a necessary madness. If you have met Susan—somewhat shy, reserved, and quiet in manner—and then read her accounts, you are reminded that this "madness" is a tool of the trade.

And indeed the schools we invented more than a hundred years ago were not designed to meet the tasks that Ohanian promotes—of reaching each and every child in an honest and serious way. Our schools are designed to teach a few "basics," to babysit, and to sort out those who are supposedly better suited for academic studies. In reality, schools are not even well designed for these misguided goals. There are better ways to babysit as there are to introduce to good scholars intellectual pursuits in more engaging ways; one hardly needs so many years of expensive schooling just to teach a few basics. In fact, some kids probably fail to learn simple basics because of the absurdity of the way we teach them—en masse, as though every child could learn to read, write, and do arithmetic on the same schedule and through the same pedagogical agenda.

But we are now claiming—from right to left—that schools aren't supposed to be in the business of sorting or babysitting, and that all kids must meet high academic standards, not just basics. In fact our schools must correct the vast and growing inequities children face outside of school (known in jargon as "closing the achievement gap"). We seem to think that our schools can both level the playing field and at the same time apply high academic standards to every student if enough outside pressure is brought to bear, if the stakes are high enough, and if those in charge of measuring success ignore the complaints and excuses of individual teachers, kids, and parents—the folks in the trenches. We're required to pretend that all children are equal outside of school and that it's only laziness preventing them from performing equally well inside school.

After reading this book, it's impossible to understand why anyone would think tough tests could transform these kids. It's equally impossible to imagine how the kinds of schools and teachers we've asked to do the job can also succeed—even with less challenging kids. To nourish teachers who can keep their focus on kids and hold themselves and the kids to truly high standards, as Susan does, will take reinventing schools, teacher education, and the relationship between kids and adults.

If and when we choose to engage in a serious discussion about what our schools are for, we should keep these youngsters and Susan in mind. We can use as our litmus test these questions: would it have helped Susan and Sylvia and Virgil? Would the odds have been better for Anita to have stuck it out had such reforms been in place?

But, of course, Susan and I both assume that the purpose of education is producing not higher test scores but more thoughtful young people capable of exercising wiser judgment, taking on tougher tasks, persevering, being curious and passionate about such old-fashioned virtues as truth, beauty, and wonderment. Consistency, as another American hero once noted, is the hobgoblin of little minds. Susan reminds us why teachers who truly reach kids cannot be fixated on consistency, cannot close their minds to other possibilities, including ones that seem in direct conflict with what they thought yesterday. It is precisely in her infuriating inconsistency, her often unspoken acknowledgment that each situation defies the conventional wisdom that worked just a day before that defines her excellence. Her superb and eclectic teaching is not a straitjacket but a stepping off place. It's okay to search for coherence, for simple explanations—even worthy—but when we're dealing with complicated human beings and complicated ideas (which high standards must always rest upon) surface coherence and simplicity must always give way to reality. Susan's response to her students is never hit-or-miss but builds on a rich understanding of kids and subject matter. The best hope lies in simple and coherent school structures so that the complexity of the kids and the adults they are surrounded by, and the learning we want them to embrace isn't sacrificed on behalf of the "system's need to align everything neatly—thus producing a kind of pseudocoherence.

If all this talk about reforming our schools is going to work, educational reformers will want to keep Ohanian's stories in mind: would Jean and Michael have flourished here? Aren't we lucky that the stories are such fun to read, reminders that although this may be difficult, challenging business, it can also be funny and joyful? Above all, a good school is a place where everybody is able to keep their sense of humor intact.

Thanks, Susan—on days when the going is toughest, you and your students will always be there with me to help me remain sane. And hopeful.

Deborah Meier
Founding Director, Central Park East Schools, New York City
Principal, Mission Hill School, Boston

Introduction

This book covers ten years of my teaching career, the time I spent with seventh and eighth graders. The reader will note scattered references to other teaching jobs I held in the district—everything from an elementary open classroom to an alternative high school—with a very brief stint as "innovator" on a team brought together by the assistant superintendent in charge of curriculum. Since she pops up from time to time in the book, this account of our brief association will set the context for what follows.

The moment the assistant superintendent in charge of curriculum picked up the phone in her office and called in an order for five turkey breast sandwiches on white bread, with mayonnaise, I should have realized that working with her would be impossible. I was among four lunch companions of the assistant superintendent: we were sitting right there—in the room—but she didn't bother to ask us if we were white bread sorts of people. I happened to know that the deli made a great liverwurst. With mustard on rye. Ever willing to see the glass half full, however, I chewed on white bread and remained hopeful.

I found myself sitting in the assistant superintendent's office on the first day of school instead of in a classroom because she had phoned me during the summer. Long distance. She told me she would soon be moving to our district to take up her new position. She'd heard about the fine work I had done that lead to my selection as one of four finalists in the New York State Teacher of the Year event. She asked for my help in "spreading innovation," urging me to leave the classroom, and join her team as a curriculum reform leader. Okay, I was flattered. I'm a missionary at heart, and for the rest of the summer, visions of curriculum reform danced in my head and, I fear, puffed up my ego.

Who could guess that Ilium would be ahead of the curve in putting a peculiar spin on the term *curriculum reform*? As my first act as curriculum reformer, I followed the assistant superintendent's orders to take standardized tests into the schools, making sure these tests were administered correctly. I handed out the test booklets and pencils; I made sure to get the pencils back; I listened to teachers complain about "one more test." For two weeks, my most significant professional act was relieving teachers of their proctoring chores so they could take a toilet break.

The other three team members were doing the same thing. Next, we brought the tests to a workroom outside the office of the assistant superintendent in charge of curriculum and, at her direction and under her supervision, we went over each test to make sure the students hadn't messed up in filling in the bubbles. While we took care of these clerical chores on thousands of answer sheets, we listened to the assistant superintendent's running monologue on how stupid district teachers and administrators are. I have taught in ghetto schools filled with plenty of rough language, but I had never heard so many curse words per minute as the steady stream spewed by the assistant superintendent.

She was particularly vehement in her denunciations of the experimental elementary school that I had left to join her team. Although she admitted she had not set foot in the building, she was confident in her judgment that those "goddamn teachers don't have a f-in' clue about what in hell they are doing." What teachers in our district needed, the assistant superintendent assured us, was her telling them what to do and us, her team members, checking to see that they did it. This was curriculum innovation Ilium style. As I said, we were ahead of the curve. This pattern of reform has since spread across the nation: Bring in someone who has never been involved in public education; proclaim that local administrators and teachers are lazy and stupid; use massive testing to force schools into curriculum compliance. Give them all the same white bread solution.

After serving three weeks on the assistant superintendent's team, I called a halt. Asking her to come to a meeting I'd set up with the superintendent, I announced, "I cannot work with this woman. Her approach to education is too contrary to mine. Please give me another job in the district—I'll accept any job—just so long as it is working with students."

Neither of them asked me what the pedagogical points of disagreement might be. They, of course, didn't care; people in power don't have to explain themselves; nor do they have to listen to teachers. But the next day I was back where I belonged—working with students. And although the assistant superintendent in charge of curriculum occasionally found ways to interfere in my professional life, she was more of an annoying gnat than a real presence; like many corporate-style reformers, she was mostly invisible and irrelevant to my real work with children.

The turkey sandwich episode is a great metaphor for the top-down, "do it our way or else" sensibility that infects too many schools today; but it is also one more proof that a teacher can just say no to Standardisto tyranny and live to tell about it.

I've been writing pieces of this book for more than a decade. I work on it for a few months and then abandon it, ever worried that my teaching career comes off as too messy, with "outcomes"—if you'll excuse a term that seems better suited to muffler and tailpipe installation than to teaching—not grandiose enough for today's oratory. The reader should know that I would sooner work at teaching my cat to play the harmonica than to spend five minutes striving for "world class standards." But finding the satisfaction in small moments as I do, I have my moments of doubt. Time after time, worrying that I may come off as a bumbling incompetent, I have consigned the manuscript to the attic. Then, rereading longtime seventh-grade teacher James Herndon's *Notes for a Schoolteacher* shows me the way. Herndon reminds us "There is no such thing as teaching school competently." He points out that anybody who thinks the trouble with public schools comes from incompetent teachers "is crazy as hell."

There it is. In these days where Standardisto rhetoric fills our newspapers, our union manifestos, our ivory towers, where professional-teaching standards boards gain credence and salary bonuses for teaching-excellence-as-measured-by-student-scores-on-standardized-tests-that-experts-decry-as-loony spread across the land, we teachers must summon the nerve to admit that Herndon got it right: there's no thing as teaching school competently.

This book is about noticing small things. It is about a teacher doing what she can, a book about trying to keep one's eye on the needs of students in a system run amok, about not giving up but coming back everyday to continue the fight. I write this book for all my colleagues in schools across the land, bearing witness to our craft, warts and all. We must recognize that acknowledging the warts does not distract from the joy we find in this craft. As teachers, we must carve out the definitions of who we are for ourselves—and for our students. Standardisto blueprints are unsatisfactory guides because they write about schools the way Hemingway wrote about Africa: without noticing the natives. Hemingway provides a neat and tidy, even entertaining, view but it's a view of not much use to someone planning to visit the continent. This is not to deny a certain allure Hemingway holds, especially if one happens to be a white, male big-game hunter. For everybody else, his stories have their limitations. So it is with Standardisto rhetoric: white, male big-game hunters will feel right at home.

I write this book most of all for students who don't measure up, not yesterday, not now, not tomorrow. We used to say some kids "fell through the cracks." It's not a great pharse, abnegating responsibility for failure as it does, but at least it has the virtue of not pointing the finger of blame at the kids. Such a phrase doesn't—unlike "raising the bar" or "instituting high-stakes testing" or "targeting kids"—give eight-year-olds nightmares. And we will all be damned if we follow the edicts of people who try to justify those nightmares. We must get back to the craft of nurturing children, proclaiming loud and clear that no curriculum silver bullet is going to enable every kid to succeed in every subject. Rather than dumping children who don't master algebra and semicolons and the intricacies of the elastic clause in our Constitution onto some refuse heap, we must help these children develop the skills and talents that will guide them in finding useful and satisfying lives in the real world. And we must strive with them to make this world a better place. I hope that the place to start is in telling the children's stories from inside the classroom.

1
▬

Legend of a Zulu Chief

Among themselves, most of the teachers refer to Sylvia as the Zulu Chief. It is not a nickname offered in affection. A tall, lanky 12-year-old, Sylvia is the leader of the seventh-grade girls, and most of the boys treat her with deference, if not awe. Nobody messes with Sylvia, not the custodian, not the principal, certainly not the teachers. Staff and students alike treat her with caution and no little degree of apprehension. Although Sylvia doesn't get into a lot of fights in school, one incident I witness convinces me that the tales of her out-of-school exploits are not merely the stuff of legend.

When I first join the other seventh- and eighth-grade teachers on the top floor of an unkempt old brick building across from the fire station in a dying postindustrial city, I don't know that I'm about to disrupt a legend. I am an outsider here, not only because of my place of birth but because I'm a woman. New to the city, I don't realize that fifteen years later I'll still be an outsider. Faculty is friendly enough in those early days. Teachers greet me with a "Good luck!" in one breath, followed by a quick "Watch out for Sylvia!" in the next.

In my first week in the building I hear half a dozen versions of how Sylvia acquired the two-inch scar running from her chin up the right side of her face. The scar is an old one and adds a certain exotic quality to the mystique that surrounds her. I later learn that none of the mythic accounts of the scar come remotely close to what Sylvia herself tells me: "I was climbing out of my high chair when I was a baby. I fell and hit my chin on the edge of the table."

As I come to know Sylvia, she shows me less of the faculty room fable and more of the preadolescent who worries about being "too tall, too skinny, and too dark." The first time I refer to Sylvia as "black" every kid in the room freezes. Then Sylvia leans into my face, demanding, "Who you be callin' black?"

1

Stunned, I try to explain that my black students in New York City referred to themselves that way. Sylvia isn't convinced, but mention of New York City carries a certain aura and she backs off.

It is 1970s, Ilium, New York. It might be the era of black power and "black is beautiful" in Berkeley, where I'd gone to graduate school, and in New York City, where I'd begun my teaching career, but the rhetoric has not reached these seventh and eighth graders in upstate New York. They value light skin tones; they refer to themselves as "colored," using "black" only as an insult. They scour the pages of *National Geographic*, looking for pictures of apes, Africans with bones through their noses, native women with bare, dangling breasts—so they can mock, "Your momma!" This exchange is typical. Sylvia warns Virgil, "You better not lean out of the window when you go downstairs. Kids up here will spit on your nappy ole black head if you do."

"Who you callin' black?" demands Virgil, pretending to be upset.

"Don' get sassy with me, boy," warns Sylvia. "Everybody knows your momma was an ape. They got her picture hangin' in the science room. A big black ape."

"Be careful," warns Virgil. "Jus' 'cause they spilled ink on you when you wuz a baby. . . ."

These episodes are sudden, violent—to my ears anyway—and short-lived. I soon catch on that students enjoy the encounters and seem to have a good sense of how far they can go. What upsets me a lot more than this "playing the dozens" is when Sylvia and the other girls start arguing about who is blackest. They echo ads in *Ebony* magazine, where *Dr. Fred Palmer's Skin Whitener* promises, "Nicer things happen with brighter, clearer skin!" "Your skin will be shades lighter, brighter, smoother, lovelier." Only one dollar for a large jar that claims to deliver "a happier, more glowing you." Although I occasionally turn a deaf ear to their exchange of insults, I come down hard on the skin-hue arguments. Sylvia always earns one of my withering looks when she starts wheedling, "C'mon, Miz O, you tell Visalia that she's blacker 'n me." She gets the look and then she gets me moving in with some no-nonsense, direct teaching.

Sylvia is a tough twelve-year-old who sneaks into my room when things get hot for her elsewhere in the school. She curls up in the corner, sucks her thumb, and listens to a tape of John Ciardi reading poems with his son. She follows along in the book. "That Benn, he reads real good," she says with a smile.

I see Sylvia lose control just once. From a distant doorway an eighth-grade girl, Virdinia, calls her a "nigger faggot," provoking Sylvia to screech down the length of the corridor, launching her body as a missile. She lands on top of Virdinia and starts pounding. It takes two big, burly men to pull Sylvia off. Even their combined strength can barely contain her rage. Never before or since have I seen anyone so out of control as Sylvia is: screaming, her arms and legs flailing, her eyeballs rolled back so far that only the whites are visible. She seems unaware of the two men trying to restrain her.

That is the one time—and the only time in my twenty-year teaching career—when I have to concede that a teacher's physical strength is an asset. It is the only time in my long association with these men that I am even remotely glad they are my colleagues. In those tense moments they behave better than I have ever seen them behave—before or since. Even as they strain to hold her, they speak quietly to Sylvia, repeating over and over, "Take it easy, Sylvia; everything is okay." The sound of their calm, quiet, even reassuring voices has stayed with me. Over the years I have tried to nurture my memory of that sound—particularly in the moments when those same men have made me so angry I could spit. Spit or sob.

Our relationship over the years has been, at best, cooly cordial. I damn them because they are so rarely passionate about their chosen work. They indulge me as the resident crackpot. For too many of them, being a teacher or a principal is not a passion; it's a paycheck with convenient hours, enabling them to moonlight at other jobs. On their bad days they are petty, vindictive, and occasionally vicious; on their good days they handle their difficult jobs better than an indifferent, even hostile, public has a right to expect. I work hard at not adopting a holier-than-thou attitude, but I long for colleagues with whom I might have some small scraps of pedagogy—or even, dare I say it, politics—in common.

So how does a bleeding heart like me end up in their midst? Nobody can figure it out, least of all me. Common knowledge among teachers, or at least what passes as common knowledge in faculty rooms, ascribes to the superintendent a specific set of requirements for teaching on the third floor of the river school. Women can teach seventh and eighth graders at the hill school, the school housing the children of college professors; until I arrive on the scene, all the seventh- and eighth-grade teachers at the river school populated by project kids are male. Burly, six-foot-tall males.

According to faculty room folklore, the superintendent sits at his huge walnut desk and stares out the window. Whenever he spies a six-foot, two-hundred-pound (white) male walking by, he races outside, asking, "Say, did you ever play college football?" If the reply is in the affirmative, he asks his second question. "Have you ever considered teaching as a career?" This may sound like an urban legend, but it is clear that size, sports savvy, and a college degree are the qualities the third-floor faculty members have in common. Once these requirements are met, the district operates on a hot-wired professionalism, requesting credential waivers and rewaivers from the state department of education. Getting those waivers seems to be the sum total of staff development at the river school. We rarely have faculty meetings, never mind in-service training.

When I first apply for a job in the district, I don't get a chance to tell the superintendent anything about my teaching experience or pedagogical beliefs. As soon as he looks at my application, he zeroes in on the fact that I received a master's degree in medieval literature from the University of California, Berkeley. The medieval literature part doesn't seem to bother him; the Berkeley part does. "Do you still believe in riots?" he asks. Not waiting for an answer, he next asks about my husband's name. "Isn't Hans a foreign name?" I have to agree that it is, have to admit that I am married to an alien with a green card. I might as well have said alien as in little green extraterrestrial; in any case, this ends the interview. The superintendent states that the fact that I have taught at the college level for two years makes me "too intellectual for this district." He adds a little homily to close the interview, advising me that if I dress properly and show up for work on time, I can probably get myself on the substitute teacher list. I wonder what it is about my current manner of dress that he finds potentially offensive. For the interview I have tucked my waist-length hair up into a bun and I am wearing a plain, dark blue suit.

Two weeks later when I go back to the district office to fill out papers to get my name on the substitute list, the deputy superintendent in charge of substitute teachers seems impressed that I taught high school in New York City and in the Neighborhood Youth Corps in New Jersey. We talk for fifteen minutes and then she takes me to meet the superintendent again. She takes charge of the interview, pointing out my experience in working with difficult students. The superintendent listens without comment. When he finally stirs, he asks, "Say, aren't you the one who is married to that foreigner?" I concede that I am, but by then he has decided to go along with his deputy and he hires me on the spot. He seems to have forgotten about Berkeley. As I am walking out the door he offers one final word. "Say, I hope you don't mind working with colored kiddos."

At the time, I am convinced that my *vitae* has impressed the assistant superintendent. Months later, I learn that I was the first person to walk into the central office after state funds came through for a new remedial position, part of an experimental program to increase the reading scores of urban youth. The phone call comes just four days before the opening day of school, and the opening is not perceived as a plum job, not by administrators, not by teachers. First, funding is ever precarious with such jobs. Every year, teachers in experimental programs are left up in the air until late August, waiting to see if funds come through for their jobs, which start the first Tuesday after Labor Day. An even greater minus is the fact that seventh and eighth graders scare a lot of people, including teachers. And these aren't just any seventh and eighth graders; these are colored kiddos.

Looking back, I can see that hiring me is just one more zany act in the zany history of remedial reading in the district. Unlike school districts that try to develop vision statements and long-range plans, this district operates on opportunism. One year they get state and/or federal funds to teach reading-through-art. The next year they drop art and do reading-through-typing, using electric typewriters so expensive that the teacher in charge can't bear to let the colored kiddos near them. When, some years after the fact, I hear about this reading-through-typing program, I try to locate the machines. As I understand it, because part of the funds for my salary came from a special federal grant, my students have the right to use anything federal monies have purchased, including those typewriters. I'm like a dog looking for a lost bone. Our district federal office is meticulous about paperwork, and I find official papers describing the reading program; I find receipts for the typewriters. But I never find anybody who will admit to having seen the typewriters in at least seven years. After months of nosing around, I match serial numbers on just one typewriter purchased for the program—the machine being used by the secretary working in the federal office. Cynics tell me most of the typewriters ended up in the same places as the paintings bought for the reading-through-art program—in the homes of principals who felt that these things were "too good" for remedial students who don't know how to appreciate them, who will just ruin them. "My kids don't get electric typewriters/free lunch/after-school jobs/preschool/dental care. Why should these kids?" is a whining refrain I hear again and again.

During my tenure I watch the district try reading through cultural enrichment (field trips to places ranging from museums to an amusement park to the circus at Madison Square Garden—truth in disclosure: I got a seat on the bus and a ticket to the circus as a chaperone, and I loved it), reading through filmmaking, reading through computer software touted as "offering impersonal feedback," reading through after-school sports programs. After I've been in the district three years, I persuade the people in charge of innovation to let me do reading through science, and I buy all the bones, bulbs, batteries, pendulums, and other supplies offered by Elementary Science Study. All the units. The district sticks with this program for just two years, but these are the best two years of my life.

My reading-through-science program, very popular with parents and given an award by the state, is wiped out when we get a new superintendent who opts for reading-by-machines, a system that eliminates something called "teacher variability," which is worse even than the plan of a nearby district offering reading through creative visualization. I'm still waiting for my district to put an official seal of approval on reading through books.

In any case, the superintendent hires me on the spot, without so much as an if-you-please to the building principal or the director of the newly formed experimental program of which my job is a part. I meet them four days later, at the special orientation for new teachers, held the day before kids show up for the fall term. At this orientation, the Coordinator of Social Studies decries the fact that 46 percent of the country's youth do not know how to rotate a globe properly—and all of us new teachers look at our neighbors, wondering who among us knows how to rotate a globe properly, while desperately hoping we won't get called on to demonstrate our abilities. The Coordinator of Physical Education gets equal time. Carrying a deflated basketball, he talks about our responsibility to teach the care for and respect of equipment. Then he pumps up the basketball. The last presentation is that of the Coordinator of Penmanship, whose talk seems to be a variation on the "cleanliness is next to godliness" theme. The coordinator warns us that the discipline of penmanship is closely tied to the development of good citizens and a stable society. "Teach students to follow directions today," she says, "and tomorrow they will obey their employers." She talks for ten minutes on the link between sloppy penmanship and juvenile delinquency. I can't make any sense of these pronouncements until, years later, I read Tamara Plakins Thornton's cultural history *Handwriting in America.* Thornton shows the long lineage of the penmanship-as-character movement. My favorite quote from her book comes from New York City superintendent of schools Joseph S. Taylor, who, in 1926, wrote, "Many hard and disagreeable things must be done by people who would rather be doing something else. The dead must be buried, sewers must be cleared, dishes must be washed three times a day. It's just as well to let children know from the start that some parts of schoolwork are not very interesting, but that they must nevertheless be done." This could serve as the mission statement for the river school where I begin a long career: Sewers must be cleared, these kids must be taught.

Once the initial surprise of seeing a woman on the third floor dies down, people figure, well, why not? After all, mine isn't really a regular job. This is remedial reading, and reading, like washing windows, is woman's work. Perhaps it's time to admit that my having been assigned the responsibilities of a remedial reading teacher is a prime example of my district's hot-wired professionalism. To get an emergency credential to teach high school English in New York City, I had gone to night school, taking the three required courses: the history of education, adolescent psychology, and English methods. For years, my husband accuses me of exaggerating my tales about that methods course. Then I wrote a piece for *Education Week* in which I mentioned the professor's fanaticism for demonstrating the correct procedure for passing out paper and adjusting the window blinds. A Washington, D.C., attorney responds, saying we must have been in the same class, as he remembers those same lectures. Sad to say, he took the course ten years after I did. Somehow, I'm not surprised that he's practicing law, not teaching.

At first I think it is my own guilty secret, what the superintendent has failed to notice—that I have a degree in medieval literature, that I have never taken a course in how to teach reading—and so I keep very quiet about it. I do, after all, need a job. My sister, a certified reading teacher, has responded to my SOS and shipped me a huge box of textbooks, manuals, research reports. Every night I go home from school and study these texts, but it doesn't take me a month on the new job to realize that in this school, people don't really expect a reading teacher to teach kids to read; a reading teacher is expected to keep those remedial readers in the reading room and out of the hallways (and out of the principal's office). Actually, the science teachers, the literature teachers, the math teachers, and the social studies teachers all have the same job: Keep control of those kids. Over and over, I hear the same words from administrators and colleagues: "We may not be able to teach them anything, but, by God, we can make them behave." The principal, a jovial, easygoing fellow who has to leave school every day halfway through sixth period (in a seven-period day) to coach junior varsity football in the fall and baseball in the spring at the high school, puts it succinctly: "Don't push 'em and don't expect too much out of 'em." Unsaid is the stronger injunction "And don't send 'em to the office."

Everybody knows that reading teachers spend a lot of time testing their students. Although a thick folder documenting each student's inability to read well travels with him through school, the test providing the latest documentation having been administered the previous May, as soon as school starts in the fall we test them again—individual tests administered throughout all of September and half of October. In April, remedial readers join the other students to spend half the month taking district-wide achievement tests. Then, through May and half of June, the reading teacher again administers special, individual tests for rotten readers. The whole process starts over the next September. I have never been able to figure out what officials think might happen to kids during the summer that we have to test students right before they leave in the spring and again as soon as they return in the fall. Now, of course, there are also the high-stakes tests for fourth and eighth graders in January and February, tests as sole criteria of whether a child passes or fails. With the thick folders documenting fourth graders' reading difficulties jamming filing cabinets in schools, why would the politicians and their state ed toadies insist that these children be terrified, humiliated, and otherwise debased by a controversial test shipped in from CTB/McGraw-Hill, headquartered in Monterey, California?

For a reason that is never explained, in my first year as a remedial reading teacher bureaucrats at the state education department decree that in February all my students have to take an extra test—a group achievement test. I try to explain to the class that the test is to help me teach better, not to hurt them. Blah, blah, blah. Nonetheless, my students are furious. Sylvia sums up the reaction to my moralizing quite succinctly: "Bullshit!"

I try to push forward with my teacher talk. "You can't fail this test; it's just to help me know what I need to teach." Then I resort to a sort of moral blackmail. "Look," I plead, "I've always been nice to you." Virgil throws his pencil out the window and then marches out the door. "Where do you think you're going?" I demand.

"Got to get my pencil," he replies. "Can't take no fuckin' test without no fuckin' pencil."

"*Ooo-eee!*" The class explodes. Virgil has said The Word. Everybody knows that whatever else you might do in school, you can't say The Word. Especially not to a teacher. Virgil's six classmates start whooping and stomping. Ned, whose room adjoins mine, rushes in to see what the racket is about. Sylvia offers this explanation: "All you teachers just want us to kiss your asses and bow and scrape. Teachers is always right. Well, you all can just kiss my black ass."

"*Ooo-eee!*" No more test taking that day. Fortunately, the bell rings and we can all retreat to a different corner. I don't report Virgil's use of The Word, and even Ned overlooks Sylvia's vulgarities. We are as upset by the test as the kids. I go home in tears, after complaining bitterly to my boss that the test has ruined my carefully established rapport. "The kids are so upset," I moan. The next morning my students show me one of the most important lessons a teacher can take from her students: In teaching, kids give us every day as a new start.

This isn't to say that Sylvia doesn't manage to get in the last word on the matter. She pulls out a tissue, wipes her eyes, and pretends to sob into it. "I've always been nice to you," she says, mimicking me. "This test hurts me more than it hurts you." All the kids laugh.

"What's so funny about that?" I ask.

"Oh, Miz O, you wuz so funny. You look like you wuz gonna cry over that rank ole test." Sylvia laughs some more, and I realize that I can laugh, too.

THOSE WERE THE GOOD OLD DAYS. These days, there is little to laugh about with respect to standardized tests. These days, the tests rule the curriculum, rule kids' lives. Condemn their futures. In the old days most of us eyeballed the test results, getting a ballpark figure for how the kids were doing, how we were doing. The tests were one of many things we considered. How times have changed. Today the Standardistos insist that these numbers that go bump in the night define us and our students.

When our old brick school, built like a turn-of-the-century armory, is abandoned in favor of a new, sprawling consolidated junior high built in a sort of Taco-Bell-out-of-control design, we find ourselves in a good news/bad news condition. By putting all seventh and eighth graders in the district in the same school, the district creates a monster of size and disunity, but we have to acknowledge that the plan isn't all bad for river school kids. For the first time in their lives the "colored kiddos" are outnumbered by middle-class kids, and their academic opportunities improve overnight. Those of us from the river school faculty find ourselves outnumbered and definitely outclassed in terms of pedagogies. And for a while old dogs try to learn new tricks; the river school veterans who have relied on macho bravado try to act like real educators—attending regular staff meetings, even talking about the needs of children and curriculum content. A few even enroll in after-school staff development courses. The sad part is that everything is hit-and-miss, with no organized attempt to improve the skills of any of the teachers. Years later when I leave teaching and begin visiting wonderful schools, I witness the reality of principals as educational leaders. As a teacher, I refused to acknowledge the importance of a principal. It is difficult to acknowledge what you don't witness.

Our new junior high has no overall plan because there is nobody in the district to devise it. There is one districtwide staff development program, one that shows teachers how to manipulate student behavior, one of those "I like the way Johnny is sitting" type things. I read the study packets given to participants and refuse to enroll in the course. After four years, I have the distinction of being the only teacher in our junior high who has not taken the course. I see evidence that the course seems to have done some good for some of my colleagues, so maybe my refusal is obnoxious. But behavior manipulation scares me. I argue that if we'd do something sensible about the curriculum, behavior would take care of itself. When teachers try to force students to read the social studies textbook, then of course there will be behavior problems. If we want to see really obnoxious behavior, we should call a faculty meeting and try to force the faculty to read these books.

I concede that the jocks-turned-administrators in our brand-new junior high try to pull up their socks. They sound as though they've been exposed to a crash course in educational jargon over the summer. Actually, the language coming from their mouths amazes me. Surely it passes from ear to vocal cords, bypassing the brain. I wonder if they're listening to tapes. Actually, I wonder if they're memorizing those tapes, maybe an Increase-Your-Educationese in twenty lessons course for principals. But as the school year wears on, in the midst of issuing memos about parameters and contingencies and individualized learning modules, the vocabulary experiences occasional meltdown, and the jocks let down their hair in the faculty room, reminiscing about those "good old days" at the river school. On such occasions, the conversation inevitably comes around to Sylvia, the Zulu Chief. For all of us river school veterans, the very name Sylvia is a *leitmotiv* signaling a tough terrain. For me, anyway, Sylvia's name evokes feelings of frustration, anger, regret . . . and hope. For the jocks, Sylvia's persona is called up as instant folk heroine, an icon with which to entertain colleagues from paler, more middle-class climates. Sitting in their shipshape new offices in this multimillion-dollar complex, these wet-behind-the-ears administrators are oblivious to the fact that their shiny new store-bought, criterion referenced objectives and their shiny new formulaic goals and curriculum mandates and student management systems are even more unreliable than their shiny new fire alarm system, which enters the spontaneous-alert mode fourteen times during the first two weeks of school. Unable to discuss adolescent psychology or pedagogy, these fellows buy their philosophies from a cut-rate catalog while polishing their river school anecdotes. Regaling wide-eyed faculty with graphically enhanced memories of the urban jungle, they make the river school sound like a nutty-but-fun place to be, a place where the kids were dumb and crazy and the faculty were men who knew how to keep them in line.

The stories get told so often that the characters and events become ritualized into a sort of stand-up comedy routine. Teachers who have never set foot in the river school soon know the patter and begin contributing details. I actually get into an argument with a hill teacher when I insist that a particularly colorful event didn't happen the way she tells it. She knows it did; she can, after all, recite its every detail. No matter that I was there. Anecdote will win out over actuality every time. Just look at tabloid journalism.

No matter how often I witness the telling of these formula tales, I am always astounded to hear Sylvia and her peers remembered so affectionately, pictured as resourceful, inventive, and even lovable in a Step'n Fetchit sort of way. The proud, hostile, and often desperate kids I remember are subsumed into situation comedy. Faculty who have never known them are entertained with stories about students' funny names, weird ways of dressing, and curious folk habits—why they don't come to school on rainy days, why they eat chalk, and so on.

One of the most popular retellings that grows to mythic proportions concerns the day, with a substitute in charge, students solve the problem of the ponderous social studies textbooks that everybody, including the social studies teacher, hates. In subzero weather, students open the third-story classroom windows and throw the books into a snow-filled gully behind the school. Seven years later, in the faculty room of our new junior high, the book-disposal story has acquired a life of its own: Time has turned the kids into folk heroes on a par with Robin Hood, John Henry, Jesse James, and Mother Jones.

I have to admit it's a story that I, too, love—up to the point where the storytellers conclude, "Boy, those kids sure got rid of those awful books!" Regrettably, that's not the way the event actually ends. True, the kids threw the books out the window. But the next day their teacher returned, and he sent those kids outside during a snowstorm, warning them not to return without the jettisoned texts. Every one of them. He has a list of which book belongs to which kid, he warns them, and the school district bill collectors will demand an accounting.

When another teacher, one who verbally humiliates and brutalizes children as a matter of course, starts getting sentimental about Sylvia, I get up and leave the faculty room. I doubt that he can actually hear his own words, sounding like he misses those kids. Maybe, in a very real way, he does miss them. After all, things were much simpler then. In the river school the absence of mayhem was considered proof that you were doing a terrific job. In those good old days everybody acknowledged that we couldn't be expected to teach those kids, because those kids couldn't learn anything but shoplifting. Small wonder that those days of nonteaching did indeed look golden in the face of the expectations and demands of middle-class parents.

I leave the room when these memory-lane narratives reach the sentence "Remember Sylvia?" because I don't want to be asked to bear witness to one more incarnation of this myth, don't want to acknowledge one more time that Sylvia was taller and braver and meaner than all the other seventh and eighth graders combined. Or that Sylvia was undoubtedly braver and meaner than most of the faculty. Or that Sylvia could tie a sub up in knots with one hand while calmly spitting pumpkin seeds into one of his pockets and lifting his wallet from another.

Actually, the legend is grounded in truth. But Sylvia's strength and her leadership capabilities and her sly cunning made it too easy for her teachers to forget that she was only twelve years old. And vulnerable.

One day I see Sylvia reading Ethel Waters's autobiographical retelling of her own tough beginnings, *His Eye Is on the Sparrow*. Sylvia is so taken with the book that I buy five more copies so she and her friends can sit around a table and read it aloud to each other.

One day the *Sparrow* readers are quietly arguing. "You ask her what it means." "No, you ask her."

Finally, I interrupt their dithering. "Go ahead. Somebody ask me. There isn't a word in that book that I'm afraid of and there isn't a word in there that you should be afraid to ask about." Sylvia then quietly asks the big question: "What's a bastard? Ethel Waters says she's a bastard."

So off we go to the library to take a look in the *American Heritage Dictionary*. A few years before, several teachers were scandalized by the dictionary, protesting that such a book did not belong in a school library, giving students easy access to "those" words. As if our students aren't already surrounded by those words. None of the dictionary bowdlerizers seem to consider how young readers are supposed to have any respect for or interest in sanitized and circumscribed school dictionaries, the ones with all the interesting words removed. Like all book censors, the teachers are more interested in safety than in curiosity. Fortunately, our librarian is a wise and committed woman, one with boundless faith in children and in books. She keeps the dictionary on the shelf.

Sylvia and her friends find *bastard* and read the definition out loud. Sylvia is astounded. "Is that all?" She reads the definition again, this time very slowly—as though a careful rereading will reveal some hidden danger. It is a word she and her peers use freely for its connotative punch; she is surprised to find its actual meaning to be so clear-cut. And not nearly so terrifying or dangerous as she's feared.

As well as being undisputed block captain, Sylvia is also by far the best reader who comes to remedial reading. In short order, she takes on the role of a drill sergeant; she organizes and pretty much runs her reading group. It doesn't take me more than two weeks to figure out that Sylvia doesn't actually "qualify" for remedial reading; I suspect that she is one of the best readers in all of seventh grade. But not for a moment do I consider trying to remove her. No administrator believes a remedial reader can become a nonremedial reader. Teachers don't believe it, either. Try to remove Sylvia and my colleagues will just figure I can't handle her. Besides the realpolitik nature of her placement, I don't want to see Sylvia go. I both enjoy and need her assistance. I know having Sylvia in my classroom is good for me; I hope I'm right in thinking it is good for her, too.

Sylvia takes charge. She puts up with no more than five minutes of extraneous chatter or obnoxious antics at the beginning of each class. Then she announces in a tone that brooks no further nonsense, "Okay. Time to READ!" And everybody reads. Time-on-task checklist keepers and advocates of other perfect and impossible behavior-management schemes will insist that I am the teacher and therefore the one who is supposed to keep the group "on task," but as James Herndon once observed of his own group of seventh-grade black girls, affectionately known as The Tribe, kids are remarkably efficient in organizing themselves. Herndon's tribe also got themselves organized to read within five minutes, and as Herndon points out, "not even an experienced teacher with a machine gun" could equal that time.

Some years later, when I submit for publication an article about how Sylvia organized the most difficult seventh graders in the school into a reading group, the editors of *Education Week* are confounded. Without asking me, they change my description of the person who showed me how to organize my reading class from "Sylvia the Zulu Chief" to a "no-nonsense African American colleague." This switch devastates me; it is such a profound distortion of the point I am trying to make. When I write a letter of protest, asking them to publish a correction, I am informed that "Zulu Chief" is an offensive racist epithet, something they would never publish. Well, of course it is. One of the points I am making in the article is that I teach in a school where teachers refer to students this way. The editors don't explain why they transformed my student into my colleague. I guess that in their current spearheading of national standards, *Education Week* editors can neither fathom nor tolerate a teacher's letting a kid take over, a teacher admitting she learned a lot about style and pedagogy from a twelve-year-old kid. Editors maintain their political correctness; in transforming Sylvia into my peer, they label her "African American colleague."

If you packed all the Standardistos in the country into Yankee Stadium in the Bronx, or maybe the Olmstead Family Mortuary Museum and Auto Detailing Shop in Heber Spring, Arkansas, or the Devil's Rope Museum in McClean, Texas (largest barbed wire historical display in the world), or maybe the Jell-O Gallery in Le Roy, New York, or the Liberace Museum in Las Vegas, their combined know-how about students and the way schools work wouldn't add up to one-tenth of the savvy of seventh-grade teacher par excellence James Herndon. I am lucky enough to encounter *The Way It 'Spozed to Be* the same week I become a remedial reading teacher. I am sure it is what saves me. Herndon teaches me that it is okay both to acknowledge and appreciate that Sylvia's behaviors and attitudes are so different from what I am used to; Herndon teaches me to give her lots of room to find her way, which means I am also giving myself room to find my way. Herndon teaches me to laugh about the predicament of being a seventh-grade teacher. His voice is so real and his teaching experiences so close to what I see around me every day, I read him like scripture, underlining passages and returning to them over and over. I learn from Herndon that one of the best teaching techniques available to us is to "wait and see what is happening." So simple and yet so hard. The temptation is always there to anticipate trouble, to miss the kids' struggles and approximations because we're so concerned with the outcomes. *Outcomes*: what a word. As though kids were volcanoes spewing forth lava. Or sewage pipes. I venture to guess that such words are never invented by people who spend their days in classrooms. Such words come from hotshot committees with something to sell.

Sylvia is as capable of fooling around—acting silly, pestering, teasing, whining, talking incessantly, avoiding work—as any other child. She is, after all, twelve years old. But in my room she doesn't cross the line between tomfoolery and trespass. Sylvia rarely shows me her legendary temper; not only does she seldom curse in my presence, she reprimands others who do. Instead, Sylvia chooses to cooperate, even to help me out. Pumpkin seeds, for example, cause major warfare in our school, and I hate them as much as any teacher. In October, I express my frustration, telling the class that our storage-closet-turned-remedial-reading-room is already overcrowded to the point of absurdity and it will be unbearable if we don't keep it clean. "It's bad enough that our lavatories are pigpens; I just can't face this room if it's covered with spit-out seeds." Sylvia replies, "Okay." And that's that. Kids don't stop chomping on their seeds, but I don't find any more detritus on the floor. I never figure out why Sylvia takes on the job as my aide and even my savior. Probably my books win her over. Sylvia loves those books, and I make sure there are always more good ones waiting for her. In return, she does her part to keep my classroom running smoothly.

At least 85 percent of a school day is stultifyingly boring for kids, particularly for adolescents who are so consumed by their hormonal spasms. I don't know many adults who could sit quietly through even one day of the dusty confines of a typical school curriculum. We should insist that our politicians try it: Let them sit for six or seven hours at a stretch, memorizing lists of arcane information, speaking only when the person in charge gives permission. The wonder is not that Sylvia and her compatriots behave so badly some of the time; the wonder is that, faced with such an irrelevant curriculum and such inadequate texts, they behave as well as they do.

Even though the writing borders on the mawkish, Sylvia and her reading group are enthralled by Ethel Waters's account of her rise from poverty and abuse to stardom. They've never heard of Ethel Waters, but the book cover shows them she is someone who looks like they do. They talk about Ethel's trouble and her triumphs in a very personal way, as though Waters were a friend or relative they are cheering on. There is no little irony in the fact that the basal readers they so steadfastly ignore in their regular literature class features highlighted epigrams of the "anybody can do anything" variety. Waters's message is pretty much the same as these exhortations, but her life is real in a way that the abstract homilies and platitudinous exhortations never can be.

Nonetheless, the book gets me into trouble. A primary grade teacher stops me in the parking lot one day, asking if it is true that my students are reading the Waters autobiography. When I reply in the affirmative she asks if she can borrow a copy. A few days later the director of the City Schools program of which I am the newest member summons me to his office. He tells me he's received a complaint that I let my students read dirty books—books with swear words, illicit sex, and God only knows what other perversions. "I'm quoting a teacher in this school," he says, "a teacher who doesn't want me to forget she's also the wife of the president of Citybank. She wants that book out of the school."

I haven't been in the job even two months, and I am the first to admit that I don't know anything about teaching remedial reading. But I am a reader, and I know what it means to like a book. I can see that this book has captured the attention of students who are chronically turned off by school materials. The combination of Sylvia's leadership and the pull of a story that touches their lives is inspiring very poor readers to work hard at reading. My boss is new at his job too. A longtime teacher, he is finding his feet as the administrator of a six-month-old experimental program funded by the state education department to develop a model for educating disadvantaged urban youth. That's what we call them: disadvantaged.

My boss has the grace to admit that he doesn't know anything about remedial reading. I decide that it might be the better part of valor to keep quiet about the fact that I don't, either. Fortunately for me and for my students, my boss is a reader, and he readily agrees with my point. "I don't know how we can raise the students' reading scores if we can't get them to read the books." I show him the impossible reading matter with which my room had been stocked: nasty little paragraphs followed by a horde of inane questions. I categorize them as the How Many Ducks Are on the Pond? genre: passages written solely for the purpose of interrogating the reader. I tell him I've been studying about how children learn to read. I quote Sylvia Ashton-Warner's insistence that forcing words that have no emotional significance onto the beginning reader may do more harm than not teaching him at all. "Such material may teach kids that words mean nothing and that reading is undesirable," I argue. And I point out that my students have already experienced seven or more years of Ducks-on-the-Pond-type basal texts and remedial workbooks, so we have a tough job ahead of us in overcoming the cement-strength obstacles the school has carefully laid down.

"It's a miracle that these kids are optimistic enough to still look at a book, never mind read it enthusiastically," I plead. "Ethel Waters isn't obscene. The textbooks are what's obscene." I tell him I am not blowing hot air. I took the social studies and science and literature textbooks home, and I read them. It was a terrible experience. "Does anybody really believe that these kids will read *Evangeline* or *Rip Van Winkle*?" I point out that although Ethel Waters provides the group text that draws kids into reading, there is also a lot of individualized reading going on. Kids are sneaking into my room for extra reading time, and the librarian reports that when they hang out in the library they actually browse in magazines and books, which is new behavior. Formerly they just "hung out."

Because he loves books, the director agrees with me—in theory, anyway. But he is in a tight spot. The banker's wife has been teaching in the school for twenty years. I've been there six weeks, an unknown quantity, and an outsider to boot. In a district where a high percentage of teachers are natives, outsiders are regarded with suspicion. Probably rightly so. After all, most teachers go about their appointed rounds for twenty or more years without ever having an official complaint leveled about the materials they use. I've been in the building six weeks and already there is a complaint about me, a loud complaint.

I invite the director to come see my students. And he does. He sees three girls and one boy crowded around a table, each holding a well-thumbed copy of the same paperback, engrossed in their oral reading; he sees two boys sitting in a corner listening to a sports biography I've taped for them. He sees two boys and a girl quizzing each other for an upcoming social studies test from chapter notes I've prepared. One boy sits by himself in a corner, reading. "I thought remedial reading classes were limited to five students," he comments. I shrug, telling him I take whoever shows up and that kids put themselves into the class for extra periods.

My boss takes the Waters book home and reads it for himself. He agrees that it has more than enough redeeming social value to offset a few swear words, even to offset the sex. He agrees that since we are funded to develop a model for teaching disadvantaged urban youth, I should look for more books kids will actually want to read. He asks me to use common sense in my choices, keeping in mind community standards and fears, but he gives me permission to "ignore the syllabus and the bank president's wife."

How lucky can a teacher be, to meet such an administrator so early in her career? In ensuing years in the district, I work in five more schools in which some fifteen other administrators are in a position to tell me what to do, people worried much more about public relations and covering their tracks than about philosophical principles or getting children to read. I watch those fifteen administrators take the easy and expedient path every time there is a policy crossroads. I know they would have told me to dump the book. A couple of them would have apologized and expressed regret, but nonetheless, the book would have gone. What is sadly significant is that in the ensuing decade and a half, I don't talk to a single one of these fifteen administrators about a single book—it never occurs to me that they'd be interested in a book that touches my life or the lives of my students. As far as I can see, those administrators are just aloof aliterates passing in the hallways. I'm almost grateful they didn't care enough to examine the bookshelves in my classrooms. To be left alone is sometimes the best a teacher can hope for.

In retrospect, I can see what an impact Sylvia, *His Eye Is on the Sparrow*, and an administrator who likes to read has had on my teaching career. Even so, I hesitate to recommend the Waters book. It is badly written, with a cloying, sanctimonious tone. I am happy that in the subsequent months the students and I find different books to champion. Of course it isn't one particular title that matters, anyway. What matters is having faith that children will read when given access to books they care about. What matters is standing up for real books instead of settling for institutional texts chosen by committees who are forever running scared, committees more concerned with politics than children.

Sylvia shows me that it is a teacher's duty as well as her mission to demonstrate to her students the power of good words. Sylvia shows me that a seventh-grade remedial reader will respond to authors ranging from John Ciardi to Malcolm X, to works ranging from The Goops to Jean Craighead George. Sylvia shows me that remedial reading shelves had better be as broad and varied as the children themselves.

Ironically, when I try to build on Sylvia's leadership abilities by arranging for her to tutor a fourth grader with reading problems, she rejects the idea of using provocative trade books. She insists on using the "real thing," the school thing. She makes an appointment to talk with the fourth grader's teacher and comes back beaming with pride; she has obtained her own copy of the teacher's edition of the basal. Every night before a tutoring session, Sylvia plans lessons out of that teacher's manual. I am surprised—and, I guess, disappointed—that Sylvia turns out to be such a traditional teacher, chagrined that she doesn't use me as her model. Then one day as she is leaving the classroom, Sylvia shows me why she can't use me as a model for her own teaching. She pauses in the doorway and says, "Gee, Miz O, I wish you was a real teacher." That phrase is one I hear repeated many times through the years. Students might like what they do in my classrooms, but none of them has ever considered it legitimate. Over the years, every student agrees: Miz O is different; therefore she isn't a real teacher. Everybody knows that the real thing is those big, ugly textbooks. Everybody hates them and nobody reads them, but everybody knows that in a real school with a real teacher, heavy ugly books are the only kind that count.

AT THE BEGINNING of the second semester my boss tells me that there is $2,500 left in the book budget, and he asks me to propose a plan for spending it. I tell him that what I'd really like to do is let the students choose their own books. We talk about this, and together we come up with the scheme of printing book coupons entitling the bearer to one free paperback book, redeemable at the local bookstore. My boss swears me to secrecy. "If the superintendent or the board of education ever get wind of this, it will mean both our jobs."

Ostensibly the students earn points toward the coupons, but I've never been good at handing out points or stickers or grades. I rig the system so that everybody gets one coupon each month. The students know the system is rigged, and they don't care if some kids work harder for their coupons than others. All they care about is getting those coupons. I talk to the kids who rarely remember to show up with a notebook or a pencil, kids who, even when they do homework, lose it before it reaches the teacher's desk. I plead with them to be more responsible about their coupons. "Lose your coupon, and you've lost your book. No second chances." Amazingly enough, as far as I know, nobody does lose a coupon. I also talk to them about the importance of making good choices. I tell them that I trust them to stay out of the adult books. "You could get me fired really quickly," I admit. The store staff confirm my hunch: The kids behave well in the store, and they don't venture into X-rated territory.

The first time I hand out coupons I arrange a mini field trip to the bookstore, which is only five blocks from the school. The students spend a lot of time considering the possibilities. And I am stunned by the choices they make. Just when I think a kid has settled on a predictable Garfield book or a rock star bio or a muscle-building book, he spots Shakespeare or Hawthorne. Someone picks up *A Tale of Two Cities* and says, "Yeah, I've heard of this." I could never have predicted what books my students would carry from that store. Not if I'd had one thousand guesses. Nearly every one of those remedial readers goes home with a classic: Shakespeare, Edgar Allan Poe, Mark Twain, *Heidi*, and *Robin Hood* are popular choices. One kid chooses *Little House on the Prairie* because she remembers her fifth-grade teacher reading it aloud. Someone else chooses *Romeo and Juliet* because "they read that in high school." So let's give a small, very small, tip of the hat to E. D. Hirsch of *Cultural Literacy* fame. Students seem happy to own these books that "everybody has heard of." I don't want to shout hosannas—just because students buy the classics doesn't mean they read them. Most of the kids never mention these books again. But even though I doubt that anybody reads them, I don't discount what owning a classic signifies. Later, when the students go to the bookstore on their own, they are still very careful about their choices, not wanting to waste a coupon on something of only transitory interest. Two sisters disprove all the blather about the inability of black urban youth to practice delayed gratification by negotiating with the bookstore owner about pooling their coupons for a more expensive title. They save their coupons until they have enough store credit to buy a hardbound cookbook. After they cover that cookbook with heavy paper, they show it off around school like a family heirloom. Sylvia complains that every time she chooses a good book, say, a crime novel, her mother takes it off to work to read. The only time I ever meet Sylvia's mother is the day she arrives unexpectedly at 8:00 A.M.—to see if she can borrow any books "like the kind Sylvia is bringing home."

The next year I invest my entire classroom book budget in coupons, and I am convinced that it is the best money any school ever spent. One thing these coupons give me is the ability few teachers have: to select books I know will appeal to my students, without bankrupting myself. I control the coupons, so I can use them right along with my students. It is a luxury never repeated in my long career, but how lucky I am that it occurs so early in my teaching experience. Being able to buy the books I want for my students and seeing their reactions convinces me never to look back. I never again rely on a basal or a canned program. Years later when my tax return is audited, the examiner questions the necessity of my declared book expenses. "Doesn't your school provide books for your classroom?" he asks. I insist that they do not supply adequate books and that I cannot do my job without buying books. I win.

As I build up my book supply with provocative titles, Sylvia begins to appear in my room more and more frequently. Nobody ever comes looking for her. My colleagues and I have an unspoken agreement: If I am willing to put up with Sylvia, then they will look the other way—with relief—when she doesn't show up for class. When Sylvia appears in my doorway at unscheduled times, it means she needs a place to let off steam, to get back in control of violent emotions. She storms into the room muttering, "I'm going to get that faggot"; usually I don't know whether she is referring to a teacher or a student, and I don't try to find out. Sylvia isn't asking me to help her solve her problems, and I am not pretending that I can. I go on with the business of the class and Sylvia finds a book and reads until she feels calm enough to face her next class. Or she pulls out the tape of John Ciardi reading poetry with his son. This big, tough, mean black girl leans back, shuts her eyes, sticks her thumb in her mouth, and listens to that tape for the eighth or twenty-eighth time while she rocks back and forth.

I stock the shelves with classics as well as contemporary books. One day when Sylvia picks up Anna Sewell's *Black Beauty*, I offer no advice. I just suggest, "Take it home and read a chapter or two and see what you think." Sylvia brings the book back the next day, tossing it on my desk. "This book is about a horse," she says, her voice rising in indignation. I tell her to try again, to make another selection. I doubt if Sylvia places much importance on that moment of rejecting a book. But certainly it is significant. Schools offer children too few opportunities to make choices in the curriculum, too few chances to reject a book.

After the success of *His Eye Is on the Sparrow*, I buy multiple copies of *Soul Brothers and Sister Lou*, a book I spot on a grocery store spindle. Sylvia organizes another round-robin reading group. Five or six students sit at a table, each one reading a page out loud. Sometimes patiently and sometimes not so patiently, Sylvia coaches poor readers through their allotted pages; she does not tolerate nonparticipation. By common consent, she usually reads twice as many pages as anybody else, just to move the story along. Every few pages a spontaneous discussion erupts—about Lou's clothes, Lou's ambition, Lou's bad sister. Because Sister Lou is so real to that reading group, because they welcome Lou into their lives as a real person who touches their lives, again I refrain from doing the English teacher thing. I do not introduce such literary elements as setting, theme, plot, or climax to a tale students see as real life.

Good news travels just about as fast in a school as bad news. Other kids hear about *Soul Brother and Sister Lou* and they stop by on their way back to class from the water fountain, the lavatory, or the principal's office, to listen to the read-aloud for as long as they figure they can get away with it. I let them linger, because what could be more wonderful than students sneaking out of class to get involved in a book?

Because I am an English teacher by trade, I worry that in my refusal to interject "teacher talk" into their reading I might be shortchanging students. But as a reader, I've always valued my emotional response to books more than a school-imposed intellectual response. This means that I listen to my students and keep my mouth shut. I don't think I've ever interrogated a student about such things as setting and rising action. Years later, when I discover Carol Bly's wonderful *Letters from the Country* and *The Passionate, Accurate Story*, I am excited to read Bly's convincing argument for not teaching literary techniques but instead reading stories for what they show about life, feelings, morals. What a relief to know that the kids and I were right all along.

So what is Sylvia doing in remedial reading? She had failed sixth grade but was moved ahead on probation because of her size. School threats and probation labels don't mean much to Sylvia; she is failing all her courses in seventh grade too. Sylvia causes a lot of disruption in class, and she refuses to memorize the provisions of the Bill of Rights, how to figure home interest rates, the name of the poet who wrote *Hiawatha*, the difference between a phrase and a clause. The regular curriculum in our decaying urban school is the same standardized, homogenized, watered-down college prep curriculum that was put in place in the last century, the same curriculum that William Bennett, E. D. Hirsch, Chester Finn, and much of the media, as well as the corporate-industrial complex claim is every child's sacred heritage—and their duty to learn. Nowadays, the Standardistos are upping the ante; they insist that every kid needs algebra and maybe calculus, a foreign language, and so on. I'm all for foreign languages and even calculus (though, increasingly, college math professors are saying that little good is served by pushing these subjects too early). But why is nobody speaking to the importance of art and music? Why do schools have to issue uniform, standardized models? I don't know why we can't offer alternatives. People unfamiliar with how schools work insist that the reason students don't know who Henry Wadsworth Longfellow is, can't locate Bolivia on a map, identify the natural resources of North Dakota, or multiply fractions is because schools stopped teaching the right stuff. People who aren't familiar with junior high students—or students in any other grade, for that matter, have the naive notion that kids learn what teachers teach. The truth of the matter is that few schools have ever stopped teaching the right stuff; somewhere along the way a lot of kids just stopped agreeing to learn it. Even at the height of the "do-your-own-thing" of the sixties, 96 percent of the teachers in this country were steadfastly refusing to make any curricular concessions for the changing ethnic and social makeup of their students, no concessions for the turbulent times in which we lived, no concessions for student interests, abilities, or ambitions. Ninety-six percent of the teachers in this country continued to teach Henry Wadsworth Longfellow, the location of Bolivia, the natural resources of North Dakota, and how to multiply fractions, because they believed that was the right stuff.

When I suggest to my colleagues that maybe we should all be reading teachers, that we should set aside the science and social studies and literature syllabi for a year, concentrating instead on surrounding our students with the most enticing reading material possible, they not only think I am delusional but that I am trying to pull a fast one. We all have a job to do and mine is to teach reading. They sure aren't going to cross that curriculum line and worry about something that is my job. These same teachers complain bitterly that students don't grasp the concepts of the seventh-grade social studies or science or literature curricula, but nobody is willing to change one word of those courses. I am not suggesting that the social studies teacher give up the discipline of social studies; I'm just suggesting that a love of history might be better delivered through, say, a few Jean Fritz, Russell Freedman, and James Cross Giblin titles than through a four-pound text stitched together by a backroom committee who have never been in a classroom. My plan seems so logical to me. It takes me years to catch on that nobody has ever expected seventh graders to understand the curriculum. That's why it's repeated in high school.

IN THE END, Sylvia is done in by ice cream. Being Sylvia, it is a lot of ice cream. Actually, it starts with doughnuts. Periodically, Sylvia arrives at school with doughnuts for math class, cookies for science, or whatever. Students and teachers alike know the origin of these treats: they are stolen from the nearby A&P. But the teacher receiving the bounty merely says, "Hey, thanks, Sylvia!" and digs in with his students.

I am grateful that Sylvia never shows up at my door with her ill-gotten gains. It is odd, in a way: she gets along with me better than with the other teachers; she spends a lot more time in my room than in theirs. I wonder if there isn't some ethical line she doesn't want to cross. I think about the fact that in my class she has the books to comfort her; she doesn't need doughnuts.

Sylvia is just as aware of our special relationship as I, and she has a way of re-minding me not to get too self-congratulatory about my own good behavior. Once, when she is being particularly intractable, I complain, "Cut it out. I don't treat you badly—I never yell at you." Sylvia stares at me for a long moment and then replies, "Well, I never curse at you, neither." Thus Sylvia makes me aware that restraint is a two-way street.

One day Sylvia organizes her cohorts on a raid of an ice-cream delivery truck parked near the school. Since I was home sick that day, I can report only what I hear later. But I certainly do hear about it. The ice-cream caper be-comes the crowning glory of the Sylvia-Zulu myth. As I've heard the tale re-counted at least half a dozen times through the years, once Sylvia and her bud-dies abscond with the ice cream, Sylvia leads the troop up and down the hallways of the third floor, delivering containers to each classroom. She ap-pears in a doorway, asking, "What do you want—chocolate or vanilla?"

Everybody, students and faculty, enjoys the ice cream, and then the next day Sylvia is expelled from school, not temporarily suspended but perma-nently excluded. By the time I get back to school three days later, Sylvia is tried, sentenced, and gone. I look at the psychological evaluation the district psychologist prepared to aid the principal in getting rid of her.

- This individual exhibits an impairment in interpersonal relationships. She exhibits an inability to recognize the needs of persons.
- This individual does not relate adequately to authority figures.
- This individual exhibits excessively hostile reactions to disciplinary actions.
- This individual exhibits behavior aberrant to social mores.
- This individual exhibits an inability to delay gratification of personal needs. She exhibits immature capacity for long-range goal setting.

Conclusion: It is the finding of this examiner that this individual suffers from mental deficiency; impairment of personal social factors as well as cultural.

I see Sylvia one last time. She sneaks into the building and comes to my room to say good-bye. She stacks up some of the books she has read that year. She runs her hand over the John Ciardi poems and smiles. She does the same thing with a volume by Robert Louis Stevenson. I am reminded of Maurice Sendak's observation about the importance of the physicalness of books. He remembers the first book he ever owned—a copy of *The Prince and the Pau-per* that his sister bought for him. He recalls being too young to understand the actual text but loving the book nonetheless—its red color, its feel, its smell.

Writing in *The New York Review of Books*, Gore Vidal makes pretty much the same point about the feel of the wonderful blue bindings of the Oz books of his childhood. Sylvia seems to be responding the same way to *A Child's Garden of Verses*, a book I've told her is one of my own childhood favorites.

Then Sylvia makes a stack of her treasures: *I Want to Be Somebody, Soul Brothers and Sister Lou, The Autobiography of Malcolm X, The Outsiders, A Hero Ain't Nothing But a Sandwich, Charlotte's Web, The Elephant Joke Book,* and three John Ciardi volumes, and she says, "You know, it just proves that people who start out bad can do okay for theirselves."

School officials use the ice-cream caper as an excuse to declare Sylvia unmanageable. They get her shipped off to an institution for wayward youth. I tell her friends I want to give her a present to take with her. They suggest a carton of cigarettes. I can't do that. Ever a teacher, I send books. I have faith that Sylvia is right, and wherever she is now, I have a strong conviction that she is proving the school wrong. Never as bad as the Zulu Chief legend suggested or school authorities were so willing to believe, she definitely has the capability to do okay.

2

Iroquois or Bust

School does one thing very well: it convinces rotten readers that reading is supposed to be a nasty chore. Rotten readers (and too many of their teachers) have never heard of Louise Rosenblatt, so they don't know about the power of "books read solely for entertainment." Few people question the notion that kids are sent to remedial/corrective/supporting/recovery reading so they can learn to decode the inappropriate texts that fill school shelves. "Decoding" is synonymous with answering multiple choice questions about the stuff in the texts. If schools would adopt standards decreeing that every board of education member, every superintendent, every curriculum coordinator, every principal, every teacher, one-third of the parents, and two or three newspaper reporters had to read the texts that fill classroom shelves, then we'd have a standard with teeth, a standard that could transform education, including rotten readers. Instead, we keep throwing more onto the compost pile of curriculum materials, pretending that the curriculum is sacred and that it's the kids who are out of joint. This is why I get myself involved with six dull little books about the Iroquois.

Even kids usually termed "cooperative" can't slog their way through the massive textbook, so Leonard Wilson, the seventh-grade social studies teacher at the river school, lobbies his curriculum supervisor to purchase copies of a paperback book billed in the catalog as "suitable for reluctant readers." Typical of the way schools work, seven months after his request, Wilson receives eighteen copies of a book about the Iroquois—to be distributed among the 129 students in his five classes. In an imaginative use of limited materials, Wilson manages to foist six copies of this reluctant-reader-friendly book onto me. Call it teamwork, or maybe professionalism-run-amok, I even promise to use the books to encourage seventh graders to "do" social studies. Eight days later, when I tell Wilson that the six copies are out on loan, he is ecstatic. "That's great. Glad to see they're circulating. At last we've found something to interest this type of kid."

"I'm not sure it's interest so much as self-protection," I explain. "The kids know you don't have enough books, so they are staking their claims. Sylvia, Virgil, Leon, Ethyl, Jimmy, and Roderick all took copies last week. They've had them ever since. I have my doubts we'll ever see those books again."

Wilson explodes. "They know the rules. I told them they can only keep a book overnight—one night. You have to get those books back!"

"Would you give up a book once you got hold of it? The kids know you're going to give homework assignments out of it."

"But those are the kids who never do the homework," protests Wilson.

"Right. But the way they figure it, if the time comes when they might do homework, they need to have the books handy."

"You just have to set up rules," insists Wilson. "A system of punishments for nonreturns. You could have fines or keep them after school, or send letters to their parents."

Right. The day our board of education provides a toilet fit to use in this school, I'll institute a system of punishments to make kids bring back those Iroquois books.

I figure Wilson has really gone around the bend if he thinks for a moment that I'll start levying fines on his books, but I manage to bite my tongue. I try to stay calm. "Look, I don't quite know how I ever came to be keeper of the books, but I hereby relinquish the honor."

"But you said you wanted to help these kids in their subject-area classes," whines Wilson, managing to sound truly surprised and hurt. As always, he takes the high moral ground. "You agreed to help students with the vocabulary so that I could move ahead with substantive issues."

Substantive issues? The Iroquois? In seventh grade? My tongue is hurting from the way I'm biting it. I do what I almost always do in the heat of great pedagogical debate: I focus on specifics. "Yes, but after reading the book, I've changed my mind. I just can't see myself putting a lot of effort into 'great coniferous forests' or 'arching boughs.'" It's not that I object to teaching about coniferous forests, exactly—what I object to are the worksheets that trail along with the book. It doesn't matter whether the subject is the Iroquois or the Egyptians or the latest rock group. Who's going to bother reading the book when filling out the worksheets is the only thing that matters? As James Herndon points out, no matter what you're studying or in what era you're studying it, "flax" is an answer that will come in handy.

Wilson reverts to the age-old complaint from teachers who claim that they have to teach subject matter. He protests that my students can't understand the material when he presents it in class. "I'm trying to teach them social studies. I don't have time to teach vocabulary."

I sigh. "I guess I can make the same sort of argument. I'm trying to teach them to read. I don't have time to teach about the Iroquois too." Wilson provokes me into saying something like this. In truth, only a bureaucrat or an ed-biz-whiz consultant with something to sell could have come up with the notion of "content reading." Kids don't learn to read in a vacuum. They learn to read by reading about specific things, even Iroquois. I just want them to have more interesting texts with which to practice. Texts without worksheets.

Despite my declaration of forsaking the Iroquois, I persuade Virgil to lend me his book. Of course he hasn't taken it home. When I ask, he digs it out of the book bag he always carries with him. Virgil might not do class assignments, but like most of the students, he keeps in close contact with a pile of books. I read the assigned chapter three times and still can't answer all the questions on Wilson's worksheet. Of course I am trying to read while Wilson is in the middle of an outburst. The converted storage area that is my reading room is situated between his classroom and Ned Murphy's, so that when either gets wound up, I don't miss a thing. Even when I want to.

"Don't you ever do any homework?" Wilson's voice rises to a screech. "This class is so far behind every other class in the city that it's pathetic. How do you expect to compete on the citywide exam? Doesn't it bother you that this school always comes in last in the city?"

What a question. I bet we come in last in the number of working toilets too. But first in the number of tiles falling from the ceiling. Last in per capita income, first in low-birth-weight children. And so on.

Nobody answers. It's funny how seventh graders talk all the time—except when the teacher asks them a question. Any question. Wilson could ask them what day it is in that snotty tone, and they'd still sit there in silence. He's a funny guy. Capable of delivering a great lesson, when he's fueled by frustration, things quickly go from bad to worse and his middle name becomes Sarcasm. "Now, I know that some of you want to increase your knowledge, but as long as Virgil and Sylvia and Jimmy continue to behave like animals, real education is impossible during regular class time. You serious students will have to come in when they aren't here. You can come in and work quietly during any free time you have. Maybe we can arrange for you to come out of your gym class. Maybe—"

Sylvia interrupts. "Who you callin' an animal?" Other kids mutter about "not missin' no gym to come to no social." Sylvia continues, "What the Iroquois ever done for me, anyway?"

"*Done* for you?" Wilson sounds stunned. "My god, why should they *do* anything for you? Why should anyone do anything for you? Doesn't welfare do enough?"

"I ain't no welfare," protests Sylvia. "My momma works. What I wan' I get for myself. Don' need no welfare. Don' need no Iroquois neither."

Wilson ignores Sylvia and continues preaching to the rest of the class. "The rest of you should be interested in the Iroquois. After all, they were a minority, but they managed to establish a fine culture for themselves, something to be proud of."

"Yeah, and then they wuz all massacred by John Wayne," announces Roderick. "I saw that movie."

"You could learn something from them. . . how to react to people with different skin colors," tries Wilson.

Sylvia won't be ignored. "Don' want to learn about different skin color," she insists.

"You may not want to learn anything, but *normal* people do."

This remark provokes Sylvia's most often-repeated riposte: "Kiss my black ass!"

I hear the door slam and figure she hasn't waited for Wilson to order her to the principal's office. Sylvia mouths off more at Wilson, who actually works hard at preparing lessons with kid appeal, than at other teachers. And she even tells him why. As she put it one day, 'You ain't got no soul. You got nothin' but white shit in your heart."

"*Ooo-eee!*" Sylvia's peers egg her on.

I wait ten minutes for the dust to settle and then go to our connecting door. "Mr. Wilson, may I please borrow Virgil for this period?"

"Well, I don't know. He can hardly afford to miss class. Can't you take him some other time?" Despite it all, despite his sarcasm and outrage, Wilson never quite gives up on teaching the Iroquois. This is a constant battle for time between us. He wants me to teach the Iroquois during reading; I maintain that at least part of this teaching should be done during social studies. And frankly, I am bewildered by his insistence on keeping Virgil.

"Actually," I say, "Virgil and I can work on the Iroquois worksheet together."

Wilson still balks. "That's homework. He's supposed to do that at home, not during class time."

I, of course, have just caused an escalation of pandemonium. Virgil stands up and announces, "I be goin' to readin'. I be read-in'." Virgil has a way of making this declaration sound like a Sunday sermon. Other kids are pleading, "Take me, Miz O. Puh-leeze, take me! Me! Me!" Wilson finally compromises by saying that six students may come with me to work on the Iroquois worksheet.

Outmaneuvered again. I must be nuts.

Such tension is ever present—between trying to relate what we do in reading with what kids are trying to do in their regular academic classes and at the same time helping kids hear words sing, helping them to discover the beauty and joy and humor of words. I doubt if there are two goals in the universe more mutually exclusive. Of course it makes sense for reading teachers to work alongside their students in regular classrooms. But pretending to kids that their subject-area textbooks are worth reading is worse than futile; it's a lie. There's no getting around it: words don't sing in seventh-grade textbooks.

To acknowledge that my tough-talking, streetwise seventh and eighth graders know all about "polluted penises" and "butterin' popcorn" is not to deny that they have a fierce hunger for the kind of poetry usually reserved for the primary grades. School texts give young children a peek at rhyme and nonsense, but for seventh graders texts are filled with "inspirational" verse by people with three names. And yet, I discover that nothing is too silly for seventh graders. We read Ogden Nash's "Isabel" out loud. In the poem Isabel meets a ravenous bear who threatens to eat her up.

> She washed her hands and she straightened her hair up,
> Then Isabel quietly ate the bear up.

"Oh!" exclaims Ethyl. "This is a poem about a colored girl. Isabel's colored!"

I am startled by this information and ask for evidence.

"Isabel straightened her hair up," reads Ethyl.

Boys are as obsessed with hair as girls. Boys grease their hair and then fight for the right to wear nylon stockings on their heads to train it to lay right. The day Virgil comes in with his hair conked, his classmates go wild. "Oooeee! Look at that straight hair! Virgil tryin' to look like the president!"

"You watch yo'self, boy," warns Virgil with a grin, "or I beat yo' black right off yo' skinny bone."

Everything always comes back to color. "Oh that Charlene," complains Mildred. "She think she so bad. Jus' 'cause she light skinned, she think she better than brown-skinned people."

"She's an octoroon," announces W. Roderick Turner. He always signs his papers with his full name. And his pals don't attempt to shorten "Roderick."

"An octo-what?"

"That means she's just a little bit colored," explains Roderick. "You can be a quatroon. That's sort of light. But an octoroon is really light."

"Well, boy, you'n me jus' be ma-roon," replies Sylvia. Everybody laughs and she smirks. "And Jimbo, he jus' a nigger, black as tar."

"I'm as light as you," protests Jimmy.

"No way!" says Sylvia. "Give me your hand. Miz O, who is lighter, me or Jimbo?"

"It doesn't really matter," I insist, picking up the Iroquois book. As always, these discussions embarrass and appall me. I never know how to respond. I know as I speak that the kids reject my pious moralism. So I get out of it the only way I know, by assuming my teacherly role. Even the Iroquois book is better than discussions of color. "Who wants to read first?"

"This black nigger don' know how to read," continues Sylvia, ignoring me. "He born in a coal bin. His mother, she look like a monkey."

Virgil decides to join in. "Black people stink. They dirty. They don' fight good. They coward. Jus' look at Jimbo. He scared, scared of a girl." Virgil dances around the table, making fake jabs at Jimmy. "See? Nothin' but an ole nigger coward."

"The colored man's skin is the sign of a curse," announces Ofelia in her precise diction. Ofelia's language leads me to research the issue of black students being bidialectal and speaking two languages. I look at the written language of my combined seventh- and eighth-grade classes. Half my students, black and white, employ many of the grammatical devices associated with black dialect and half don't. I become convinced that the language elements of dropping the s on third-person verbs and plurals, dropping the final t on words, and so on, are more a result of economics than race. Even the "he be" construction is used by about the same percentage of whites as blacks. Poor kids talk and write using these elements; middle-class kids don't. Educated blacks sometimes enjoy dropping into the patois among friends, but uneducated blacks seem trapped in a language without options. Educated blacks may well be bidialectal; I don't see much evidence that ghetto kids are—until and unless teachers teach standard dialect.

Ofelia, the daughter of a Baptist minister, speaks precisely as she explains the sins of blackness. "Eve had two sons: Cain and Abel. Cain was black and Abel was white. Cain killed Abel and now all the black folks are bad. The darker we are, the badder we are."

Oh my god. Spoken by the darkest kid in the class. And she makes this pronouncement with a smile. How do I respond?

Before I can get out a word, Sylvia announces, "Let's read." She motions to Virgil. "Sit down, nigger."

Finally I find my voice. "What's all this *nigger* talk? I don't like it. I want it to stop."

Sylvia shrugs. "Tha's what they be—always messin' things up."

THE BULK of our classroom materials was purchased before school opened, and some unknown person had made an attempt to buy materials relevant to urban students. A set called *Cities* is billed in the catalog as appropriate for urban reluctant readers. It has six copies of several novels, including Herman Wouk's *The City Boy*. According to the synopsis in the teacher's guide, the hero is "twelve, fat, and intensely romantic." On the first page I find such sentences as "The anodyne in this boy's life was food. No anguish was so sharp that eating could not allay it." The book has 320 pages of this sort of thing. Somehow, I don't think Herman Wouk was writing for reluctant readers. The set also includes six copies of *Up the Down Staircase*. I read this book right before I started teaching in a New York City high school larger than my hometown, and I was stunned to learn that "up staircase" and "down staircase" were not just figures of speech. They have to regulate staircases that way in city schools for the simple expediency of crowd control. I loved this tale of a New York City teacher, but somehow I don't see my seventh graders getting involved in a book written from a teacher's viewpoint.

My classroom also comes equipped with all the old chestnuts: *Moby Dick, Silas Marner, Wuthering Heights, Robinson Crusoe, Lord Jim, Treasure Island, The Deerslayer, David Copperfield,* and the *Iliad*. Later in the year I discover how other reading teachers got rid of such stuff: they give the volumes as prizes. One day Roderick shows me the reading prize he received in sixth grade: a shiny new paperback copy of *Ben Hur*. His prize for fifth grade was *Robinson Crusoe*. What a reward for ten- and eleven-year-old rotten readers who are polite and do their worksheets. Coincidentally, when I am forty-two years old I decide to reread *Moby Dick*, and I discover what I didn't realize when I was forced to read it in college—that it is indeed a great book. What a shame that so many great books are wasted on the young. Rereading and rediscovering Melville at the age I did convinces me to campaign for forbidding *Moby Dick* to anyone under forty.

I know that for every classic I denounce or even poke mild fun at, there will be sixty-three people who recall their reading of the volume as a transcending moment of childhood. Well, good for them. Sometimes a teacher who is as sensitive as she is enthusiastic can take her own favorite books from childhood into today's classrooms, but it is a technique that must be practiced with great care. When I taught third grade I did not attempt to introduce my own third-grade favorite, *The Secret Garden*, mostly because I've always been reluctant to reread books that I loved as a child, fearing they might lose their magic. My own reading as a seventh grader, while omnivorous, was also undistinguished. I read everything from Zane Grey to *Forever Amber*. At times I regret that, because nobody guided my reading, I missed out on so many classics. At other times I wonder if I should be grateful. In *Stand Still Like the Hummingbird*, Henry Miller recalls that being told to read the "indispensable epic" Spenser's *Faerie Queene* caused him to quit college. It's probably a good thing I didn't encounter this work until graduate school, where a student doesn't expect to enjoy what she reads. Years later, Miller decided to give Spenser another try. His experience was not quite as sublime as my second try with Melville. Of the Spenser opus, Miller says, "Let me confess that today it seems even more insane to me than when I was a lad of eighteen."

I feel the same way about many books commended to children. Recently I set myself the task of reading all the Newbery winners. It's enough to turn one off reading. A few are great, really great; roughly half are unreadable. If the National Council of Teachers of English and the International Reading Association had the nerve to publish a list of works that are insane for children to read, the world would be a better place. Trouble is, too many of their members insist on teaching the great works, insane or not.

Along with novels with an urban setting, the *Cities* collection has a short story collection, and the kids hate it. These rotten readers, whether they speak black dialect or not, are indignant that the stories in the collection are "written bad." As they read aloud, students correct the colloquial language of the text, substituting as close to standard dialect as they can manage. If a character in a story says, "I ain't got no pencil," the student reads, "I haven't got no pencil." It is an amazing process to witness.

Finally, when Sylvia makes one of these translations from the black dialect text to a mostly standard dialect delivery, I ask her, "Is that what it says in the book?"

"No," says Sylvia, "but the book is wrong. They don' talk right in the book."

"Why do you suppose the author wrote it that way?" I ask.

"Because he don' know no better!" Sylvia glowers. "This book is sank."

"Really?" I ask. "Who is talking like that in the story?"

"Samuel."

"How old is Samuel?"

"Twelve."

"Okay." I zero in. "Do you know any twelve-year-old boys who talk like Samuel does in the story? Any boys who say 'I ain't got no pencil'?"

"Sure," agrees Sylvia. "Everybody." She laughs. "Everybody 'cept Roderick 'n Ofelia. But *books* ain't—aren't—s'pozed to be like that. Books s'pozed to be right. People talk one way. Books s'pozed to be the right way." Sylvia pauses and then adds, "I *talk* like that, but if I write like that, I get a bad grade. They give these books to colored kids. White kids don't get these sank books."

For me it is a moment of truth. Good intentions aren't enough. I put the class set of short stories in the closet and never take them out again. Instead, I look for high-appeal books that are "written right."

Kids on our floor hear themselves referred to as "Zulus" so often, I decide to read them a story about Albert John Luthuli, Zulu chieftain and 1960 Nobel Peace Prize winner. Kids like the following description: "Heavily muscled, his head was large and set majestically on his strong neck." They also like the fact that Luthuli received a $43,000 prize. I am worried that in an era of mega-million-dollar athletic contracts and corporate bonuses, kids might sneer at Luthuli's award. Instead, they are in awe. Nor are they unimpressed when I bring in an article I've published. After reading the article Virgil asks me if I got paid to write it, and my heart sinks. I just know they'll think $75 is pitiful. I am wrong. They are amazed that someone would pay me that kind of money to write about what they are doing in school.

Nonetheless, no matter how many times I bring in uplifting stories about black people, the kids again return to their arguments about shades of blackness and degrees of ugliness. Marilyn, a child of solid family background whose parents are professional people, points to a picture of Floyd Paterson in the newspaper: "You want to see ugly? Look here and see just how ugly a colored man can be. Look at his baby. That baby is so sorry. It looks like a monkey." When I'm not battling the "ugly nigger" issue I am confronting amazing misconceptions. When Jimmy reads aloud to me about the boyhood of Booker T. Washington, I try to relate it to the students' social studies. Jimmy reads, "While a young boy, Booker was aware of the war to end slavery."

I interrupt. "What war was that, Jimmy?"

"Uh—Uh," Jimmy stammers, then gives me his big, foolish "Who, me?" grin.

"What war freed the slaves, Jimmy?" I prompt. "You know, the one fought between the North and the South."

Jimmy gazes at me, putting on his exaggerated "thinking" expression and replies, "World War II?"

"Jimmy!" I know I'm screeching but I can't seem to stop. I regard myself as pretty much unflappable, but in his social studies class Jimmy has been studying the Civil War for eight weeks. "Jimmy," I say. I force my voice to be calm, helpful, "World War II ended in 1945. Do you think there were still slaves in 1945?"

He once again assumes his thinking stance and then exclaims, "World War I!"

"Jimmy, did you ever hear of the Civil War?"

"Civil War?"

"You know. Social studies. The War Between the States. The North against the South." I don't know why I persist, but I guess every teacher occasionally gets caught up in the obsession to dig out a right answer. "So what did the North and the South fight about in the Civil War?" Jimmy begins to wiggle in his chair; he rolls his eyes to the ceiling and twists his hair.

"I know you know the answer. Just think about it, please." I am like the person trying to communicate with someone who speaks another language, talking slower and louder, as if decibel level will suddenly transform foreign words into something recognizable.

"Uh, well, the German wuz helping the South, and the Jap wuz. . . "

"Jimmy! Forget about Germans and Japanese. Which side had slaves, North or South?"

"Slaves lived in the South," intones Jimmy, his voice expressionless as though reciting the line by rote.

Of course I know better, but I can't seem to help myself. I am driven by some wild demon, a demon who collects clichéd answers to clichéd questions. "Very good! So why did the North fight the South?" Even as I ask the question I make my silent realization: "Oh my god, now I'm trying to get him to learn stereotypes. What am I doing?"

"They wanna get the slaves for theirself?" Somehow Jimmy's answer seems to get to the heart of the matter at least as well as the pat response I've been pushing him into, so I drop my frenzied interrogation. I tell Jimmy that he can stay in my room the next period and watch a library filmstrip about the Civil War. I figure the whole class will profit from the information.

The first image on the screen is a skinny black man lying in bed, his limbs exposed. Virgil takes one look at the screen and laughs, "Ooo-eee! There that black Jimbo." Everyone laughs—except Jimmy. He might pretend to enjoy the role of being a carefree fat clown, but he isn't about to be called a *black* clown. "Don' you call me black, you nappy bitch!"

Sylvia interrupts. "Hey, stupid, don' talk like that in here." She turns to me. "Sorry 'bout that Miz O."

The next frame in the filmstrip shows slaves huddled together on a ship bringing them from Africa. And so we get the "Yo' momma" comments. Two frames into the narrative and I wonder what has possessed me to show this filmstrip. Every time a picture appears of an Aunt Jemima figure in the mansion kitchen or an Uncle Tom picking cotton, the kids snicker and poke each other. They don't listen to the narrator's explanation of the injustices or his theories about the strengths of black people. They just laugh at the pictures of those funny-looking colored people, insisting all the while that Jimmy might be related to these sanky oddballs, but not them. I decide to abandon social studies, figuring I'm not doing any better with it than is Mr. Wilson. No better? I'm doing a whole lot worse.

But the kids' incredible lack of history—or reality—keeps intruding, compelling me to keep trying to find a way to reach them. Students enjoy browsing through a collection of postage stamps I've amassed, because I let them use the stamps as a reason to go to the library. The idea is to pick a stamp, research the person depicted, and give an oral presentation containing at least three facts about that person. My hope is that in working with the stamps, kids will learn rudimentary use of research tools and gain a bit of cultural knowledge as well. One thing that surprises me is how much students love architectural monuments: the Eiffel Tower, Taj Mahal, Westminster Abbey. I encourage browsing; I also encourage them to find stamps that gain them extra credit in their academic classes. Ofelia does her research on Booker T. Washington and reports back to the group that he was famous and "the first Negro president of the United States."

I ask her where she got this information. "In the encyclopedia." Sure enough, she shows me. Booker T. Washington was a president, all right, president of a university. And in Ofelia's thinking, a president is a president is a president. Ofelia's class, which is about half white and half black, doesn't believe me when I tell them that there has never been a black president of the United States. Roderick insists that there is a chart on the wall in Mr. Wilson's room showing all the U.S. presidents and asserts that for sure one of them was a Negro. The other kids agree.

I guess with the lighting and the poor-quality reproduction, Chester Arthur could "pass." When I flat out tell the kids that Arthur was white, they flat out don't believe me. What amazes me is that these kids, for all their intensive study of the Civil War, the civil rights marches and sit-ins, for all their singing of "We Shall Overcome," for all their Black History Week pageants, for all their "yo' prejudice" accusations against teachers, have no notion of the larger implications of racism, no notion that we Americans, at this point in history, are incapable of electing a black person president. I can say what I like. They look at Chester Arthur's smudged picture and figure I just don't know a black man when I see one.

I wonder what we can do to fill out their fragmented notion of history. They pick up bits and pieces and try to piece them together. One day I ask Tammy, a dutiful student who always does her homework, how someone gets elected to Congress. She tells me, "You have to be famous. You have to invent something—like a lightbulb or a cotton gin." Funny thing: across the country, history and social studies standards declare that fourth graders "understand the structures, functions, and powers of the local, state, and federal governments as described in the U.S. Constitution." Is Tammy's confusion a result of nobody teaching her differently? I don't think so. Tammy doesn't "get it" because too many people have tried to teach her too many inappropriate concepts too early. I wonder why we don't fill elementary history courses with the good stories of history and leave the three parts of government for high schoolers.

W H E N I R E A D A L O U D to the students, Jimmy inevitably interrupts the best part, whining, "I gotta go to the bafroom." Although it is my policy to let students leave the room without question, Jimmy is the principal's prime suspect as perpetrator of a series of small fires set in the school over the past few weeks, and faculty is under administrative edict that Jimmy must be in our sight at all times. So I tell Jimmy that he has to wait until the end of the period when I can accompany him to the lavatory door. He jumps up, clutches his belly, and whines, "But I gotta go bad!"

Virgil grins, "Jus' pee on the floor, man."

Funny that Virgil should give this advice. Virgil is sent "'way" later in the year. According to faculty gossip, confirmed by students, Virgil walked into Woolworth's, a few blocks from the school, asked to use the restroom, and—when he was denied permission—opened his fly and peed all over the merchandise. In February 2000, the Associated Press ran a story about the arrest of a substitute junior high math teacher who encouraged a thirteen-year-old boy to urinate in a classroom trash can. The kid repeatedly asked the teachers for permission to use the bathroom. After he asked a third time, the teacher told him to use the wastebasket. The boy took the trash can to a corner, wrapped a jacket around himself for privacy, and peed. The teacher was arrested for contributing to the delinquency of a minor and released on five hundred dollars bail. It's a weird story, but I am—strangely perhaps—just a bit sympathetic with the teacher. I know how a teacher, particularly a substitute, could be provoked into such outrageous behavior. Anybody who hasn't been a substitute in a seventh-grade classroom should take a deep breath before condemning that teacher. Kids are adept at using bathroom requests to send a green teacher beyond the bend.

Expanding on the theme that "they" would rather have chitlins than sirloin, Wilson insists, "These kids like being sent away. They know they'll be treated better at reform school than at home. They eat better and they sleep better. They *want* to go."

I protest, "But Virgil isn't a neglected child. The situation with his mother wasn't great, but he's with his grandmother now, and she provides a good home. His clothes are well cared for—you could slice pie with the crease in his pants. He looks well fed, and he has good manners, when he chooses to use them." I pause to take a breath, and then continue. "Virgil may like to raise hell, but he doesn't do it out of ignorance. Someone has taught him how to behave. And he's part of a large, loving family. When the kids wrote about how they celebrate Thanksgiving, his story was quite wonderful. His grandmother really put on a feast, drawing in family from six states."

But good family or not, Virgil gets the boot. "I'm goin' to Rome, Italy," he informs me one day.

"You're going to Rome, New York, Virgil," insists Roderick. "Not Rome, Italy."

"Listen, punk," Virgil threatens. "I ain't goin' to no Rome, New York. I'm goin' to Rome, Italy. See? I'm gonna eat lots of spaghetti." Virgil says he'll be gone for eight months. "I don' mind gettin' out of the city for a while. I'll like livin' in the country. I'll learn to speak Italian."

IF WILSON CAN BE SARCASTIC about students, Ned can be brutal, using his physical size and strength to intimidate them. Periodically, Ned decides to make an example of Jimmy, whose behavior usually ranges from goofy to goofier. Ned comes up with the blackboard strategy, initiated with the following command: "Boy, get your face against that blackboard."

"I have a name," Jimmy mutters, trying to copy Virgil's aggressive stance.

"Oh, you don't like to be called 'boy'? Well, listen here, *boy*, if you don't get your black nose against that circle on the board and shut your big fat black mouth, I'll shut it for you. You understand that, boy? Do you? Well, you'd better, boy. You open that fat mouth one more time and I'll shove your woolly head right through that wall."

Later, around the coffeepot, Ned explains his technique. "That Jimmy is such a goddamned nuisance, eating those goddamn pumpkin seeds and dropping them all over the floor. Never sits still a minute. Never stops talking and jitterbugging around. Today I made him go to the front of the room where I'd drawn a little circle on the board. He had to bend almost double to reach it with his nose, but that's what I made him do: stand there with his goddamn nose in the circle. That'll teach the little bastard."

"Jimmy's not such a bad kid," I offer. "He's squirmy and pesty, but he's not mean. He's an okay kid."

"Okay kid!" Ned explodes. "My brother is a cop. Last year that 'okay kid' took a hammer to half the parking meters downtown. He and another kid took their loot to the A&P and tried to get bills. What a dumb shit! That's how the cops caught him—trying to cash in five hundred quarters at the A&P, the stupid jerk."

I wonder if Ned is sneering at Jimmy less for stealing than for getting caught, which is my perception of how the whole city works. I can't resist commenting, "Well, this city has the most corrupt political system in the North-east. Even James Bond novels mention our insurance fires in commercial establishments. Can you imagine? A British author has heard about Ilium insurance fires. Of course you have to be Italian or Irish to get away with crime here."

"You defending that sneaky little bastard?"

"Not really. I'm just wondering why we're ready to crucify Jimmy and Virgil but we ignore the widespread corruption of politicians in this city."

Ned has a habit of being absent on Fridays or Mondays during golfing weather. One Monday his substitute is a graduate student from the local university. The sub starts the day by trying to teach. Fifteen minutes into the period, he abandons this strategy and just tries to keep order. At least he lasts the day. We had one sub who left at lunchtime and didn't come back. We figure he spent the afternoon in one of the bars conveniently located just three blocks from school.

We learn the next day that when the sub was otherwise occupied, some of the boys went fishing in Ned's newly installed fish tank. Ned seems on the verge of tears when he sees that tank the next day. Not only are the fish dead, the kids have dumped great quantities of pumpkin seeds, paper clips, chalk, and other junk into the tank. "I just can't figure it out," Ned says, shaking his head. "I work like a dog for three weeks to build these kids a decent aquarium. Then when I'm out for a day, they destroy the whole thing.

"I thought they liked the damn fish. Why would they kill the fish? Besides all the chalk, I found a razor blade in the tank. And you want to know the really ridiculous part? I have to stock the tank again. The feds are paying for it, and they want to see fish. They buy fish like there's no tomorrow. I don't know how fish are supposed to help ghetto kids improve their skills, but it's the first item on any 'enrichment' budget. This school must have at least thirty goddamn fish tanks for the bastards to destroy."

"Did you know Jimmy went swimming in your aquarium yesterday?" offers Wilson. "He came into my room looking like Moby Dick, dripping water all over the place. Delmore told me he'd caught four fish."

"I'll kill that fat little bastard."

I try to talk to the kids. "Why would you want to wreck that beautiful fish tank?"

They counter with a variation on the *Cities* anthology dispute, revealing that even fish tanks have an element of social class distinctions. "It wasn't beautiful," they counter. "Mr. Murphy had too many weeds growin' in it."

Ned may express disdain for federal funding for fish tanks, but he is very proud of the variety of fauna that he finds and then carefully places in the tank. For him, the fauna is scientific art. But the kids continue their critique of the tank. "That tank was too messy. Besides, that ofay teacher think he so bad. He think his fish so bad." Okay, part of their fish tank rampage is a way to get back at a detested teacher, but another part can be seen as a critique on art. What middle-class kids at the hill school see as a pretty display of flora, kids at our school see as "a mess," another affront to the way things are s'pozed to be.

Ned enters teaching in a career shift from work in industry as a chemical engineer, and he moonlights in a part-time job after school. At first, he has no reluctance about teaching in a ghetto school, because he thinks he can do a good job and make a difference. I think the trouble starts when, discovering he can't teach the kids the curriculum he's been handed, he has no notion of how to improvise. Ned cares about science and he is certain the kids will be better off for learning the curriculum. He never questions the curriculum, and the curriculum clouds his ability to see the needs of the kids. Then, as their resistance to the curriculum grows, he dismisses the kids as animals. Before long, Ned hates the kids and they hate him. All Ned has left to cling to is the curriculum.

There are plenty of days when I hate Ned, too. But then I see flashes of possibility. I see Ned sitting one-on-one with a kid, trying to help him understand an assignment. I remember when he tried to break up the fight between Sylvia and Virdinia, how he held Sylvia and spoke to her so gently. I am convinced Ned's main obstacle to becoming a good teacher is that he thinks it is important to teach the stuff some outside forces told him he should be teaching. It never occurs to him that the curriculum, not the kids, might be wrong.

"Set firm standards and train teachers to teach to those standards," the corporate bigwigs and their political cronies, the media pundits, and the educrats intone. Ned buys into this agenda. And when the kids don't learn what he teaches, he gets bent out of shape, personally aggrieved. And nobody ever shows up to give Ned or any of the rest of us advice about how we might teach either the curriculum or the kids. Insisting that memos in our mailboxes tell us all we need to know, our easygoing principal prides himself on not holding more than two faculty meetings a year.

None of the official curriculum is essential for kids to learn, not now, not this minute: not igneous rocks, not Iroquois, not apostrophes. The only important thing for a kid to know at the end of eighth grade is how to read well. I'd like him also to have some notion of how math works, but I'd settle for reading. But since all the people in charge know how school is s'pozed to be, they try to ignore the reality of seventh and eighth graders' psyches and hormones, and they insist on Iroquois, igneous rocks, and apostrophes. Like Ned and Wilson, I drift in and out of becoming obsessed with teaching something. Sometimes I even choose Iroquois or apostrophes. And when the kids don't learn it, I sometimes let myself become the injured party, give in to feeling victimized by the kids. But I also seem lucky enough to be visited fairly regularly by the revelation that never comes to Ned and Wilson: Most of the

time I can see that it's the fault of the Standardistos and the sychophant educrats who lick their boots, not the kids.

I SHOULDN'T SAY my colleagues and I never receive anything to support our teaching. The district office sends out inspirational posters, posters
rooted in the values and skills of Noah Webster's spelling book, Ben Franklin's
almanack, and Reader's Digest, posters preaching the gospel of success. We
are supposed to hang them on our walls.

Look for Diamonds in Your Own Backyard

Faith Can Move Mountains

God Helps Them Who Help Themselves

The Early Bird Gets the Worm

I try some of the proverbs on my students. In response to "The early bird
gets the worm," serious, literal-minded Wendell, a boy who had not an ounce
of irony in his bones, complains, "Who wants a worm? I'd rather stay in bed."
That starts a whole discussion concerning who'd get *stuck* with the worm, not
who would be lucky enough to possess it. The worm becomes like the Old
Maid in a deck of cards: none of my students want to be left holding it.

With "A stitch in time saves nine," kids want to know "Nine what?"
Then Virdinia adds her wit. "Ain't nothin' gonna save those clothes you buy at
K-Mart. When they goes, sister, they just goes." This starts another round of
playing the dozens. "Yo' mother, pickin' the garbage fo' yo' clothes."

"People who live in glass houses shouldn't throw stones" elicits a number of responses: "Who writes this stuff? I don't know nobody living in no
glass house"; "Everything just gets broke in some old glass house"; "They need
to keep they clothes on. How do they go to the bathroom?"; "Better not throw
no rocks at me or I bust 'em in they head!"

Kids are indignant that some proverb writer could claim that "might
doesn't make right."

"Sure it does! Just ask any cop!"

"You don' have to ask 'em, they be showin' you."

Ofelia tempers this sentiment with, "It might not be right, exactly, but it
doesn't matter."

Sylvia agrees. "Yeah, what good is it to be right if you lose anyway?"

Mildred responds to "A penny saved is a penny earned" with, "A penny's
not going to do you much good. You need lots more than that."

I suggest that maybe a penny just represents money in general. "It could
be ten dollars saved, or one hundred."

"If I had ten dollar, I be buyin' me some candy and some hot dog and some for my friends too," offers Jimmy. "Then when they gots ten dollar and I don', they be givin' me some of theirs."

Jimmy's statement that a penny shared with others now is a penny shared with him later comes back to me a few years later when Carl arrives at school with a big bouquet of flowers for me and candy for the students. For a variety of reasons, my policy is not to accept gifts, but Carl pleads with me to take those flowers. "I didn't steal them," he says. "See? I got a receipt." Carl finds the popularity he yearns for that morning as he hands out gum and candy. Then his father arrives at 11:30, steaming mad, convinced that Carl has stolen a twenty-dollar bill out of his wallet. Apparently Carl took money to buy things he could give away. I try hard not to sentimentalize the impulse that drove him to spend the larger part on flowers for me. His fellow students certainly don't sentimentalize such an act. Particularly the black students. Carl, a white kid who lives in their midst, is pretty much an outcast, not because he is white but because he's sneaky and lacks style: Fat, scruffy, sloppy, and often just plain dirty, Carl's clothes aren't as clean as theirs and, according to the students, his father is a whole lot meaner than theirs. "Carl is crazy to steal from that man. He's mean." "That Carl gonna get beat bad." "Carl shouldn't be stealing from his dad just to give out candy."

On another occasion, upset by a fight with his father, Carl begs me to take him home with me. "I could live with you and do chores—you know, mow your grass, wash the dishes and stuff." When I turn him down, he tries his wiles on an aide in the office. He is so woebegone she almost takes him home.

Some years before, one of my students did get taken in by a colleague. I had taught Alyssa in a GED course for the Neighborhood Youth Corps and then helped her get a scholarship to the local community college where I taught. Sixteen years old, she was living in one room, sharing a cot with her one-year-old son. She didn't live at home, because her stepfather "bothered her." One day she appeared in the doorway of my classroom, saying she needed to talk to me. I invited her for a cup of coffee. As I started to sip my coffee, she blurted out, "I just can't do this any more. I took a bunch of pills." She was vague about how many pills—forty or fifty, she thought.

I had taken the bus to school, and I had no idea where the hospital was. So I ran to a pay phone and called the police. I rode in the back of the paddy wagon to the hospital with Alyssa, holding her hand and telling her we would come up with a plan to improve her life. As hospital personnel started to pump her stomach, I asked them to keep her there, promising to return after my next class. As he drove me back to the college, a police officer told me he had met Alyssa the year before when he had helped deliver her baby . . . on the street.

My office mate heard all my frantic phone calls, trying to find a social worker or student counselor who would take some interest in this girl on a Friday afternoon. He took Alyssa home to meet his wife and children, and Alyssa lived there several months. It gave her a break from her problems, gave her a chance to concentrate on her studies and to be part of a family.

Every year I get a Christmas card from Alyssa, a chronicle of her education through a master's degree, her jobs from entry level to executive, her marriage and second child, a child whose nursery looks like something out of *Architectural Digest*. Alyssa insists I saved her life, not because I took her to the hospital but because I trained her to get her high school equivalency certificate and got her started on her college career. I feel lifelong gratitude toward a fellow teacher who had the compassion to take a risk and take a kid home.

Alyssa offers a constant reminder that we teachers don't have the luxury of knowing about many of our successes. Alyssa, after all, dropped out of school when she was fifteen. Probably if her teachers remember her at all, they remember her as one of their failures, a poverty-stricken, pregnant failure. When I met Alyssa, I thought she was a middle-aged cleaning lady: It wasn't just her dirty, matted hair, her sweater with big holes in it, her skirt held together with a safety pin. Alyssa looked very tired, middle-age tired. I would have put her age at forty, not sixteen. And yet this girl triumphed. She told me about teachers who had encouraged her along the way, teachers who will probably never know that they made a difference.

I ACTUALLY FINISH the year on a fairly good note with my colleagues. In April I introduce them to James Herndon's *The Way It 'Spozed to Be*. They'd been infuriated when I brought in Kozol, but they love Herndon, who acknowledges and illuminates the wonderful wackiness of eleven-to-fourteen-year-olds in a way that leaves child psychology books dithering in the dust. One morning before the regular coffee klatchers have the lids off their Styrofoam cups, I plunge in. "Listen to this." And I start reading. Herndon's funny, gritty narrative stuns these men into silence. And interest. And laughter. After that, until the end of school, individual teachers pick up the book now and then and read a couple of pages. Once, the principal even picks it up. "So this is the book I've been hearing about." He settles down at my desk and reads for ten minutes, surely a personal record. My other boss, the urban ed director, reads a few passages and then buys his own copy. He loves that book, appearing in my doorway and reading passages aloud to me.

Okay, they are intrigued and amazed by Herndon's irreverence, his daring acknowledgment of the wacky seventh-grade girls known as The Tribe.

But I figure that these fellows also have to be taking in a bit of Herndon's concern for children, his practical savviness, his willingness to let the official curriculum go, his good heart.

But if I end the year thinking positively about what I've taught, I am also mindful of what I've learned. Sylvia, of course, stands forever in my mind's eye. And Virgil. Right until the end, when he gets shipped off to Rome, Virgil never lets up on tormenting Wilson. In the words of the guidance counselor, Virgil is an "acting-out kind of kid." Wilson calls him a raving lunatic, a raving retarded lunatic. Of course I have to admit that Virgil is a handful, but he isn't a mean kid and I remain grateful for what he taught me about discipline. One day I say to him, "All right, Virgil, enough is enough. You've been in here two periods today. Now you get out and go to another class."

"Write me a pass to the library and I leave," bargains Virgil, chewing on the toothpick he habitually has hanging out of his mouth as a badge of cool.

"Go. Get one from your classroom teacher, the place where you are supposed to be," I insist. "You know I can't write you a pass when you don't even belong here."

"Sure you can," Virgil smiles. "Here's the paper. Now jus' write 'Virgil E. Thompson to the library.' That's V-I-R-G-I-L."

"Out!"

"Look, lady,'" snarls Virgil, the smile disappearing. "You don' write that pass by the time I count to three, I smash your face in!" He shakes his fist for effect.

"Can he count to three?" I ask Jimmy. Jimmy doesn't say a word. His eyes get very big.

"One. Two," begins Virgil.

"Two and a half," I say, taking a step toward Virgil.

Virgil smiles, "Two and a half." He picks up a chair and raising it over his head, he warns, "Watch out, lady . . . two and nine-eighths . . ."

Virgil and I start laughing at the same time. Jimmy looks at both of us and grins. Virgil puts down the chair and says, "Come on, Jimmy, we gotta go to class."

Virgil teaches me that underlying many crises, humor is possible. He also teaches me to take a step forward.

3

In Search of a Text

Since I am the reading teacher and I have the self-assigned role as the link between kids and curriculum, I decide to do what nobody else in the school does: I read all the books that make up the official curriculum. I'm sure I am the only person in the school who has ever done this. Actually, Mr. Wilson probably read the social studies book when he began his career. He is the kind of teacher who would do that sort of thing. Wilson is pleased that I want to work with him, want to help students read his books and pass his tests. He invites me to sit in on a few classes—"So you get an idea of what we're dealing with here." I think that by "what we're dealing with here" he means the kids, not him or the books.

Since my classroom is a converted storage closet connecting the social studies and science classrooms, it is easy for me to slip in and out of both. Wilson presents a very professorial stance: he dresses well, his stack of overhead transparencies are color coded, with fancy overlays. He's proud of those overlays.

"Now, boys and girls, let's review the material you read for homework last night, 'How Nature Molds New York.'"

"New York be moldy all right," offers Virgil.

"Yeah, moldy and broken. My mama don' want me goin' to no school with broken windows and plaster fallin'."

"Any of that plaster fall on me and my mother will sue the board of education," announces Ruby, pausing in her careful application of gold-speckled green nail polish and looking up at the ceiling above her desk.

"In our reading we learned something about the mountains, plains, and rivers of New York," continues Wilson. He tells me that if his tenure at the river

43

school has taught him anything, it is to ignore 95 percent of the stray remarks thrown out by students. "Once you let them divert you, you never get back on track," he advises.

"Of course, you already know about an important river of New York. You can almost see the Hudson River from our window."

"Aw, who wants to look at that rank river?" mutters Virgil.

"As your book points out, the Hudson was a very important trade route and it is still a mighty river."

"But Mr. Wilson, you can' swim or fish in the Hudson," complains Leon. "Would *you* eat a fish that come out of that polluted ole river?"

"Well now, pollution is another problem," sighs Wilson. "If we have time at the end of the year, we might be able to go into it. But first we have to finish the book." He holds up the heavy tome for emphasis. "And right now we're concerned with the history of this great river. Who can go to the map and trace the route of the Hudson River?"

His query meets with silence.

Roderick raises his hand. "Yes?" encourages Wilson. "Do you want to come to the map?"

"Mr. Wilson, I just want to report that someone has written a nasty word on my desk. I don't want to be blamed for filth."

"Well, uh, we'll take care of that later. Right now I'd like a volunteer to find the Hudson River. Surely someone must know where it is. Can you find your own city on the map? If you can find Ilium, you can easily locate the Hudson."

Silence.

"Virgil, take the pointer, go to the map, and locate Ilium."

Virgil walks slowly to the front of the room. Taking the pointer in his left hand in a javelin position, he stabs New York City. "Right there," he mumbles. "Right *there*." He jabs so hard the pointer pierces the map.

"That's New York City," protests Wilson, his voice rising in exasperation. "Right on the Atlantic Ocean. Have you ever stood anywhere in Ilium and seen the Atlantic Ocean?"

"Mr. Wilson, I saw the Atlantic Ocean once," volunteers Roderick. "It was very nice."

Virgil walks back to his seat, muttering, "I don' care nuthin' 'bout no map. Don' care 'bout no Atlantic Ocean neither."

"Well, now," smiles Wilson, "that's my job. I'm here to teach you how to use the maps. If you pay close attention, you will find that it's not so difficult." He takes the pointer and indicates a small spot in upstate New York. "Here's where we live. And see this blue line? Well, boys and girls, that's the Hudson River!"

Virgil, arms folded across his chest, makes a point of turning his head ninety degrees from the board.

"I thought that's where it was," smiles Roderick.

"As your book points out on page seven, boats can sail from the Atlantic Ocean up the Hudson River, clear up to Albany and Ilium. Maybe some of you have seen them unloading bananas over at the port."

"Banana for yo' monkey mother!" Delbert says to Virgil.

"Yo' mother be eatin' coal," responds Virgil. My mentioning these remarks both overemphasizes them and doesn't emphasize them enough. The remarks are a running subtext in Mr. Wilson's classroom, but because he is what is known in the trade as a "good disciplinarian," the remarks rarely gain the upper hand.

Because he works in an officially labeled disadvantaged poverty school, Leonard Wilson's classroom is filled with special materials that promise to stimulate student interest and increase their understanding. To supplement and enliven the text presentation of how nature molds New York, Wilson's curriculum supervisor has given him forty-six multicolored transparencies of rock formations to use on the overhead projector, put a special rock collection in the media center, and bought two movies on the Ice Age. He also provides class sets of map kits that encourage students to make their own maps, filling in whatever distinguishing characteristics are under study. Despite the curriculum coordinator's pushing hands-on involvement, Wilson draws the line at having his students make papier-mâché relief maps. "Let him cite me for insubordination, I refuse to provide papier-mâché with which students can supplement their chips-and-soda diet. If they didn't eat it, they'd smear it over each other." Papier-mâché is the one topic on which Wilson and I find a meeting of the minds. My one regret is that I didn't take his word for it but insisted on discovering truth for myself.

Wilson is also unenthusiastic about the new talking globes on order. "What I really need," he pleads, "is a change in curriculum. These kids can't read. Let's throw out the textbooks and try a more project-oriented curriculum." His supervisor reminds him that every eighth grader in the city takes a final exam in the spring, so all students must learn the same curriculum. "You'll really like this talking globe. It's the latest thing for this type of student."

"This type of student" is a phrase we hear a lot at the river school. And at least 50 percent of the time it is said with good intention. The trouble is, too often the phrase is uttered as definition, not as observation from the classroom, never mind an observation from the real world. Once an explanation for a child's behavior is decided on, that explanation is very resistant to change, which is one reason so few kids ever get out of remedial reading or low tracks. By and large, we believe what we already know; we also hear what we already know, protecting our narrow knowledge by ignoring contradictory information. We all do this, liberals and conservatives alike. In the last couple of years I have worked hard at shifting my knowledge base. I join a conservative listserv, and because they charge more for "respond to group" privileges, I opt for "no response" and thereby save money and prevent myself from trying to answer the silly, stupid, demeaning remarks they make. As frustrating as it is, being rendered mute is very good for me. It forces me to stew in silence, to listen. I notice this "take time to think about it" slowly transfers to my behavior on listservs populated by progressive educators. As I look back over the number of posts I made when I first joined and the number I make now, I see that not only do I talk less, I rarely respond immediately (and when I do, I often regret it later). I suppose the "instant response" capability afforded by computers offers great convenience, but instant gratification also carries serious pitfalls. In the jargon of our trade, we call this "wait time." It is a critical concept.

When Wilson announces the first test, he tells the class, "To help you out this first time, I am going to give you the actual questions to study tonight. All you have to do is take home these questions, look up the answers, and then answer the very same questions tomorrow. Everybody can get 100 percent on this test!" He grins a big grin. Turning on the overhead projector, he fills the screen at the front of the room with bright blue questions and announces, "Write these questions in your notebooks. Remember, these are the exact questions that will be on the test." The students follow his exhortations and write down the questions.

1. What are Grenville rocks?
2. What did the ice sheets do to the surface of New York State?
3. Why do the Finger Lakes have such peculiar shapes?
4. What are the chief drainage basins of the Empire State?
5. Define: lava, moraines, plateau, erosion

Two days later the class looks expectant as Wilson pulls the test papers out of his briefcase. "Did I pass, Mr. Wilson? Did I?" the voices clamor.

"Did you pass?" screeches Wilson. "I really don't know how you even have the nerve to ask that question!" He slams the papers down on his desk. "How can you possibly expect to pass a test when you don't listen in class, you don't take notes, and you don't read the book?"

He waves a paper at the class. "Someone in here doesn't even know his own name, let alone anything about social studies. Here's a paper with no name." His voice grates with sarcasm. "I can't say that I blame you, though. I wouldn't want to put my name on any of these papers, either." He grabs another paper. "I can give this person credit for getting the date right and the name of the school right. Congratulations. Most of you didn't even do that much." Wilson scoops up the stack of papers and tosses them in the trash can. "That's the only fit place for these. Except for Roderick's. Roderick, you did pass. You may come get your paper."

"It was a very nice test, Mr. Wilson," offers Roderick.

"No fair," complains Ruby. "My momma bought that paper. You can' throw my paper away. My momma be suing this school if you damage my property."

"Somebody stole my book. I can' study if I got no book."

"I bust my glasses. Can' do no test with bust glasses."

"My sister had her baby. Can' read 'bout them Finger Lakes when my sister havin' her baby."

"My mother frien' come by. She tol' me to go to the movie. Can' study in no movie theater."

"There was a fire in my building. I couldn't study with the firemen running around."

The class continues playing with their test-taking form of the dozens, mocking Mr. Wilson by mocking his test. Finally, Virgil wins the game. "I wuz in jail, man. I tol' that po-leece man I be needin' to study for a test 'bout them Finger Lakes, but he jus' wouldn' listen."

Interrupting their banter, Wilson refuses to rise to the bait. "You'll have a chance to do better on chapter two. Take out your books and look at the title: 'New York Is the Most Important Business State.' A lot of you didn't seem to understand what you read in the last chapter, so let's try reading this one out loud together. Suppose you start, Virdinia. Right at the top of page seventeen."

"Aw, she can' read," mutters Virgil.

"Better 'n you, boy, so shut up."

"What page?"

"They's a page missin' from my book. Lousy book. Don' haf enuf pages."

"Everybody shut up and let me read!" threatens Virdinia. Then she begins to intone, "The Empire State offers more opportunities for jobs at good wages than any other region in the world."

"All right," interrupts Wilson. "Let's stop right there. Who can tell us what 'wages' are?"

Stony silence greets his query. Even poor readers like to read out loud, and they hate to be interrupted by a teacher's questions. "Come on," urges Wilson, "surely someone can define that word."

"The wages of sin is death," pronounces Ofelia.

"Yes, but what exactly are wages?" insists Wilson. "Do any of your parents have jobs?"

"Sure they does!" exclaims Virgil. "My mom work. She ain' no bum."

"Well then, she collects wages. Wages are salary, payment for work done."

"Yeah," complains Virgil. "But it say here in the book that in New York you get good wages. My mom, she works in New York. She don' get no good wage."

"Well," explains Wilson. "It doesn't exactly say that everyone's wages are good. It says that New York offers the *opportunities* for good wages."

Murmurs of disgust greet this comment, but no one directly disputes the issue.

"You know," continues Wilson, "my grandfather came to this country as a young man with forty-three cents in his pocket. He worked as a bricklayer until he had saved enough money to buy a small grocery store. He never went beyond third grade in school, but he worked hard, and so far six of his grandchildren have finished college."

"I want to know jus' who in New York get the good wages they talk about in the book," mutters Virgil. Then he speculates, "The governor?"

"Yeah," agrees Delmore. "The governor. Nixon, he get all the money."

"Nixon?!!" screeches Wilson. "Don't you even know who the governor of our state is? Who the president of the United States is?" He paces back and forth across the front of the room. "What's the use?" he mutters. "What's the use?"

"Whitey get 'em, that's who," offers Virgil. "You jus' get yo' black ass down to welfare, boy. Whitey collectin' all the good wages, and there ain't none left for you, nigger." He spits a pumpkin shell into the aisle for emphasis.

"Let's continue reading," announces Wilson. "We have a lot of material to cover this year. Ruby, will you continue, please?"

"That ain't fair!" protests Virdinia. "I only got to read one sentence. Then everyone start hollerin' an' I didn' even get to read. Everyone shut up and let me read."

"Mr. Wilson told me to read," insists Ruby, tearing the book out of Virdinia's hands even though she has one of her own.

"Get your black hands off my book!" shrieks Virdinia. "I'll pull every hair out of that nappy black head if you don' let go!"

"Who you callin' black? You bathe in tar ev'ry day." Trying to keep Virdinia from getting the book, she scratches her.

"Ooo-eee," croons the class.

"You's bleedin, girl," urges Virgil. "You gonna let that bitch do that?"

Virdinia jumps on Ruby, carrying both of them to the floor. The class gathers around the two combatants, stamping the floor and hollering encouragement. Wilson walks to the hall phone outside his door. "Is Mr. Riley there? Tell him the Zulus are at it again. I can't separate them."

The fight stops as suddenly as it began when Ruby bites Virdinia on the forearm. Virdinia jumps up and screams, "She bit me! You some cannibal? Bitin' people? You belong in Africa!"

"Yo' blood on my blouse," counters Ruby. "My mother will sue if yo' rank blood don' come out!"

Wilson orders the girls to the office and tries to continue. "Wilson, please continue reading where we left off."

"I don' have my glasses today."

"Aw, Wilson can' read. Why you pick him?" asks Virgil.

"Well, Virgil, maybe you'd like to read?" offers Wilson.

"Naw," shrugs Virgil. "I give somebody else a chance."

"Virgil can' read neither," Sylvia laughs.

"You better watch out, girl," warns Virgil, jumping out of his chair, puffing out his chest, and swaggering over to Sylvia's desk.

"Yo' bedtime eight-thirty," laughs Sylvia. "When you can' stay up pas' ten, you let me know, boy."

"Listen, girl, you know who the bigges' 'n the bes', don' you?"

"Well, who can read?" insists Wilson, trying to ignore the byplay. He makes it a policy to avoid speaking directly to Sylvia and she returns the favor, addressing most of her comments at inanimate objects: the f-in' book, the f-in' pencil, the f-in' globe, the f-in' movies, the f-in' encyclopedia.

"I'll read, Mr. Wilson. I'd be glad to," offers Roderick. The class groans. Roderick reads with expression, sounding like a TV evangelist just before he begins laying on hands. "Today the railroads and highways *roar* with traffic," he begins dramatically. "The Empire State enjoys excellent railroad services. Railroads serve all sections of the state. Aircraft fly overhead—"

"But we ain't goin' nowheres," interrupts Sylvia.

"Those trains are always late," offers Ofelia. "My mother went to New York City once. You know how long she waited in that station? Three hours. That train was three hours late."

"You gotta have a differen' kind of money down in New York?" asks Delmore.

"Don' be stupid. They use our money in New York City. That the same state."

"You mean I can spend this money in New York?" asks Delmore. He seems amazed as he looks at the two quarters in his hand.

"You gotta car, Mr. Wilson?" asks Virgil. "What kin' of car you got?"

"Aw, he only got an ol' Volkswagen. They ugly. My mother gonna buy a Buick. Soon she get the money."

"My uncle, he got a Cadillac. A purple Cadillac," offers Delmore.

"Yeah, but we know where yo' uncle got the money," sneers Virgil.

"How do you expect to get through this book?" insists Wilson. "Let's get on with the reading."

"In New York there is one passenger automobile for every four persons," intones Roderick. "This shows New York is a wealthy state."

"So? Nine people in our family," complains Virgil. "Where our car? We should have two car. This book full of lies." He throws the book on the floor and stares out the window. "Jus' lies," he mutters.

Roderick continues to read. "In New York are some of the largest stores in the world. However, most of the retail stores are small. Usually they are run by the owner. Probably you know at least one retail merchant."

"Yeah, Moretti. He own the store on our block. He sell rank hamburger. Nobody know what in that meat."

"Cats. He catches stray cats and grinds them up."

"But he gives credit. The A&P don' give no credit."

"Yeah, Moretti ain't so bad. My mother can' pay her bill for a while. She been sick. Got no money. So we jus' pay interest. Two dollar a week interest."

Roderick continues reading from the text. "Think of the money the retail merchant has spent to buy the articles he hopes to sell to you."

Sylvia interrupts. "He don' *spend* no money for us. He *take* our money. This book sucks."

"What you complainin' about, girl?" demands Virgil. "We know you don' buy no articles. You steal them articles. Every lunchtime you run downtown an' steal them articles. They see you comin' in that door at Woolworth an' they ring for the poh-leece."

"Shut yo' mouth, black boy," Sylvia says with a grin.

"Take out your notebooks," announces Wilson, hoping to forestall another round of the dozens. "Answer the study questions at the end of the chapter."

"We ain't finished readin'," complains Virgil.

Leonard Wilson would have to possess the sensitivity of a begonia not to know that things aren't going well with the class. But he blames the disorder on not having the right books for this type of kid. I wonder what would happen if Wilson ever had the opportunity, like me, to sit in the back of the room and watch what is happening. Wilson is smart and he works hard. I'm not willing to dismiss him as a racist either. That's too easy an answer. I think if he had the chance to view what happened today from the outside, he'd see that, contrary to what he believes, the kids have a pretty good grasp of the chapter. If he could try following his students' lead and teach against the text, the students might even learn that history is important to their lives. But instead of attending to his students' remarks, which belie the text's assertions that New York State provides good jobs for all as well as good transportation and other resources, Wilson feels compelled to defend this book that he despises, and to test his students on information that they are convinced is false.

DONALD DOESN'T PARTICIPATE in classroom antics. Curiously formal, Donald is pretty much of a loner. Donald refers to his stepfather as "Mr. Simpson" or "my half sisters' father." Although always polite, he is never willing to concede that he learns anything in my class. He wants us to believe that there is nothing he doesn't know. For example, the other kids are fascinated by my fountain pen. They ask a lot of questions, not knowing whether the item is the latest new gadget or something I'd brought with me on the *Mayflower.* A high percentage of kids come back from Christmas vacation carrying their own fountain pens. But Donald remains Donald and dismisses my pen with the kind of remark I have come to expect of him. "Oh, I know all about those. My grandfather had one." Donald talks a lot about this man, who taught him everything from skinning a deer to forecasting the weather. When I express wonder and amazement at all the things his grandfather knows, Donald tells me, "Well, you know, he was a full-blooded Cherokee."

Donald is thirteen going on forty-five. He is slight in stature and always seems to be hunched over in deep concentration. Rarely smiling, he takes a solemn approach to most every topic. My students and I exchange notes every day, and Donald's notes to me reveal that he longs for the good old days when he lived in the country, cultivated his own garden, went hunting with his own gun. Donald has an effective means for ignoring the present; because he has an extreme hearing loss, all he has to do is turn off his two powerful hearing aids. When I complain about this trick, he insists that batteries are low, implying that when I do something worthwhile, he'll turn them back on.

Donald never lets on that he likes anything about the class, the work, the students, or the teacher. His favorite remark is that he "knew that already." He doesn't announce this with any belligerence or sarcasm; his delivery is always quiet and matter-of-fact. He is neat and self-absorbed.

And punctual. Donald is never late, an important element in the story of what happens on the day I gain my fame as a disciplinarian. Soon after the bell rings Kevin tells me, "I have to go see the principal." A few minutes later, the principal comes in and nods to Donald. "I'll see you in my office." Donald doesn't say a word but picks up his books and leaves. Later the principal tells me that Donald had stabbed Kevin in the lavatory during the passing period between classes. It was just a pocketknife jab that, though not serious, broke the skin.

"But they were both on time!" I exclaim. The incident seems unbelievable. Kevin is something of a bully, though more of a loudmouth blowhard than a real danger. He pesters and even threatens kids but usually backs off when anybody stands up to him. I can almost picture Kevin stabbing Donald; I cannot fathom the reverse. For one thing, Donald is four inches shorter and thirty pounds lighter than Kevin. The principal gets the story out of them. Frustrated by Kevin's taunting him about the unsavory reputation of his sister, Donald told Kevin to meet him in the boy's room. Once there, Kevin kept up his taunts, and Donald pulled out his pocketknife and stabbed him in the arm. Honor satisfied, Donald rushed out of the lavatory to get to my class on time, with Kevin following close behind. He, too, didn't want to be late.

I can't resist pointing this out to the principal. "I bet you never knew I ran such a tight ship. Donald doesn't worry about your wrath over pulling a knife, but he doesn't want to face the consequences for being late to my class. And Kevin figures that flowing blood isn't enough of an excuse to be late either." Fortunately, we are operating in the pre–No Excuses era. The boys get a one-day suspension and are soon back in school.

THE DAY WE READ Langston Hughes's "Landlord," the students' enthusiasm fills the hallways. They stamp their feet and exclaim "ooo-eee!" They want to read it again and again. Leon memorizes it, which enrages Mr. Latimer, his English teacher. "It's nothing but propaganda, doesn't give a balanced view. It certainly isn't a fair picture of the landlord. The guy who doesn't pay his rent always tries to find excuses." Funny thing. Mr. Latimer is himself a landlord. Professional courtesy restrains me from calling him a slumlord.

"Who says a poem has to be balanced?" I ask. "The kids had a positive reading experience." We'd actually had a good discussion, too. Leon points out, "You can sue the landlord if the rats eat the baby. Otherwise you can't sue him for just having rats around." Suddenly I realize why New York City black congressman and proven crook Adam Clayton Powell is reelected time and time again. He puts his success on display. As he likes to boast to his constituents, "When you come to Washington and walk into my new office, you'll see nineteen rooms . . . two kitchenettes . . . four sanitary facilities." Imagine, an office with four toilets. I long for one toilet in our entire school building that is fit to use. When really desperate, I walk six blocks downtown and use the department store facilities.

Mr. Latimer claims that "my" poetry puts kids in an uproar for the rest of the day. "I thought they were always in an uproar," I counter. I have no real quarrel with Mr. Latimer other than the fact that he sticks to Henry Wads-

worth Longfellow and those writers dished up by the committee who com-
piled his text. The kids' reaction to "Landlord" cheers me when I need cheering. Ever after, I have wished I'd had the nerve to invite them to dramatize it.
They loved putting on plays. I should have told them to stage some of Langston Hughes's poetry instead of what I did choose.

I decide that my students should participate in the annual Christmas
"do" at our school. Traditionally, seventh and eighth grades attend the program
(unless they do something that really annoys their homeroom teacher and he
refuses to take them), but they do not themselves perform. I decide to change
this tradition: I announce that the rotten readers are going to put on a play. I
write a playscript from a novel, *J.T.*, the story of a poor black city kid who
steals a Walkman from an open car window. Lots of things happen to the kid,
and in the end he returns the radio.

My students like the book and are enthusiastic about putting on the
play. They come in during lunchtime to rehearse. As the day of the performance
grows closer and I grow more and more frantic because they haven't learned
their lines, they even follow my request to come after school for rehearsals.
But they still don't learn their lines. Since only Leon and Sylvia bother to
memorize any dialogue, and since they are both able to project their voices,
they get the starring roles. When the day of the program rolls around, everybody seems to have memorized enough to make the whole thing doable. But
I am nervous. I want these kids to look their best, do their best—to show the
rest of the school what they can do. I suspect I also worry about looking like a
fool in front of my colleagues.

The auditorium is packed, and since performers go on by age, we are the
grand finale. Most classes get up on stage and sing a few songs. There are a few
skits about Santa and his elves. Then comes The Play. It goes pretty well until
the end. I don't think Leon and Sylvia planned their subversion ahead of time.
I don't think they knew what they'd do until they were up there on the stage
in front of the whole school. Then, instead of sticking to the sweet, moralis-
tic, virtue-rewarding ending of the original story and my script, they make the
play true to life. Not only do Leon and Sylvia substitute black dialect for the
language of my script, in their ending Leon's character steals the radio—and
keeps it. Sylvia's character has her radio stolen—and gets even by stealing a
radio from someone else.

From the wings, at an ever increasing decibel level, I keep feeding them
the lines from the script I had written—and they keep ignoring me, substituting their own dialogue. While trying to control my hysteria as I watch their version unfolding, I look out at the audience. The kindergarten teacher is sitting
in the front row, outrage oozing from every pore in her stiffly held body. *Her*
students' performance had been letter perfect. Of course all kindergartners

don't get to perform. Only those who learn the lines perfectly—with perfect enunciation—are allowed up on stage; eight others are left sitting alone in the first row. Her rules for performing are similar to her rules for joining The Handwriting Club. When kids can produce a perfect copy of a passage she writes on the board, they are inducted into the club. The last week of school, club members are invited to her house for a party. She calls this "standards of excellence." I call it tragic. Just because Harvard is exclusionary doesn't mean kindergarten should be. Or seventh grade either.

The kindergarten teacher definitely doesn't approve of the Christmas play we are offering. Then I look at her students. They are ecstatic. Their soul brothers and sisters are putting on a play in their language, telling about life as they know it.

Even if I couldn't have seen the similar response from older children in the audience, I would have heard their laughter—and their cheers. I confess: even though I realize that the kids love the play as it is performed, I am still mortified—and worried about my colleagues' reaction. Oddly enough, no colleague ever mentions the play. Not one. Thinking about this later, I realize that my colleagues undoubtedly think the "in your face" quality of the play is my deliberate intention, that I put the kids up to it. It has taken me a while to get here, but by now, I don't mind this judgment of my peers at all; I am even proud of it. Unless we subscribe to the notion that children should be seen and not heard, then certainly we must see that one of our jobs as teachers must be to help students find their voices. And to be heard outside their own small world, students must learn the language of power. I happen to believe that speaking the language of power means learning how to use standard dialect, but a bigger part is learning to speak one's mind rather than memorizing someone else's script.

Children need the opportunity to use their language—and public places like the school auditorium stage are a good place to start. I now realize that in writing the script for the Christmas play, I had assumed all the power. Leon and Sylvia took a little bit back. It has taken me a long time to hear what they were telling me, but at last I think I have. Not that it is a simple, clear-cut message. After all, these are the same kids who rejected textbooks written in dialect. The real point is that students, like their teachers, need lots of options.

WHEN I'M NOT PANICKING over my students learning their lines for the play, I am trying to keep my boss from finding out that someone has made off with my second stopwatch. I suspect Virgil; he is so crazy about that stopwatch, and it came up missing right after he was using it. Inexplicably, Virgil loves the SRA reading kit I've inherited with the classroom. The box is filled with cards color-coded for reading difficulty, cards filled with paragraphs to read and questions to answer. Virgil times how long it takes him to read each card, announcing to the world: "Two minute, thirteen second, Miz O, an' I only miss one." I can't believe my own voice when I tell him to do two more cards and then he can go on to the next color. Here I am, feeding into Virgil's notion that reading is a constant race to beat his own best time. Maybe it doesn't suit my definition of reading, but before he invents this contest, I have not realized that Virgil can read. Whatever the merits of having a kid treat reading like a racehorse being put through its paces, part of me thinks maybe Virgil should carry the stopwatch to all his classes. If nothing else, his performance will amaze his teachers, force them to see him in a new role. Virgil the reader.

When I tell the coffee klatchers about this amazing turn of events, their scoffs are loud and mean. Wilson flat out insists, "Virgil can't even write his name with any consistency, never mind read." Ned grouses, "What kind of work is this, anyway? I'm serious. You tell us Virgil is reading on a fourth- , maybe fifth-grade level and that Sylvia is on the ninth-grade level. But they can't do the work in our classes. I ask them to read out loud in class, and they mispronounce every word. They can't pass any of the tests."

Wilson adds, "They don't have to pass the tests. Don't you know about the Civil Rights Act of 1964? Every child will be passed into high school, regardless of race, creed, ability, or effort. We don't dare fail these kids, and they know it. They've got a free ride, handed to them by the NAACP, the unions, and the state education department." He laughs. "And now the president wants to send them all to college."

The task of educating the urban poor is simple: follow the manual and blame failure on low motivation, broken homes, welfare, late-night TV, potato chips, and chitlins. Or there are alternative lists, blaming children's academic failure on low birth weights, their mother's cocaine addiction, landlords' failure to remove lead-based paint, and an oppressive socioeconomic structure. Too few people are willing to look at the curriculum. And too many insiders associate good manners with academic success.

Anita Hampson is a perfect example. Very neat, very polite, this black girl is also a very hard worker. She never misses a homework assignment; she always raises her hand to answer all the questions with the textbook answer. Anita earns high nineties in all her classes. When we learn that one of our students can get a scholarship as a day student to the local posh, private school, Anita is the hands-down faculty choice. Anita reads on a sixth-grade level. But there is no chance I'll ever get a scholarship for Sylvia, who reads on a ninth-grade level, so I suggest Evelyn instead. Like Sylvia, Evelyn reads on a ninth-grade level. Although Evelyn is not the troublemaker that Sylvia is, neither is she popular with the staff. "Moody," "absent a lot," "sloppy," "not very co-operative" have been teacher comments on her permanent record card since she was in first grade. Evelyn is also a poet, keeps a vocabulary notebook, and has ambition. She tells me she can't wait to get out of school and move to New York or Chicago or Atlanta. "Someplace else," she'd say. "I'm going to live someplace else."

When we are invited to propose a scholarship student to the prep school, the principal, on faculty recommendation, sends in Anita's name. "She doesn't read well enough, and her math ability is nonexistent." Anita has never been put in remedial reading—too polite and too much of a teacher pleaser for that. But once our school chooses her to take the entrance exam, I coach her for six weeks. She does poorly on the test, but based on our school's recommendation, the prep school decides to take her anyway. I ask Evelyn if she will take the test. "Huh! Now you know nobody is going to let me in their fancy school."

Evelyn is, of course, right. When I bring up her name to the faculty, they start talking about her family. "Don't you know about her mother? Her father's a drunk and her mother's worse." The faculty refuses to acknowledge that the family background baggage that she carries make it all the more remarkable that this girl has done so well for herself. Evelyn is bright, tough, sensitive, curious, rebellious. I think she is stubborn enough, and mean enough, to have done just fine in that posh prep school. Evelyn would have seen that it was a two-way street: able to receive the good they had to offer but also determined to give a little attitude back. Of course what they want is a good nigger, and that's what we offer them. Sweet, compliant Anita lasts one semester. Then she gets pregnant and drops out.

What is a meek and mild child who is used to following orders, not asserting herself, to do when she's thrust into the elite, arcane environment of an upper-class boarding school during the day, returning to the ghetto at night? I wonder if getting pregnant seems like the only option in a school where good behavior isn't enough, a school where English classes consists not of copying definitions out of the dictionary but of sitting in a group of eight discussing Faulkner short stories. Which tragedy is worse, that we sent Anita there—or that we failed to give Evelyn the chance?

Amazingly enough, I do get the second stopwatch back. The kids know who took it, and I think my frenzy over losing it provokes them to threaten the thief into returning it. A white kid took it and the black kids made him bring it back. Ned claims it would never have come back if a black kid had taken it because blacks stick together. In the three days before I get it back, just about every teacher in the school gives me advice on the care and preservation of stopwatches. My favorite is the suggestion that I lock it up in the safe in the principal's office.

The most stupid thing about the whole affair is that the stopwatch is superfluous to my reading agenda. It came with the room, and, by chance, I discovered that some kids love it. I don't see a virtue to speed reading, but then I watch Jimmy and Virgil labor over those color-tabbed cards and think, "Well, maybe." I don't hold up the SRA paragraphs as great literature, but I don't damn them either. The questions and word analysis on the backs of the cards are problematic, but the paragraphs themselves provide lots of interesting tidbits of information. And for some kids those cards seem to provide a sort of legitimacy to our class, proving this is really reading. My colleagues, after all, aren't the only ones who have doubts about me. The kids, too, know what a real reading teacher is supposed to do. A reading teacher is supposed to fill her room with boxes of disembodied paragraphs with questions and controlled reader machines that force a kid to read down a page at a certain speed, preventing him from looking back at what he reads; a real reading teacher is supposed to give tests, lots and lots of tests.

The cards are, of course, merely filler; they aren't real reading, not the stuff to get kids hooked on books. My colleagues think I am crazy to spend the curriculum budget on paperback books. Two arguments prevail: "Why buy books for kids who can't read?" and "The students will just steal the books." I wonder why kids would steal books they can't read, but as it happen, my students agree with the second argument. Kids are always warning me, "Kids will steal these books." Maybe someone should do a study of what books get stolen. And fill classrooms with more of those kinds of books. Then, in the end classrooms shelves will contain nothing but *Moby Dick* and *Hiawatha*.

Leon starts coming to remedial reading because he wants to borrow my books. An imp of a boy whom I suspect of spearheading the tossing of the social studies books out the window into snowbanks below, he is a good reader. Nonetheless, he has no trouble getting out of other classes to come to reading. Ned says Leon is sneaky and Wilson says he is nothing but trouble. Since these are the unofficial requirements for going to remedial reading, Leon becomes a remedial reader. Later in my career I use the Leon Principle when setting up an innovative reading program: Delabel it, provide interesting materials, and let everybody come. Only classroom teachers and I know who has to come, and when the good students beat a path to your door, the stigma is erased for remedial readers.

From time to time Leon tells me he is writing a play and an autobiography. He occasionally gives me small glimpses of papers he carries around, but I don't get to read much. He always puts me off, saying he wants to work on it some more before I read it. The Christmas play has shown me that Leon is a real ham. At the spring concert I witness his musical leanings.

For all his ranting about students not doing the required work, not accepting responsibility, Leonard Wilson is vocal about refusing to come to school on the days when concerts and other special outings are scheduled. Once a year we walk with the students over to the music hall where a symphony orchestra performs a special children's concert.

Maybe the principal is getting even with Wilson for missing this concert for the third year in a row, but he assigns Mr. Hogue to be the substitute. Mr. Hogue is infamous for his impassivity. He pretty much stands at the front of the room behind the teacher's desk with his arms folded. All period. All day. We suspect he's asleep on his feet. With his eyes open.

The kids love Mr. Hogue. "Hi-ya there, Mr. Hog. Good to see you again, man." Kids stand on desks, hang out windows, go through Wilson's desk drawers. I swear it. I saw it. Mr. Hogue just stands there with his arms folded across his chest. He looks like a Buddah, a penguin, a sitting hen. He never says a word while kids continue to climb, shout, snoop, commit petty vandalism.

Finally, after months of substituting, Mr. Hogue does speak when he finds out that he will be responsible for escorting twenty-five homeroom students to the concert. "What these kids need is discipline, not culture," he announces just as we start to herd kids down the stairs. I am so startled to hear him speak that I forget to spit in his eye. And the night before I had made a solemn oath to spit in the eye of the first person who said, "What these kids need is discipline, not culture."

The kids have a wonderful time. Somehow Mr. Hogue's group gets into the front row center. I am eight rows back and off to the side, but I have a good view. Mr. Hogue promptly falls asleep. Leon has come prepared. Sitting right next to the sleeping Hogue, Leon pulls out his harmonica and accompanies the orchestra. At one point the conductor turns around and Leon's buddies, not wanting him to get in trouble, put their hands to their mouths and pretend to be playing harmonicas. It is a wonderful moment.

A few weeks later, Leon disappears. Kids tell me he's been sent south to live with an aunt. I worry about trouble with the law, but I never hear another word about Leon, not for some twenty years. Then, one Saturday morning, I am wandering around the Boston Book Fair. A very tall, very dark man comes up to me and asks, "Say, didn't you teach reading at the river school? You taught me to love books." It is Leon. He introduces me to his girlfriend and hands me his business card, saying he hopes the next time I'm in Boston I'll let him know so that he can take me to dinner. Leon is a television producer. Of course I'm overjoyed to know that he is working in a field he likes, a field that lets him exercise the creative talent that was visible in seventh grade. But the deep, abiding joy, the joy that sets me grinning every time I think of that seventh grader, the kind of thing a teacher so rarely finds out, is knowing that the boy who messed up my Christmas play grew up to be the kind of man who spends a Saturday morning at the Boston Book Fair. I wonder if he still plays the harmonica.

EVERYBODY HAS ADVICE for Leonard Wilson and me and all the other seventh-grade teachers in the land. Most governors, corporate executives, media pundits, and everybody's Aunt Mabel insist that their own graduation signaled the end of some golden age of education; school standards have been falling ever since. This, of course, is nothing new. We can find screeds from the ancient Greeks on the sorry state of children's education. But one of my favorites is more recent. Early in the 1990s, Jacques Barzun addresses himself to seventh-grade teachers. In *Begin Here: The Forgotten Conditions of Teaching and Learning*, Professor Barzun talks about what a seventh-grade history class should look like. He would have seventh graders read Prescott's *Conquest of Mexico* and then write a précis. Students who write the best précis, advises Barzun, will read them aloud to their classmates. Barzun does not say how many times he's tried this ideal lesson plan with a pack of twelve-year-olds. Being locked up in a room with twenty-five seventh graders and a stack of *Conquest of Mexico*s is as good a definition of hell as I've come across.

Jimmy shows me he doesn't need the *Conquest of Mexico*; he needs *Little Red Riding Hood*. When the librarian offers me some captioned filmstrips of fairy tales for which the sound no longer works, figuring that they might give my students good practice in reading, I can't imagine my rough-and-tough rotten readers watching fairy-tale filmstrips. But being a teacher, I don't refuse any free materials. I just dump the set on a shelf. Then the principal asks if, since I rarely leave the building during the one-and-a-half-hour lunch break, I'll keep tabs on Jimmy. Jimmy has been stealing from Woolworth's during the lunch break, and the manager says that if it happens again the store will prosecute.

Why does our school take one and a half hours for lunch? That's how long it takes to bus kids home and then pick them up and bus them back to school. We do this because our board of education is steadfast in its opposition to federally subsidized lunch programs. I attend board meetings and listen to board members orate on the privilege of every mother to welcome her children home for a midday break, the joy of providing a lunch for them. The night I watch the board vote down free milk for kindergartners as an intrusion on family values, I vow to stop attending board meetings.

My agreeing to ride herd on Jimmy during our lunch break is not entirely altruistic. I figure with Jimmy in the room, my colleagues will find somewhere else to hang out, so I agree. My colleagues are getting me down. I'm tired of their politics, jokes, and small-mindedness, not to mention all the sports blather and betting pools. They bet on everything, including the arrival date of staff babies. In the course of nosing around the room, Jimmy discovers the box of filmstrips and he soon proves that Bruno Bettelheim is right: People who don't get fairy tales when they are young will find them later, find them and take from them what they need. Like Charles Dickens, who said that Little Red Riding Hood was the love of his life, Jimmy is entranced by the little hooded girl.

For a while Jimmy keeps his fascination secret. He watches the filmstrips only during the lunch break. He watches *Little Red Riding Hood* over and over, finally moving on to the others. Then one day during reading class Delmore asks if he can watch that story about those little pigs. Then Venetia wants *Cinderella*. The cat is out of the bag. Who could predict that Jimmy would be the purveyor of good curriculum news? Everybody is engrossed by those filmstrips, chanting the words in unison off the screen. I rush out and buy books of fairy tales, a collection that has grown to gigantic proportions, including forty-three versions of *The Three Little Pigs*.

THESE DAYS we hear a lot of blather about educational parity, about every student having an equal opportunity to study hard, to read that text, to write those term papers, to pass that test. And to get one of those good jobs and one of those fancy, big cars too. No one can deny that our school is not a good place for kids or their teachers to be, but I don't know what it would take to make it better. I mask my disquiet and work pretty well with students because my classes are small and I have a boss who lets me choose the books kids need. Small classes help me recognize my students' strengths and allow me to help them build on those strengths. I have no illusions that I can step in and herd Leonard Wilson's classes through a one-assignment-fits-all curriculum. With an eye on the citywide exams in the spring.

I complain a lot about the lack of opportunities for professional growth, but the one time our district provides us with "development," I wish they hadn't. The course is billed as a combined-curriculum model integrating social studies and language arts. The promise is that we'll learn how to plan a lesson. They offer us a sample lesson on teaching students about the parts of a newspaper. The motivation—or, in the jargon of the trade, the anticipatory set—is to ask students, "How many of you get a newspaper at your house every day?" What kind of motivation could that possibly be? Maybe one family in ten in our school gets a daily newspaper; not one twelve-year-old in five hundred cares.

But in-service participants are not supposed to question the basic premises of the advice nomadic consultants offer. We are told that after the teacher is sure her kids are motivated about newspapers, she can spread out the parts of a newspaper and explain them. Again, who cares? It seems typical of the school consultant circle that they deliberately deform and dilute the power of newspapers. Certainly, the importance of the newspapers is not the fact that they are divided up into sections.

It just so happens that the newspaper has always been an important part of my curriculum. A teacher who wants to get kids interested in newspapers needs to show them there's something in it for them, not proceed on the basis of definitions. We kill a curriculum for kids the minute we make them define it. For twelve-year-olds, anyway, definition must follow function, not proceed it. If there are no dramatic crimes or spectacular car crashes in the headlines, then the classified ads are a good place to start. I'm also on the alert for the offbeat story. I remember the time I challenged kids to find the weirdest story in the paper. Gennaro kept pestering me to provide a hint. I assured him, "Hints aren't needed: you will know it when you see it."

About ten minutes later he yelled, "I got it! I got it! It *is* weird!" He turned to other kids and said, "Would you believe a man shot his lawnmower?" Of course it helps to have offbeat stories, but such techniques work a whole lot better to create newspaper readers than to require them to study—and memorize—the organizational structure.

One of my favorite examples of the absolutely wacko lack of understanding of what schools need comes from a state education department that publishes guidelines of the skills needed to qualify as a master teacher. I don't see any point in naming the state because so many states have nearly identical criteria. Here is a small sample:

5.1.1 Keeps his/her desk tidy because he/she expects students to keep theirs tidy

8.1.0 Invites the child to be more specific

16.3.1 Begins instructional task promptly

36.1.4 Relates today's lesson to the next day's lesson

42.6.3 Avoids outbursts

51.2.6 Provides grammatically correct bulletin board displays

Who wants to be first in line to invite Virgil to be more specific? People who can talk like this about the craft of working with children have no shame.

None. But of course they don't talk about teaching; they talk instead about "facilitating learning." These people have a lot to answer for. Maybe it's because my own desk is always such a mess, but I wonder who could, with a straight face, say that the condition of a teacher's desk has anything to do with who she is as a teacher. Of course I admit to being suspicious of people who keep too neat a desk. When my principal regularly complains about my mess of a desk with the observation "Cluttered desk, cluttered mind," I regularly respond, "Empty desk, empty mind."

Michael Winerip once wrote a piece for the *New York Times* about a woman who is paid top dollar for organizing peoples' closets. She belongs to the Association of Professional Organizers. Winerip asked to see the professional organizer's own closet. For every piece of clothing, this woman keeps a note card of matching accessories. With her green suit, for example, she always wears her green shoes, amber pin, and beige pocketbook. "I never have to think about anything; it's great," she said. I have used this bit a few times in talks to teachers, trying to make the point that we have to clean our own closets; we can't hire somebody to invent and arrange our curriculum. Teaching isn't neat and tidy and predictable; we can't depend on always wearing the green shoes with the amber pin. Or expect kids to learn about the formation of the Finger Lakes.

Closet organization is a pretty good metaphor for teaching as a profession that is not predictable, capable of being pigeonholed, a metaphor for a profession where you have to think about a lot of things at the same time and can never depend on being able to present the same lesson twice. But every time I include this item about the closet organizer in my speeches someone comes up afterwards, asking for the address for the Association of Professional Organizers. Maybe this is an even better metaphor for teaching. We teachers are ever tempted by the elusive promise of a neat and tidy classroom.

Even though plenty of people support Professor Jacques Barzun's contention that "knowing a subject and wanting to teach it are the chief prerequisites to success" in teaching, I'm not given to making similar or even opposite contentions. I do know, though, that teachers who endure and even triumph need to be smart. They also need a sense of humor, a tolerance of ambiguity, a capacity to love and be loved, a willingness never to reach, please pardon the term, *closure*. God, what a term. The grave, a neat and tidy place, is where we will find closure.

When an administrator comes back from a conference that abuts a fancy golf course, I'm not sure exactly where he acquired the wisdom he imparts to us. He decrees that he wants to see teachers circulating, that he doesn't ever again want to catch a teacher sitting behind her desk when there are children in the room. As though being on your feet is synonymous with being on your toes.

Because I am new both to teaching and to seventh and eighth graders, I sign up for a workshop "presenting the realities of classroom management in the urban school." The first night, the consultant passes out a handout titled "Strategies for Developing a System for Maintaining Classroom Control." There are twenty-five precepts. Here are six of them.

- Explain your discipline policy to students. Reason with them about the consequences of cause and effect.
- Make sure students understand your threats. When you make a threat, follow through on it immediately.
- Discuss a student's misbehavior with him in private.
- Be aware that students respond to nonverbal communication cues. Use your eyes, posture, feet to good advantage.
- Find out the discipline policies of your colleagues and administrators.
- Remember that you are a role model for your students.

I kind of wonder why a teacher is making threats. My experience is that threats always land me in a worse situation than the one that provoked the threat. Why should I check in on my colleagues' discipline policies? So I can behave as badly as they do? And just how would I use my feet to good advantage? To kick my students? Or my colleagues? Admittedly, sometimes, when I'm at the end of my rope, kicking someone in the rear would no doubt feel good. In the long range, sure I hope I can offer students an important message that means something to them, but mostly teaching is minute by minute, and I have to remember that I am not a role model. My students don't want to be like me: they want to drive a Cadillac or a Cherokee; they want leather jackets; they want to eat potato chips. They want to go dancin', not sit home readin' and eatin' yogurt.

It's hard to choose a favorite precept from the list of "Strategies for Developing a System for Maintaining Classroom Control," but this one rates high:

- Away from classroom pressures, diagnose specific problems and plan prescriptions for remediation.

I don't know who first came up with a medical model for education, but it was a bad idea, a notion that has done a lot of harm. Assuming that students are a disease that teachers can and should diagnose and remedy reveals an arrogance of position and a contempt for children that is soul-searing. One hears it most often from people who have never sat in a teacher's chair. And second most often from those who haven't sat there for decades.

These days, teaching seems to be divided into two camps: those who think schools should be clinics and those who think schools should be boot camp. Seventh graders have shown me that we could all take a lesson from Garrison Keillor, who describes himself as "a serious man with a knack for the long pause." In our profession, we are well served by not jumping in but, instead, standing back. Teachers' development of a knack for the long pause might well be the best hope for our schools.

Along with cultivation of the long pause, here are a few more rules for classroom management.

- Being fair doesn't mean treating everybody the same way.
- Clean up your own mess. When you cry for help you have to live with the help that's offered.
- Do what you have to do, but don't make threats.
- Losing your temper is better than holding a grudge, but be quick to say you're sorry.
- Don't trust anybody who tries to define or organize what you do.
- Don't worry about the big picture: do good today.
- Laugh every day.
- Cry at least once a week.
- Remember that a seventh grader is a person between the ages of eleven and thirteen who is thinking about sex every three and a half seconds, a person you probably cannot beguile into thinking about the formation of the Finger Lakes or compound interest or the importance of setting in *Johnny Tremain*.
- Don't worry if you gain five pounds; that's only 2.8 Celsius.

4

Making Words Count

In the courses teachers are required to take, professors and textbooks dispassionately report on prepubescent mind-body conflict, on heightened environmental stress, on physical and emotional turmoil, on the significance of being a middle or only child or raised in a one-parent family. The experts report that preteens are insecure, that they suffer from identity problems, that they need to test their limits, and so on and so on. Somehow they manage to make it all sound clinical, antiseptic, predictable, and maybe even manageable. Until you get shut up for six hours a day with a pack of these kids, you cannot begin to imagine, never mind appreciate, what teaching seventh graders is about. Talk to seventh- and eighth-grade teachers who like what they do, and they'll tell you they relish the great exaggerations their students provide. Most longtime teachers of this population acknowledge that you have to be a bit off-center yourself to tarry in seventh grade. For someone who has enjoyed the challenge of seventh grade, ninth and tenth graders can actually seem too staid, too settled.

IT HAS ALWAYS struck me as odd, even contrary to the nature of the enterprise, that administrators and a good many veteran teachers continue to give new seventh-grade teachers that old chestnut of advice, "Don't smile until Christmas." Nothing could be more inappropriate in dealing with kids struggling to make peace with this age of aching vulnerability. Better advice would be, "Don't be reluctant to throw away your lesson plan. Be ready to smile, laugh, howl, guffaw." I have never met a seventh-grade teacher whom I judge "successful" who doesn't have a good sense of humor, a fondness for nonsense, an ability to fool around. Taking affection for children as a given, nothing is so much required of a seventh-grade teacher as adaptability. You just never know who will walk through that door each day. And even when you have gauged the mood of the day correctly, you have to be ready for the climate to change in the time it takes one kid to say "Yo' momma," or otherwise insult, tease, poke, steal from, flirt with, or ignore another kid.

No definitions or case studies can prepare a teacher for the reality of seventh and eighth graders. Ear-blasting laughter one minute, hysterical sobbing or silent pouting the next; the need to be cuddled and comforted in one moment, and the stiff, don't-come-near-me hauteur the next. I learn to react to Shari's dressing and behaving in *Little House on the Prairie* mode on Monday and then showing up on Tuesday looking like a hooker. And acting like one too. As a matter of fact, when Shari's attendance falls way off, I begin to nose around. I find out that she and a friend are spending a lot of time in the nearby college dorms. The counselor phones the dean of students and points out that Shari and her friend might look nineteen on any given day, but that they are only thirteen and the university is on the brink of a scandal. Soon after, Shari grumbles about getting kicked out of the dorms, but her attendance in my class picks up. And she still looks like someone out of *Little House on the Prairie* half the time.

To teach seventh graders is to enter a state of incessant disquiet and incertitude. That's why, when a test I take as part of a National Endowment for the Humanities–funded project to train teachers in art theory indicates that I have a high degree of tolerance for ambiguity, I'm not surprised. Actually, I can't think of a better description of teaching seventh grade: perpetual ambiguity. Nonetheless, neither this university seal of ambiguity sufferance nor ten years of working with difficult students prepares me for Tiffany. Tiffany whines and wheedles her way through each day. Starved for attention and rejected by her peers, Tiffany clings to every adult in the building. When her favorite teacher of the moment becomes exasperated and exhausted by her demands, Tiffany winces and moves on to another teacher, or the nurse or the principal or a hall monitor or the food server in the cafeteria. Whenever any adult offers Tiffany either praise or reproof, she darts back through the same circuit, repeating the details of her encounter. Two weeks into the school year Tiffany has an established retinue of adults she can play for attention.

When Tiffany takes two steps toward me, I have to steel myself not to back away three steps. Give Tiffany even a smidgeon of the attention she craves and she'll adhere to you. Some days I am sure I can feel her tentacles contracting around me. Answer one question and she'll ask sixteen more. Not that Tiffany cares about answers. Most of the time she operates on automatic pilot: She isn't listening—not to her own questions, not to the adult's answers.

Her sole goal is to get—and keep—the teacher's attention, to keep herself in the spotlight. I wonder if Tiffany fears she might disappear if an adult isn't looking at her.

Tiffany responds pretty much the same way whether the adult notice is positive or negative: She blinks rapidly a few times, purses her lips together, and then grins. I can be saying "Good work" in my most congratulatory tone or, "Sit down!" in my most severe; Tiffany invariably grins that little grin. Regardless of my reaction, Tiffany pops up twice a minute with inane questions—"Does a period go here?" "Does this look all right?" "Is the nurse here today?" "Do you know what we're having for lunch?"—until I decree, "No more questions! None. Do not get out of your chair again this period." More often than not, Tiffany gets the last word, whining, "What if I have to go to the bathroom?" But as I come to know Tiffany better, I see the pain behind that grin. And I, who prides myself on letting kids move about as they want—to sharpen their pencils, talk quietly to their classmates, go down the hall to the lavatory, get a drink—wonder how this poor, scruffy, desperate waif of a child can reduce me to such frustration. She is, after all, just twelve years old.

I AM FOREVER GRATEFUL to Tiffany for the way she shows me the folly of an "assertive discipline" type behavioristic scam that entices me for a couple of weeks one desperate February of my discontent. I've been teaching ten years, certainly long enough to know better. I excuse myself by again pointing out that it was February, always a low point in the school year for me. This particular February I become fixated on the fact that not all my students are participating in what I consider to be one of our most important classroom practices—the daily exchange of notes between students and teacher. Some of the kids are slipping through the cracks. Tempted by a journal article about the importance of student accountability, I make a giant chart listing everybody's name alongside a grid of squares. According to my dictum, every time someone hands in his little three-by-five spiral notebook with the day's note inside, he colors in a square next to his name with a magic marker. Students seem to like this system a lot, enjoy seeing those squares colored in next to their names. There is a renewed flurry around the can that holds the notebooks.

But it doesn't take me two weeks to see that kids seem to be spending more time counting how many colored squares they have amassed than chuckling over my notes to them or writing their responses. They begin to accuse each other of cheating—coloring in squares without writing the notes. I notice that Tiffany, always a faithful note writer, has more squares colored in than anybody else. The only problem is, she has more squares filled in than there are days since we've been following this procedure.

So I set a new rule. I am the only one permitted to color the squares. I bring in a special bright purple magic marker. When a student hands me a note, I drop what I am doing, go to the chart, and ceremoniously color in a square next to the student's name.

It doesn't take Tiffany two days to figure this one out. She brings in her own bright purple marker and colors squares in as she feels the need. She doesn't just color squares opposite her name but uses the marker as her ace in the hole. Classmates who are nice to Tiffany can use her bright purple marker. I've always felt a bit proud that I am the one teacher in our district who stands firm in my refusal to take in-service training in a behavioral course in positive thinking, a course which directs participants to stand in front of a mirror and practice saying, "I like the way Jane is sitting quietly." Nonetheless, I now have to admit that the purple marker is just about as demeaning to me and my students as those pat positive phrases. I have taken one of the joys of our day, sharing notes, and turned it into a numbers game. Hats off to Tiffany for showing me the error of my ways. No student protests when I dump the chart in the trash can. Tiffany just grins.

SCRAPPING THE CHART doesn't turn Tiffany into a model student. When we are working on recording the first signs of spring, Tiffany turns in a typically careless, lazy piece of writing: "Flowers make me happy. Warm weather makes me happy. I am happy in spring." I can't hold back my sigh of exasperation. We'd been working on this project for two weeks. We've had some terrific discussions, looked at some beautiful books, searched the newspapers for signs of spring, read spring poems, taken an observation walk around the neighborhood. As homework, students have conducted fun-filled and information-packed interviews, asking people in the community what they notice about the emerging season. After two weeks of just being awake in our classroom, this is Tiffany's product? I figure that Tiffany had remembered the assignment was due the period before mine and dashed off this piece in the locker area between classes—an effort that would still have given her plenty of time to clean her locker and get a drink.

I am a rather relaxed sort of teacher, eager to recognize and accommodate the special needs of students, refusing to impose external guidelines on what the children and I need to do. I try to stand up to unreal expectations sent forth from national commissions on excellence or local syllabus-drafting groups. But I am fierce about some matters. I give a lot to my students, and I expect them to exert a similar level of effort. I do not allow them to take the easy way out. I have plenty of seventh graders who read on a first-grade level, and I expect them to work hard with those first-grade skills. From Tiffany, who reads fluently at a fifth-grade level, and, when inspired, can handle more difficult texts, I will not accept such careless, thoughtless *happy/sappy* drivel. In telling Tiffany very directly that her work is not acceptable, I know I've probably violated sixty-two tenets preached in articles on adolescent development, not to mention writing process. One problem is that I have never seen *my* students pictured in those neat, cheery little articles, those articles showing kids holding conferences with their peers and then earnestly going off to a quiet corner of the room to revise their work. My curriculum coordinator, who has never taught elementary or secondary students but has a degree in curriculum development and issues edicts such as "Students will utilize writing process to revise," hasn't met Tiffany. I haven't met a seventh grader about whom I can announce that the student will utilize anything. *Will*, indeed. The best one can say about seventh graders is that on a good day, *the student might.*

For starters, Tiffany has no peers who will come near her, never mind conference with her. Tiffany is unkempt and often unwashed; she is also bossy, sneaky, and whiny. She deliberately provokes rejection and even violence. I think of the day Tiffany walks into the girls' locker room and complains loudly about the "dirty niggers" in our school. Then, after she escapes from two students who confront her about this remark, she runs to the office in hysterics. When the principal finally gets her calmed down enough to be able to understand what she is saying, Tiffany insists she has no idea why two black girls would suddenly jump on her and pull her hair. When he has heard the whole story, the principal tells Tiffany that she has gotten off pretty lightly, but she remains adamant in her refusal to acknowledge that she has done anything to provoke anybody's anger.

I halfway suspect that the principal had been busy earlier that day and had brushed aside Tiffany's perpetual round of questions when she dropped by his office on her daily rounds. Unable to get his attention, she headed off to the gym and caused a near riot to make it impossible for him not to notice her. I'm speculating here, but this scenario is very plausible. It is the way Tiffany works.

No seventh grader will sit cheerfully—or even begrudgingly—with Tiffany and advise her on her writing, but I'm not going to let her manipulate me into rewarding her once again for unacceptable work by sitting with her one-on-one and discussing her "piece." I tell Tiffany her work is unsatisfactory. "What's wrong?" she whines. "It's spelled right." Ah, does she know that there is a history of wrong-minded pedagogy in such a remark? Get them to spell it right and the world will beat a path to your door, offering riches and fame.

"That's not nearly good enough," I insist. I tell her that stringing a few correctly spelled words together doesn't mean that she's said anything. "*You* aren't in this writing. You need to show what you think, show your opinions through an example." Tiffany, of course, is immediately hurt. She grabs her paper out of my hand, wads it up, and starts to walk away, not able to hear my suggestions for the next step. The product of five years of remedial reading, Tiffany sees the sole object of any assignment as simply turning it in. Get something on paper so that the page isn't blank, and then get rid of it fast. If you spell everything correctly, you're home free. Years of working through workbooks and mountains of skill sheets have conditioned Tiffany into producing paper piles. Quantity counts for everything; nobody expects quality from remedial kids.

Not much is expected of remedial kids in other classes, either. Students are given an easy out: do your pages and you're off the hook. I once watched Tiffany and her classmates sitting in the library, copying out passages from the encyclopedia. And I saw firsthand what I had long suspected, that students had good reason for their cynical assessment of what school expected of them. I asked Tiffany what she was writing so furiously. "Four pages," she answered.

"No," I persisted. "I don't mean how long. I mean what topic?"

"Oh, our teacher doesn't care. It just has to be four pages." I don't think Tiffany has it in her to be cynical enough to make that up, but I don't see how she can be right either. So I ask her teacher. He patiently explains to me that her interpretation is indeed correct. "It teaches them self-discipline," he intones. "These students can't possibly understand the sophisticated and abstract concept demanded in our social studies text or our departmental guidelines. That's hopeless. But students can learn to follow directions and to hand assignments in on time. They learn that when I say four pages, I mean four pages. If they hand in three and a half, they fail." He goes on to explain the other requirements that teach his students self-discipline. Papers have to be written in blue ink on blue-lined college-rule paper with a red margin down the left-hand side. It is a simple formula. Form is all. Content is nothing. Get the form down, and you are guaranteed an 80 on the report card.

Students interpreted these edicts literally. Laurie, also one of my students, is copying the encyclopedia entry on Patrick Henry and only manages to fill 3 pages of her college-rule paper. Not one bit fazed, she finishes copying the last word in the Patrick Henry entry and goes right on with half a page about William Henry, British physician and chemist, the next entry in the encyclopedia. I am sure Laurie has no notion of the accomplishments or the era of either Henry. Her charge, after all, is to copy, not to comprehend. And copy she does—no more and no less than the assignment requires. When she reaches the bottom of the fourth page of her college rule paper, Laurie stops in the middle of a sentence. Assignment completed—proof she is a self-disciplined, upstanding student, able and willing to follow directions, proving herself worthy to pass social studies.

I may be disappointed in her teacher, but I don't hold him in total contempt. He is a decent fellow; he treats children decently. He even cares about them. But he is handed an impossible curriculum and impossible texts and told that "all students can learn it." If a teacher has the habit of mind to follow rules, then what is he supposed to do with such a mandate? I doubt that we can insist that everybody be a revolutionary. And when our education leaders finally acknowledge that children like Laurie and Tammy aren't learning anything, they step in to solve the problem by raising the standards for all, making wrong-headed curriculum even more wrong-headed.

I READ our district language arts syllabus, which has been lifted without acknowledgment from the state department of education language arts syllabus, and then I bury it in a paper pile in a cupboard, never to cross my line of vision again. I can't say I find it ridiculous; I find it incomprehensible. Such a document has no meaning to my life with seventh graders. If students are to make some sense out of school, even find some moments of intellectual satisfaction, then we must get beyond the politics and bureaucratic bumbling of such paper piles.

What I do next with Tiffany is unplanned, strictly an act of frustration and irritation. In retrospect, I wonder if my plan wasn't inspired as much by a desire to be rid of the sound of Tiffany's whining and wheedling for a few minutes as anything else. I grab her arm and say, "Bring a pencil and a piece of paper. You are going to the library." She looks scared. My irritation is obvious and, with her social studies assignments in the library as a frame of reference, I'm sure she has visions of copying six hundred pages out of the encyclopedia before I'll be satisfied. By the time we get to the library my irritation has vanished. I remind myself, "This child has known more misery in twelve years than most of us will know in fifty. She doesn't know who her father is, and her mother pretty much abandoned her, showing up at odd moments and then disappearing again. She lives with an old woman she calls Grandma, but there isn't any blood relationship. Grandma has some sort of arrangement with the county welfare system to provide Tammy a residence. How does a twelve-year-old cope with the knowledge that everybody who is supposed to care for her has abandoned her and that someone has to be paid to provide her a home?

I put my arm around Tiffany's shoulders, saying, "I am going to show you a very special book. What you do with it is up to you, but it could turn into a real treasure chest if you let it." I sit her down in front of a thesaurus and turn to the word *happy*. "You used the word *happy* in that short paper you wrote. Take a look at all the other words that mean happy." Tiffany starts reading the words aloud. She is astonished. She loves *whooped with joy* and *purred*. "Can I have them?" she asks me.

For a moment I am taken aback. *Have* seems an odd word for her to use. But then I realize that Tiffany, who doesn't understand the first thing about prewriting, composing, and revising, just might have discovered a vital writing concept all by herself. She has intuitively grasped the necessity of taking charge of words, of holding them close and possessing them. She sees that if you like the look and the sound of a word, then you want to own that word, to carry it off to some private place and admire it. For the first time in her schooling, Tiffany has encountered some words that she wants to own. It is a breathtaking moment—for both of us.

"Sure," I respond. "Pick out any words you like. Once you find them, they will be yours, for as long as you want them." I give her another squeeze, adding, "And can remember them. To own words, you have to know them. Once you forget a word, it disappears."

"Oh, I'll remember them." Tiffany's reaction combines the typical emotional intensity of a seventh grader with her own instinct for survival, which includes a certain canniness. As a practical matter, I'm sure Tiffany figures it can't hurt to try to please a teacher who just a few minutes before was in a snit. But Tiffany's reaction mostly transcends all that. It is one of those crystal moments of discovery, awareness, an opening of new worlds. All these years later, I still get goose bumps just thinking about it. I like to think the feeling, if not the precise circumstance, has stayed with Tiffany too.

Tiffany treats those words as though they are the secret code to mark a hidden treasure. She writes down *whooped* and *purred* because she likes the sound of them and because, she adds softly, her cat is her one true friend. Then she picks *rhapsodize*. She asks me to pronounce it and then tries it out a few times on her own. She likes the way it sounds too, but she picks it mainly because it is long and complicated and she is sure none of the other kids will know it. "If I rewrite my story, can I use *rhapsodize*?" she asks.

"Sure, if you want to," I agree, trying to sound offhand, trying not to whoop a bit myself. It seems important that I treat Tiffany's sudden desire to rewrite a piece as a natural, commonplace event. It seems especially important that I not intrude on her independence and discovery with praise. The realization that it must be the student's work, the student's piece of writing, the student's independence is not an insight that comes automatically or easily to me. Maybe being a writer myself makes me a meddler, makes it harder for me to restrain myself from jumping in and inflicting some hard-core editing on my students. I shudder to think what havoc some heavy-handed, tone-deaf editors I've known would wreak in classrooms. But in any case, by the time Tiffany and I arrive at that moment in the library, I've had more than a decade in classrooms to work on my own self-restraint, and so in that moment I do the right thing: I step back, warn myself to keep "hands off," and leave Tiffany to deal with her moment of opportunity.

Tiffany is assigned to Language Arts Tutorial for two consecutive periods, and when she returns to the classroom an hour later, she asks if she can go back to the library and show Melanie "that treasure chest of words." Melanie looks doubtful about going anywhere with Tiffany, but a chance to get out of class, to socialize in the halls, to check out who is in the library, is not to be missed—even if Tiffany is the one providing her ticket out.

I'm sure Tiffany makes her selection after due deliberation. Melanie is a star attraction. Amiable, pretty, full of fun—everybody likes Melanie. Even teachers. A with-it, confident kid, Melanie is the first one to deliberately wear mismatched kneesocks, the first to sport seven rings on her fingers and three earrings in each ear, the first to wear her sweaters inside out. When Melanie steps outside the borders of convention, we know we are witnessing the start of a trend.

My heart goes out to Tiffany, wishing she hadn't been quite so ambitious in the pal she's picked to take to the library. I figure that as soon as they get there, Melanie will drop her fast. I am wrong. When they come back half an hour later, I hear Melanie thank Tiffany for showing her "that neat book." Tiffany later tells me that they had started with *happy* and then looked up a few more words. Before the end of the day, Tiffany has informed half the school about *rhapsodize*. The librarian, the nurse, the hall monitor, and even a few more kids she's managed to coax into the library, all know she has found a great book.

The next day the principal stops me. "I can't believe it. When Tiffany appears in my office, I always want to duck. I know there's either going to be a riot or hysterics or just a whole string of lies to work my way through. And when she comes in wearing that goofy grin, I know I'm really in for it. Yesterday when she started going on and on about *rhapsodize*, I was sure she'd been eating silly pills for lunch." He sees me stiffen. "Only kidding. I even went to the library with her and looked at that book. Actually, I'm wondering if we should get it gold plated. At the very least we should get steel covers. Tiffany's going to have it worn out in a week. She had half the school traipsing in there to look at it. Knowing Tiffany, I expect the whole South End to be lining up today."

At the end of the year Tiffany does well enough on standardized tests to make her ineligible for my class in eighth grade. How's that for news: a remedial reader gets delabeled. Actually, about 30 percent of our seventh graders score out of the program at the end of the year. Tiffany is gone but not forgotten. She still writes me notes. Occasionally she adds a P.S.: "I still have *rhapsodize!*"

Okay, I confess. I had half a dozen thesauruses in the classroom. I showed Tiffany the one in the library as an excuse for getting her out of sight for a while. More important, the thesaurus lesson worked well for a particular kid on a particular day. That did not inspire me to rush out and plan thesaurus lessons for all the other kids. One of the mistakes we make over and over in education is trying to universalize the particular. Here and there over the years, I have shown quite a few students how a thesaurus works. Nobody else ever took to it the way Tiffany did. I'm proud I thought of it at that moment. I'm proud it worked for Tiffany. That's enough. Let the politicians and the educrats make their pronouncements about "all students." For me, being a teacher means taking pride and pleasure in the particular. One student on one day. Having a storage chest full of ideas and strategies at the ready isn't enough. Being a teacher means having the savvy to know when and how to use each one.

EMILY IS ANOTHER of my students for whom words acquire a special meaning, though I'm not at all sure I will ever understand just what that meaning is. Emily is one of those quiet, pleasant, passive children who sit in classrooms year after year, never volunteering a word. Emily is such a good, polite little girl that by the time she reaches junior high, she has never been in remedial reading. Her eighth-grade science teacher is astounded that Emily is not receiving extra help and sends her to me. Emily sits with her vague little smile all day, not understanding an assignment but never asking for help. If I ask her directly, "Do you understand this?" she just looks at me, reluctant to admit incomprehension. I'm not at all sure that Emily understands what she doesn't understand. Asking questions about some elements of a text is a sophisticated process, one requiring comprehension of the surrounding text. Even though I know better, some days I plead, "Emily, *please* ask for help when you don't understand something. That's what I'm here for—to help you. Besides, I like helping you." Emily blushes and hangs her head. And sits there quietly until the next time I check on her.

Emily never misses a day in our note exchange. Our exchange seems unexceptional until the day I pose to Emily this question: "What is your favorite flower?" This introduces a theme that lasts for months. Emily replies, "Red rose, yellow rose, blue rose, and pink rose or zinnia."

I am delighted to have struck a chord and answer,

Dear Emily,

Here's a poem for you by a woman named Elizabeth Coatsworth. I like it a lot and hope you do too.

> Violets, daffodils
> Roses and thorn . . .

From that point on, Emily's note to me consists of lists of flowers. One day her note is

Carnations, sweet william, baby's breath.

Emily

That's it: the whole note. The next day it is

Daisies and marigolds.

Emily

I always sign my notes, "Your friend, Mrs. O," and most of the kids copy this format. But Emily doesn't give me any salutation, just her name. I write Emily questions about some of the flowers in her lists, but she doesn't answer me. She just keeps writing those lists:

Bloodroot, pansy, tansy, tulip, dandelion, milkweed, iris, baptisia.

Emily

Dogtooth violet, lady's slipper, jack-in-the-pulpit.

Emily

Wild rose, gold rose, honeysuckle, cactus, black-eyed Susan, sweetpea, four-o'clock, Queen Anne's lace, butterfly bush, morning glory, lily of the valley, harebell, thistle, bardock.

Emily

I can't imagine where Emily is getting all these names. Then one day I see her taking a big, fat *Encyclopedia of Gardening* out of her book bag. Sometimes her lists are short; sometimes they are long, but no matter what I say in my notes, Emily just keeps giving me more flower names in hers. One day I don't answer her note, figuring it doesn't really matter; after all, she doesn't seem to be paying any attention to what I say. She isn't answering my questions or commenting on any of my funny stories. Emily, however, is quite indignant when she doesn't have a new message from me. She drops her memo pad on my desk and complains, "You forgot to answer my letter." I apologize and write her a note.

Why don't I just ask Emily what's going on? I don't know—except I have a feeling something cosmic is occurring. Students and I rarely talk about the content of our note exchange; the real beauty of the notes is that we do our "talking" in the notes. I don't question Emily about her notes, never ask, "Emily, why do you write all these flower names?" because I don't want to jinx anything. I just treat our exchange as a regular part of our day and continue writing her notes, letting Emily work out whatever she's working out. I guess I operate on the principle that "the mystery will be revealed one day." And in the meantime, don't meddle.

Finally, one Thursday a couple of months after Emily wrote her first flower list, she sends me a hint that she is indeed paying careful attention to my notes. I write,

Dear Emily,

Peony! I love peonies. I'd forgotten about peonies until you mentioned them in your note. Thank you for reminding me.

How about *butter*cups, sweet*peas, milk*weed? Would you like to eat them for dinner?

Your friend, Mrs. O

Emily replies:

Dear Mrs. O,

Houseleek, stapelia, arrowhead, wild columbine, halachoe, tritoma, clover, may*apple, strawberry* geranium. No I do not eat plants.

Emily

After this one small breakthrough, Emily's lists continue as usual. The lists, in fact, get longer. Every day I write Emily funny stories about my cats, complaints about shoveling snow, what I did over the weekend. Every day she gives me lists of flowers. Then I begin to write about how much I am looking forward to spring, and Emily surprises me again.

Dear Mrs. O,

It is supposed to get to 65° today.

Your friend, Emily

The "Your friend, Emily" is in tiny letters, almost too small to decipher. I want to whoop with joy. I write her a spring poem in reply, and then ask her a question. "If you had a choice of any place in the world, Emily, where would you like to visit?" Over the months, I have asked Emily fifty or more questions in my notes, all of which she calmly ignored. But here comes another answer.

Dear Mrs. O,

> Portland, Oregon.
> Brown and furry caterpillar in a hurry,
> Take your walk to this shady leaf or stalk,
> May no toad spy you
> May the little birds pass by you;
> Spin and die,
> To live again a butterfly.

Christina Georgina Rossetti and Emily

What a gift. Of course I am thrilled. I write back, telling Emily how much the poem delights me. I include a short poem about butterflies in my note and ask Emily another question: "What do you like about butterflies?" And here comes another answer:

Dear Mrs. O,

They look pretty and all the different butterflies and special colors and it would be nice to fly.

> In spring the chirping frogs
> Sing like birds . . . in summer
> They bark like old dogs.

Onitsura and Emily

This is the last question Emily answers for another two months. Every day she gives me a poem in her note, and I give her one back in mine. And I always ask her a question, not knowing what may spark another response. One day Emily reads my note and storms up to my desk. "You just took *my* poem," she complains. "I was going to give that one to you today." We agree that it is pretty nice when two people like the same poems so much that they want to give them to each other. Emily shows me that she has started a scrapbook of poems, a hoard of poems she likes and hopes I will too.

Sometime during the flower list notes, Emily begins bringing me a flower every day. Some days they are silk, other days they are real. Emily lives with her grandparents and works in their nursery. In class, she opens up a bit, revealing her extensive knowledge about flower cultivation. One of our class projects is for students to prepare a talk for their classmates about something they know how to do. To my surprise, Emily, who rarely communicates with other students, is enthusiastic about this project. She brings in a lot of material and demonstrates how gardeners graft plants to produce new species. Emily is knowledgeable and articulate, and her classmates are amazed—and interested. Emily's demonstration goes so well, she agrees to present it to all my classes. She also gives the talk in her science class.

When Emily is in high school, she drops by occasionally "just to say hi." I always ask her how she likes her courses. She always smiles her vague little smile and replies, "Fine." When Emily is a senior she brings me a poinsettia at Christmas. "I hope you still like flowers," she smiles. Then she asks the question that every student who comes back to visit asks: "Do you still write those notes to kids?" It is the part of the curriculum that most returning students ask about. My answer continues to be yes.

After Emily graduates from high school, and yes, she does get a diploma, something that dismays the current corporate-politico power brokers, she starts sending me a card at Christmas and another one in April, a Happy Spring card. For a few years she includes a short note, and these notes break my heart. Each year I can see diminished verbal facility. The spring cards drop off. Then one Christmas, there is no note. Emily sends a huge, elaborate card with a poem copied out on a separate piece of paper stuck inside. This pattern continues for another few years: No personal message about how she's doing, no comment on what I have written her, but always a poem. Twice a year I send her a card. I always tell her something about what I'm doing, tell her about my cats, and I always ask her a question. I know she reads the cards because she has paid attention to my changes of address. Her address hasn't changed.

Most years Emily has signed the cards, "Your friend, Emily." Last year her salutation was, "Your friend always, I love you, Emily." This year her card makes me weep. No poem. No salutation. Just the one word: Emily. Her name is written in the tiny letters I remember from our note exchange fifteen years ago. Emily haunts me forever. I never did figure out what poetry meant to her. I can only hope she still has it.

5

Writing Because We Want To

a note from Susan Ohanian

6/6
TO: Dr. Marcella White, Vice Principal
RE: Next Year's Schedule

This is just to confirm our recent conversation about my planning period running back to back with my supervisory and lunch periods so that I can conduct a writer's workshop in the upper level of the media center during that time. I very much appreciate your support of my efforts.

a note from Susan Ohanian

9/6
TO: Dr. Marcella White, Vice Principal
RE: Writer's Workshop

I am ready to begin writer's workshop. Over the summer I scrounged two more manual typewriters from the business department at the high school. Do you think we could get typing stands for them? I would also appreciate your directing the custodians to move the two file cabinets in my classroom to the writer's workshop area of the mezzanine.

Teachers Association Alert

9/10
TO: Susan Ohanian
FROM: Ann Burke, Building Rep

The policy of the teachers association is that teachers should not volunteer to teach extra classes. It sets a dangerous precedent.

WHAT IS VOLUNTEERED TODAY MAY BE REQUIRED TOMORROW.

cc: NYSUT Regional Field Representative

a note from Susan Ohanian

9/10
Ann,

I am not volunteering to teach an extra class. I am asking that I be allowed to run a workshop during my supervisory period rather than spend my time guarding the lavatories against kids' smoking. I would point out to the association that these two activities take the same amount of teacher time and attention.

Susan

Teachers Association Alert

9/16
TO: Susan Ohanian
FROM: Ann Burke, Building Rep

Please be advised that the teachers association is going to protest your assignment during your contractual supervisory period to the upper level of the media center. Contractually, you can be required to monitor lavatories; you cannot be required to supervise students.

WHAT IS VOLUNTEERED TODAY MAY BE REQUIRED TOMORROW.

cc: NYSUT Regional Field Representative

ENLARGED CITY SCHOOL DISTRICT
OFFICE OF THE SUPERINTENDENT
THOMAS C. MANCINI

10/3
TO: MS. SUSAN O'HANIAN
FROM: THOMAS C. MANCINI
RE: RELEASE FROM SUPERVISORY PERIOD

IT HAS COME TO MY ATTENTION THAT YOU HAVE REQUESTED TO BE RELEASED FROM YOUR SUPERVISORY PERIOD. I WILL AGREE TO ALLOW THIS ON A ONETIME BASIS ONLY, WITH THE STIPULATION THAT THIS ACTION SETS NO PRECEDENT.

PLEASE SIGN ALL FOUR COPIES OF THE ENCLOSED AGREEMENT TESTIFYING THAT THIS AGREEMENT IMPLIES NO REMUNERATION FOR EXTRACURRICULAR ACTIVITY, ESTABLISHES NO PRECEDENT, AND CAN BE WITHDRAWN WITH TWENTY-FOUR HOURS' NOTICE.

THE TEACHERS ASSOCIATION REPRESENTATIVE IS BEING ASKED TO SIGN THE SAME AGREEMENT.

CC: TEACHERS ASSOCIATION
    J. B. FENSON, ATTORNEY AT LAW

ENLARGED CITY SCHOOL DISTRICT
COORDINATOR OF LANGUAGE ARTS
JOHN PARACHINI, ED.D.

10/19
TO: FACULTY
RE: WRITING CLUB

SUSAN O'HANIAN IS CONDUCTING A WRITING CLUB EVERY DAY IN THE UPPER MEDIA CENTER FROM 11:40 TO 12:50. STUDENTS ARE INVITED TO COME ANY TIME DURING THIS PERIOD. THEY SHOULD PLAN TO STAY AT LEAST 15 MINUTES. THEY SHOULD COME AT LEAST ONCE A WEEK, MORE OFTEN IF THEY WISH AND IT FITS YOUR SCHEDULE.

MRS. O'HANIAN WILL WORK WITH STUDENTS ON AN INDIVIDUALIZED BASIS, BUT A BOOKLET HAS ALREADY BEEN DISCUSSED BY THE GROUP. CLUB PARTICIPANTS HAVE ALSO DISCUSSED THE POSSIBILITY OF VISITING ELEMENTARY SCHOOLS TO READ THEIR WORK.

Whew! As E. B. White once confessed, "I don't know which is more discouraging: literature or chickens." Every teacher who has ever tried to get her schedule changed must know what he means. It has taken nearly a year to convince school officials to let me run a writer's workshop during my hall-duty period and my own lunch break—about one and a half hours a day in total. Of course, I've been working in the district more than ten years and they still haven't gotten it into their heads that my name is spelled without an apostrophe.

It has been a difficult, solitary struggle against bureaucracy. I guess I shouldn't be surprised to learn once again that a union can be just as bureaucratic as any bunch of administrators. It is neither the first nor the last time my union will demonstrate this fact to me. I began my teaching career quite literally in the middle of another teacher's lesson plan in New York City. I began on a Wednesday, replacing a teacher who moved on to a union job. That Wednesday happened to be parent conferences, so I found myself in the rather unique position of meeting the parents of my students before I'd laid eyes on the students. I've never had a whole lot of respect for anybody who could pull such a stunt. Couldn't he stay in the classroom one more day?

Then, in that same first year of teaching I complained to the United Federation of Teachers (UFT) that the New York City Board of Education was refusing to pay me at the master's-level salary rate because I hadn't signed the right form. I didn't sign the form because I didn't know it existed. The union invited me to its office on Park Avenue South, where I confronted this ocean of desks manned by people talking on the phone. It looked even more bureaucratic than the school board offices at 110 Livingston Street. A UFT official had called me there to inform me, "Hundreds of teachers are in the same fix. There's nothing we can do." Somehow, the logic of this explanation escapes me. Shouldn't hundreds of teachers being in the same fix provoke union action? I took the matter into my own hands, writing a series of letters to the *New York Times*, accusing the paper of accepting false advertising, since they printed board of ed ads stating a certain salary, and they continued to print these ads after I informed them that teachers were not being compensated accordingly. Four months later, I received a check from the New York City board of ed. No explanation. Just a check.

In Ilium, nobody, administrators or unionites, wants me to do the writing workshop, but I finally wear them down. Wouldn't you think that everybody would be delighted that a teacher wants to spend an extra one and a half hours or so a day encouraging seventh and eighth graders to love writing? Not so. The administrators worry that I've hatched some devious union plot to subvert teachers' contractual obligations. The union worries that I have become the unwitting tool of some administrative scheme to subvert the same contract and trick teachers into teaching an extra period. Nobody trusts Freud's

observation that sometimes a cigar is just a cigar—that I simply prefer organizing a writer's workshop to patrolling the lavatories.

What actually happened is that I woke up one morning and decided
that five years of lavatory duty was enough. I also felt demeaned and demor-
alized by my vagabond status during the lunch break. A schedule reorga-
nization claimed my classroom, and I can no longer sit in there during lunch.
This leaves me the choice of hanging out in the faculty room or venturing
into the cafeteria. So offering up my twenty-seven-minute lunch break for
writer's workshop is offering more of a sow's ear than a silk purse. Even so, the
union and the administrators dither. And no colleagues line up to support
my cause. Those who don't think I'm out of my mind are threatened by my
volunteerism, agreeing with the union that it is the first step on a slippery
slope leading to some sort of teacher gulag. The sad fact is that many teachers
would rather patrol the lavatories than sit with kids. But that's their problem.
Not mine.

I have no idea who might show up to writer's workshop, but by the end
of the second week a pattern begins to emerge. Four eighth-grade girls come
every day. I quickly figure out that the lure of writer's workshop is not the
prospect of writing or using the typewriters but rather the promise of peace
and quiet. The girls hate the noise of the cafeteria as much as I do. After this
group has been attending for a couple of weeks, their honors English teacher
gives them a pass to attend for half their English class period, so I see them
several hours a week. Not that they take all that much note of me. This tal-
ented clique spend much of their time talking over eighth-grade facts of life,
ignoring all other workshop participants—and me—as much as they can.
Nonetheless, because these girls are long used to producing work schools
judge as excellent without expending much thought or energy, they also manage to be major contributors to the anthologies the workshop produces. And
they don't even have to interrupt their conversations for long to accomplish
this end.

Jolene appears every day with a pass from her seventh-grade science class.
She always brings her science text with her and copies out passages in response to questions on a worksheet from her teacher. Jolene works on science
for about half the period and then watches other students in the workshop.
She watches a lot and eventually writes a little. Jolene's teacher expresses enthusiasm about her being in workshop, but neither he nor Jolene ever explain
just why she comes here to do her science assignments instead staying in science class. Many years of hanging out in schools have shown me that sometimes you're better off not asking. As usual, I have a theory: Jolene's teacher is
a nice enough fellow, but he is as loud and excitable as any seventh grader, always talking in exclamation marks. I suspect Jolene craves the peace and quiet

of workshop, and he's good-natured enough, and kid-savvy enough, to let her do what she wants to do.

Lots of kids come by the workshop once or twice just to check things out. Once they find out that nothing much is happening nor likely to happen, they disappear forever. Three wannabe hoodlums show up the second week. They spend their time pestering the honors English girls. Two move on to the greater possibilities for mayhem available in the cafeteria, but one, Rick, stays on. The girls continue to ignore Rick, and I manage to outlast his nonstop high jinks and even prod him into an occasional piece of writing. Although his production remains sporadic, he is so amazed at seeing his work in print in our first publication that he begins to get passes from his English class to come sit in writer's workshop. I say "sit" because Rick is, after all, an eighth grader, and he is always more interested in pestering the girls than in writing. Nonetheless, his teacher insists that Rick's workshop attendance spurs a "miraculous transformation" in his class work. This inspires me to develop a construct elucidating the relationship of change of scenery to miraculous transformation of eighth-grade performance.

One of my theories about being a teacher is that those of us who stay the course are sustained and even exhilarated by minuscule shifts in student behavior. We become expert at noticing those tiny transitions. Other people see adolescents as a menacing, undifferentiated mass. We teachers notice individual tics. Not since my first year as a reading teacher have I believed in or been willing to stake my reputation on the "two-years-growth-in-seven-months" claims of the hucksters. I have two questions about such claims:

- If those remedial readers really make those kinds of gains, how come they never get out of remedial reading?
- What is a year's growth in reading, anyway? What does it mean when people label a kid a 4.6 in reading? What do we know about him that is different from a 6.4? Let us talk about these differences rather than continue to count the numbers.

FROM THE OPENING DAY, Cindy is a workshop regular, and she is the one who makes a lasting impression, another one of those kids who leaves her mark on me forever. Cindy teaches me that seventh graders need not be tricked, cajoled, menaced, or bribed into performing. I am both chagrined and ashamed to admit that for a while I totally misread Cindy because I harbor a certain prejudice; after all, I taught two of her older brothers. I knew the boys when I taught at an alternative high school. They were pushed out of the regular high school because they were, in the lingo of the guidance department, "reluctant to conform to minimum academic standards." They were, to borrow again from Herndon, a pair of nasty little shits. Despite the fact that there were only forty students in our school—with two teachers and one counselor available to offer an individualized curriculum and a lot of personal attention—and they only had to sit in class for three hours a day, the boys didn't succeed with us either. Succeed? They barely made it through the front door.

The boys' parents, one an eighth-grade graduate and the other who completed ninth grade, were caring and concerned. They came to our alternative high school a number of times and talked over the problems their sons were having both at home and at school. Our conversations consisted mainly of mutual commiseration and hand-wringing. No matter what anybody says, you can offer as enticing a program as possible, but nobody can make anybody do anything. Not without cattle prods, anyway.

Looking at Cindy, I remember the conversations with my colleagues after the parents left the school; we repeated a line familiar to so many teachers: "If the parents don't read, how can you expect the kids to read? If the parents sit in front of the TV [or out at the bar], how do their children learn to behave differently?" And so on. We were earnest teachers. We cared about our students, we worked hard, we tried to "keep up" professionally, and we tried to reach those boys. But after seven months of resisting our every effort to lure them into our curriculum, the boys dropped out of school and concentrated full-time on their lives of crime. So when I meet Cindy six years later, I make the mistake of thinking I know quite a bit about her as soon as I learn of her family connections. Cindy proves me wrong. I have since read *Born to Rebel* by Frank Sulloway, the MacArthur Genius Award recipient who documents how different siblings are from each other—a person tends to have more in common with any randomly chosen person of their own age than with a sibling—and why this is so. Cindy demonstrates this phenomenon to me before I read the research, convincing me that birds that flock together are definitely *not* of a feather.

Six years after Cindy's two brothers drop out of our alternative program, I am back in a mainstream school. I might be doing my job as irregularly as I think I can get away with, but I am a regular, tenured, certified English teacher. Well, almost regular. I teach something called language arts tutorial, a class for the seventh and eighth graders with bottom-of-the-barrel skills. In the language of the trade, they are "reluctant readers." Premier reading researcher and practitioner Dick Allington once called such kids rotten readers, a term I like for its directness. It cuts to the bone, unmasking the euphemism and the jargon. These kids have one thing in common: they can't read. We sympathetic experts can talk till the cows come home about their street smarts, their resiliency, their other intelligences, their creativity, athletic ability, manual dexterity, sense of humor, ability to bet the horses, or whatever. But their deficiency in being able to get any meaning, never mind pleasure, from the printed page scars them.

Cindy is not a great reader, but she isn't a rotten one either. Cindy shows up to writer's workshop on the first day because she's heard about the big old Royal manual typewriters. Like every kid who gets free use of a typewriter, she types her name and her friends' names over and over, trying to see how fast she can do this. Once she has typed her name and her siblings' names and her friends' names 116 times, she is willing to try a writing project I suggest. I look at her first feeble attempts and mentally peg her "dull average." I give workshop participants the task of updating Mother Goose verses. Cindy draws a blank. To her, a printed text is final. The idea of altering it is too revolutionary to consider.

But she enjoys reading the efforts of other participants. The clever revisions of some of the honors English crew inspire Cindy to try rewriting "Mary Had a Little Lamb," but she can't bring herself to break away from the original enough to change either the words or the situation. Finally she copies the original nursery rhyme and—with great derring-do—changes the words at the end of each line.

Cindy comes to workshop every lunch period. Then she extends her stay by persuading her social studies teacher to let her out of class. Other children are also prying passes out of their teachers, but Cindy is the champion. I keep the writer's workshop open one and a half hours a day. Those who come only during the lunch break spend approximately two and a half hours a week in workshop. Before long, Cindy is averaging from five to seven hours a week.

If I don't directly "teach" Cindy to write, I nonetheless insist that I am her teacher. Most often, one's teacherliness is manifested in ways that won't show up on one of those tapes hopeful applicants mail in to the professional standards board. The best moments in teaching are a result of knowing when to keep quiet as much as anything else. Rather like that classic movie of Andy Warhol eating a mushroom, to outsiders not a whole lot seems to be happening. We teachers need to know when to step back instead of stepping in. When not to help, when not to explain. An important part of who we are is what we choose not to do. But this silent attention is the opposite of passive behavior. I'm always conscious of myself as an important, if indirect, catalyst for what happens in a classroom or in a lunchtime workshop. Call it potential catalyst. Always waiting for the ready moment, ever watchful for what David Hawkins calls the bird in the window. As Hawkins points out, if we aren't ready for that bird, ready and able to capitalize on its unexpected appearance, then it never happens.

At first, Cindy doesn't seem to do much. She practices her typing and reads everybody else's work. Then she begins to write a letter. Some days she writes only a sentence or two, types them, and maybe shows me. I might tell her a particular word seems especially effective or suggest that a phrase reminds me of a poem. Cindy might then read the poem. As with so many children, poetry provides the breakthrough to creativity that Cindy needs. She understands that the only reason I give her poems is because I enjoy them and think that she will too. There is no pressure of questions or accountability—no standards, if you will. Certainly there is no bastardization of poetry such as appears on a CTB/McGraw-Hill fourth-grade high-stakes test. There, children are given a delightful poem by Valerie Worth and told to "find the noun in the sentence." Plenty of fourth graders know that poems aren't filled with sentences. Plenty of teachers know that poetry should not be degraded in this manner.

Gradually I notice that Cindy no longer relies on me to suggest poems. She begins exploring my bookcases and my file drawers. I call these drawers my "good words" drawers. They are filled with snippets of poems I like, interesting news items I've clipped, and activities I've written to provoke word play. Cindy loves being invited to snoop in a teacher's files, and these files become both her inspiration and her sustenance. Cindy begins taking activity sheets home and writing there. During workshop she continues to read everything the other students write.

The honors English crew are so wrapped up in their own conversations and ideas, they have neither the time nor the inclination to pay attention to anybody else. But Cindy pays close attention to them, carefully reading what they write. She reads, and then she reacts with me. When Cindy likes something, she says in a marvelous way, "This is excellent." A reviewer for *The New York Review of Books* could not pronounce judgment with any more certainty.

Cindy develops a fondness for X. J. Kennedy's amusing verses. "That 'Exploding Gravy' is excellent," she tells me. "I am using it as a model, but it isn't easy." Cindy chooses a picture from my picture files of nineteenth-century clip art. It shows two grim-faced children sitting at opposite ends of a table, a big bowl in front of each. She writes this poem as a caption to the picture:

SAD KIDS

Johnny and Cindy look discouraged.
For they don't like porridge.
For supper they'd rather have Veal Parmigiana.

I like this poem almost as much as Cindy does. I show her Edward Abbey's opinion of porridge: "The two vegetarians in our group . . . prepared their breakfast oatmeal, a viscous gray slime." Cindy tells me later that she forgot "that nasty word," but she enjoyed telling her mother that oatmeal is "gray slime."

Cindy hadn't been able to come up with a clever adaptation of "Mary Had a Little Lamb," but months later she is intrigued by an activity sheet on lipograms. She tries writing the verse with no *a*'s—Merry got this little pet, its fleece so white, so soft—and no *l*'s: Mary had a tiny pet, its fur as white as snow. And so on. She keeps experimenting with different letter omissions, and then, inspired by my extensive collection of alphabet books, decides to try a missing-letter alphabet book based on the verse.

A: Merry got this little pet, its fleece so white, so soft.

B: Mary had a little sheep, its fleece as white as snow.

C: Mary had a little lamb, its pelt as white as snow.

And so on. Cindy discovers the thesaurus, a book that immediately entrances her.

One day I am watching Cindy working by herself on a project she has found, and I realize that she isn't "dull normal" any more. She is able to exercise a degree of literary judgment, making critical choices based on word usage and rhythm and other literary devices. Even more, she exhibits a sense of humor, originality, and persistence. She has developed an appreciation of language that she nurtures and extends outside school. The girl who was too timid to change "Mary Had a Little Lamb" is now eager to try all sorts of literary forms.

Two or three times a week Cindy brings in work she had done at home. She doesn't produce any five-paragraph theme papers, but she brings in funny epitaphs, picture captions, limericks, hippopotamus shopping lists, recipes, interviews, and fables. Sometimes she says, "My mother really liked helping me with this one," or "My mother would like to try another one like this."

Yes, Cindy's mother is also writing. In the household we alternative high school teachers had given up on six years previously as not providing "appropriate literacy support," a parent is reading and writing alongside her daughter. Cindy and her mother teach me to stop and take another look. They make me realize that even I, who pride myself on rejecting the deficit models of student achievement set up by ed-whiz-biz consultants, have fallen prey to the "What can you do with these (inadequate) offspring of (inadequate) parents?" scenario. Cindy forces me to step back and see again how crucial is the literacy stimulus the teacher provides. After all, given engaging prompts, Cindy's mother is moved, not only to help her child with written assignments but to try her own hand at them.

Cindy makes progress in writer's workshop, but it isn't a progress that I can prove to anyone with a checklist mind-set. I don't know if Cindy can write a business letter or a five-paragraph persuasive essay. I don't much care. Cindy does not get a grade from me, so neither she nor I have to worry whether her work is a 98 or an 89. Neither she nor her mother ever ask me to grade the work. They are working hard on writing because in so doing they are able to find joy in words. Amazingly, Cindy's regular language arts teacher, a stickler for punctuation, syntax, and the whole ball of wax, is convinced that I am teaching "skills." She expresses enthusiasm for the great improvement in Cindy's writing. But even she doesn't ask what we do in workshop. No teacher or administrator ever asks.

OUR DISTRICT might be said to operate on a "don't ask, don't tell" policy. Good thing for me; it means I can do pretty much what I want. I know that in such a system, bad teachers are ignored as much as good ones, but I have my doubts whether imposing a uniform curriculum in the name of standards ever saves a district from bad teaching. H. L. Mencken pointed out that an idealist is one who, on noticing that a rose smells better than a cabbage, concludes that it will also make a better soup. He could have been talking about the Standardistos. On noticing that roses bring a higher price in the marketplace, Standardistos prize them over cabbages, insisting that the entire garden be turned over to the cultivation of roses. I won't carry the analogy to painful ends, but I do worry that teachers are being pushed to keep their plants in neat and tidy rows by people who have never set foot in a garden. And the reasons given always have something to do with the marketplace.

The only administrative interest in writer's workshop appears in the form of sabotage. Long angry with me over the union newsletter I produce each month, one of the three principals finds it particularly reprehensible when, during a protest for lack of a contract and in defiance of an administrative edict banning union T-shirts on school property, I wear a T-shirt emblazoned with the message SUPPORT TEACHERS. Trying to forestall charges that this attire is "unprofessional" and hoping to spearhead a free-speech action, I sew lace around the neck and sleeves. The principal is not amused. When he orders me to cover up the T-shirt, I point out that the PE teachers are wearing T-shirts with inscriptions and ask him to delineate exactly which letters on mine are forbidden. So he issues a memo banning all clothing with writing on it. Alas, the union is not interested in the free-speech issue. In any case, not content with putting an official letter of reprimand in my personnel file, the principal brings fifty-five seventh-grade boys from the cafeteria to the workshop, announcing in his booming voice, "Hiya, Missus Ohanian! Here are some young men who want to join your writing club!" With that, he disappears, leaving a swarm of pubescent boys carrying trays overflowing with spaghetti and meatballs, green beans, vanilla pudding, and cartons of chocolate milk.

What makes this throng a catastrophe waiting to happen is the location of our workshop. Seven years previously, when our new, multimillion-dollar middle school was still in the planning stages, faculty tried to get involved in its design. For starters, they recommended against the configuration of the locker area and expressed distress and disbelief that the architects planned an open mezzanine extending around three sides of the media center below, billing it as a "quiet study area." Administrators squashed teachers' worries with the assurances that these prize-winning architects were going to produce a building "at the cutting edge" of school design. And so the locker areas and open mezzanine went from shopping mall blueprint to schoolhouse disaster. It took six years for the administrators finally to scrap the wacky locker setup, but student access to the mezzanine was short-lived. On our second day in the new building, an eighth grader left his classroom at the end of third period, took a detour through the mezzanine, tossing a chair over the railing as he headed to his fourth-period class. The chair crashed into a table below, just missing a teacher and three students. After that, the mezzanine doors were kept locked; no students are allowed up there unless accompanied by an adult.

Since our workshop is located along one side of this mezzanine overlooking the media center, it is inevitable that the feverish horde quickly discover the fun of making food drops onto students sitting in the media center below. As I confiscate the tray of one kid, who was dropping green beans one by one, three more kids begin flipping pudding with their spoons. A descending sauce-covered meatball misses its intended victim but leaves a long red smear down the ecru wall.

Since the principal himself is as impulsive and self-centered as any seventh grader, I don't choose to dignify his actions by complaining. Instead, I ask the industrial arts teacher to print up a batch of writer's workshop passes. Then, unilaterally, I decree that no one can come to writer's workshop from the cafeteria without first securing a pass from me. Neither the principal nor I ever refer to the day he launched the multitudes onto writer's workshop. We find new battles to fight.

The spaghetti/vanilla pudding bombardment is the only real glitch writer's workshop encounters for months. Student enthusiasm continues to grow. By December, we are averaging seventy-eight students a day. We've produced one book, *Mother Goose Revised*, and are working on a second. Since the copy machine is so unreliable, I talk to the industrial arts teacher about getting several hundred copies printed. He explains that he needs a requisition from the central office, and that's when we hit our second glitch. This one proves to be major. Two days after I send a printing request to the central office, a memo is issued.

ENLARGED CITY SCHOOL DISTRICT
OFFICE OF THE ASSISTANT SUPERINTENDENT
IN CHARGE OF CURRICULUM
MARY J. COCHRANE

TO: DR. PARACHINI, DR. WHITE, MRS. O'HANIAN
FROM: MARY J. COCHRANE, ASSISTANT SUPERINTENDENT IN
CHARGE OF CURRICULUM
DATE: JANUARY 27
RE: WRITING CLUB

SINCE MY RETURN FROM SICK LEAVE IT HAS COME TO MY ATTENTION
THAT A NEW WRITING CLUB HAS BEEN FORMED AT THE JUNIOR
HIGH BY MRS. O'HANIAN.

I WANT TO MEET WITH THE THREE OF YOU IN DR. WHITE'S OFFICE
ON FEBRUARY 2 AT 3:45 P.M. TO DISCUSS THIS MATTER. THE DIS-
CUSSION, AS I PERCEIVE IT, SHOULD INCLUDE, BUT NOT BE LIM-
ITED TO, THE FOLLOWING ITEMS:
1. ORIGIN OF THE PROJECT
2. GOALS, OBJECTIVES, AND LEARNING OUTCOMES OF THE PROJECT
3. NUMBER OF STUDENTS PARTICIPATING
4. COST PROJECTIONS THROUGH JUNE

MJC:DE
CC: SUPERINTENDENT MANCINI

a note from Susan Ohanian

2/7
TO: Miss Cochrane, Dr. Parachini, Dr. White
RE: Writer's Workshop Meeting

I don't see how I can break my promise to members of writer's workshop, who have worked hard since September. Since I donate the supervision and typing time, the only cost for publishing their work is for paper and photocopying. I have been successful in finding alternative paper sources and will look for funding to subsidize printing costs. Please inform me—in writing—what the district will charge per page for photocopying or using the high school print shop facilities.

Contrary to charges leveled at me in the meeting, I can offer assurance that I do care about correct spelling. Although I have published articles honoring students' invented spelling, one should not infer that I would ever publish student writing with misspelled words. As you can see in our first publication, the students and I are committed to excellence in any publication we undertake.

Teachers Association Alert

2/8
TO: Susan
FROM: Ann Burke, Building Rep

The association herewith donates five reams of paper to the writing workshop. We have a ream on order for you. When you need more, let me know; I am sure the state association will kick in too.

cc: NYSUT Regional Field Representative

Memorandum from the Office of the Vice Principal Marcella E. White, Ed.D.

BULLETIN #587
2/10
TO: All Faculty
FROM: Marcella E. White, Ed.D.
RE: Use of copy machine

To expedite use, the copy machine is being retooled to record user numbers. Each faculty member will receive a user number. After 2/8 the machine will not operate without this number code first being punched in.

Memorandum from the Office of the Vice Principal Marcella E. White, Ed.D.

2/10
TO: Susan Ohanian
FROM: Marcella E. White, Ed.D.
RE: Writing Club

Please be advised that according to instructions from Assistant Superintendent Cochrane you are not to use the photocopy machine at any time for the purposes of reproducing work of members of the writing club.

cc: Assistant Superintendent Cochrane,
Dr. Parachini

2/15
Dear Susan,

I feel really badly about what's happening. My niece is in your writing workshop. If I happen to see student work lying around, I could photocopy it during my lunch break. Since I do copy work for the office when I'm not working in the cafeteria, I have their access number. BURN THIS NOTE!!!! (But don't give up.)

Josie

NEWS FROM NICK

2/15
Dear Susan,

Joey Rinatti has made remarkable progress in writing, and I know part of it has been through seeing his work in the writing project publication, which I've been using in class. Since these materials are part of my lessons, I will continue to photocopy class sets, and "extras" for contributors to share with friends and family.

Nick

2/25
Dear Ms. Ohanian,

We have just read the book produced by students in the writing workshop (including our son!). We are amazed and thrilled that he is so interested in this project. Imagine, a thirteen-year-old boy who doesn't have much good to say about school giving up his lunch period to write.

Thank you!
Ann and Chris Sheehan

Students come up with the idea to sell future booklets for twenty-five cents—to cover the cost of printing. I take this idea to the vice principal. Three days later I am called to another meeting with the vice principal, the language arts coordinator, and the assistant superintendent in charge of curriculum. The assistant superintendent announces that she is sure I will end up publishing an article about "the writing club," and she wants me to know that the school district has no interest in subsidizing or otherwise promoting my "private business enterprise." She dismisses what she insists on calling "Mrs. Ohanian's writing club" as an attempt at producing "elaborate literary products" that are not appropriate in our school district. "This is not New York City," she announces. I'm amazed that she knows that students in New York City publish their writing.

Despite these pronouncements, the assistant superintendent recants just a smidgen. She decrees that we can publish one small anthology at the end of the year—no more than ten pages. "Publish only the best," she insists. "I know you don't care about bad spelling, but I do." Ironically her obsession with an article I'd written three years previously, a piece that mentions invented spelling, is my only indication that any administrator in the district has ever read anything I've written.

I obey all the official restrictions on photocopying student work, but I do not obey the edict that we should publish only "the best." Publish only the best and the honors students will see their work in print and kids like Cindy won't. I continue to type up everything the kids turn in, and they develop quite a black market for getting copies run off. The hall monitors prove to be their best resource.

The students are disappointed that they can't publish a big anthology. This edict against publication does, in fact, slash the numbers attending writer's workshop. Our daily membership of over one hundred drops to forty-two. I have to admit that the assistant superintendent and her lackeys have done me a favor. Trying to manage that many students had brought me to the point of quiet desperation. I was so thrilled with the turnout, I was unwilling to admit I felt overwhelmed. The remaining forty-two students dig in, and we come up with an innovative way to get their work out to a larger audience.

The small group from honors English continues writing personal narrative and a variety of poems ranging from concrete verse to odes on love. But the other students, students who, like Cindy, fall into the category of the overlooked, decide that they want to write a mystery. They divide up into eight teams that vary each day from three to six members, depending on who can get out of which classes. Except for Cindy. Not a collaborator, Cindy works solo on her team of one, definitely a kid after my own heart. She exemplifies what too many of the sunny writing process adherents either fail to realize or refuse to admit, what Paul Theroux calls "the loneliness of the long-distance writer." The fact is that writing, real writing, requires time, silence, and space—all by one's self. Alone. This is why schools are such singularly poor places to get any writing done. It is why I am particularly impressed when children manage to pull it off.

Nonetheless, I encourage teamwork among the seventh and eighth graders, because as a teacher I have to juggle various goals and the writing project is just one among many. The original plan is that each team will write one chapter of the story. But there's a snag in such a plan because kids come to workshop at different times, and since I am forbidden to use the copy machine, it is difficult for one team to see what another team is doing. Finally, students figure a way around this impediment: They decide to call their mystery *Murder at the Junior High*. Each team will write a chapter independent of the other chapters. In these innocent, pre-Columbine-tragedy days, we are happy with the book structure: each chapter will be about a different murder set in our school.

I offer each team the option of taking five photographs with my Polaroid camera to illustrate their chapter. Once they get caught up in writing their mysteries, kids bring in their own cameras loaded with film. The mystery-writing caper turns into one of the wildest six weeks of my teaching career. And all I do is sit on the mezzanine, hand out the camera, and listen to excited talk about how the various murders are progressing.

Cindy's chapter involves an English teacher, who murders a student during a grammar lesson. I swear I didn't give her the plot. I caution the students that they can't accuse any adult of murder—or let any adult be murdered—without that person's permission, so they draft a very legalistic "permission form." I am impressed that they persuade eighty-three adults in our building to agree to participate as murderer, victim, or whatever role individual plot circumstances might require. I ask the mystery writers if they really intend to have so many murders occur. They say no, but they want to be ready "just in case." The fact is, they love the permissions form they've created; mostly they love traipsing around school collecting all those signatures, talking with the signers about their writing plans. The permissions process takes up close to two weeks. I figure that it's time well spent. Who, besides the assistant superintendent in charge of curriculum and the principal, can fail to acknowledge that it is a very good thing for seventh and eighth graders to be talking to lots of adults about a writing project? Maybe you have to be a seventh- or eighth-grade teacher to recognize the marvel of a student initiating a conversation that is even vaguely curriculum-oriented and doesn't include one of two phrases: "Do I have to?" and "This sucks."

I must admit that this small band of kids, most of whom are, at best, mediocre students, turns our school of twelve hundred into something between a street fair and a madhouse. Being chosen as a murder victim becomes a faculty badge of pride. A normally staid and proper teacher rushes by me in the hall, exclaiming, "Your kids have me scheduled to die in the locker room in five minutes!" She is clearly exhilarated by the notion. The custodian asks me, "Those girls who say they need to take a picture of someone floating face-down in the swimming pool belong to you?" Ron, deemed by his teachers as "totally irresponsible and undependable," chooses to be accountable for a lot of details when he arranges for his chosen victim to die in the school elevator. He makes an appointment for his math teacher to be at the crime scene at a specific time, arranges with the principal's secretary to get the elevator key, gets the camera from me, gathers up the props to position around the body in the elevator. In short, this undependable boy conducts the entire murder in a highly organized, responsible fashion—and this extends to his writing.

Four girls team up to write about a crime taking place in the cafeteria. "As if the food weren't bad enough already," writes Kelly, "someone is actually poisoning it." She and her cohorts borrow the nurse's handbook of medical terms and lift a lot of impressive-sounding phrases to describe the poison and the condition of the bodies. The girls squabble for days about what food they should choose to be poisoned, finally settling on pizza because "everybody eats it." Kim quarrels with this scenario, saying that it means only kids will die. "Teachers don't eat pizza," she insists. Janella seizes on this assertion: "That works! It means the murderer has to be a teacher, somebody out to get kids."

I show the cafeteria team a death certificate and a police report concerning the death of a shooting victim, asking them to contrast this language with that found on a bereavement card. The official forms inspire the girls to talk about "the deceased" for days. The materials also inspire them to create their own official form. They devise a questionnaire for faculty suspects, which, when finished, provides another excuse for kids to walk around the school soliciting information. "Where were you at 12:45 P.M. on March thirteenth?" "Was the deceased in any of your classes?" "Did you see the deceased on March thirteenth?" "Did the deceased ever cause any disruption in your classes?" "Did the deceased turn in homework regularly?" And so on. The questionnaire is three pages long.

There isn't a corner of our school building that isn't used as the scene of one crime or another. At least half the faculty and staff get caught up in the flurry of activity, letting writer's workshop kids out of class to take photos and conduct interviews, posing as victims, offering ideas and props. Curiously, the administrators keep conspicuously aloof from the proceedings. I think they are missing a golden opportunity for positive exchanges with kids with whom they have plenty of negative contact, but that's their problem, not mine.

After six weeks or so, the crimes are committed and the chapters are written. And because the assistant superintendent in charge of curriculum, bless her dried up, suspicious little mind, has forbidden me the use of the copy machine, we come up with the idea of posting a chapter a day along the glass wall that fronts the media center. Students walking by in the hallway between classes, on the way to PE, on the way to lunch, can read the chapters. There isn't a time during the day when clusters of students, faculty, and staff aren't gathered around that wall. To keep up, you have to read and reread every episode, because kids keep adding new material.

This project cements my suspicion that school really isn't a good place in which to get much writing done. During writer's workshop the kids talk and plan what photos they need to take. Some people may call this prewriting, a term I've never warmed to. Pretty much of a pragmatist, I figure you're either writing or you aren't. I try to avoid junking up what I do in the classroom with hocus-pocus language that is incomprehensible to people in the real world. I'm neither ashamed nor secretive about giving fledgling writers plenty of time to discuss their writing, take pictures, and knock on teachers' doors with questionnaires in hand. But I don't know what is served by surrounding such activity with abstruse pedagogese.

Those questionnaires take a lot of time—time to write and lots more time to distribute. When you give seventh graders permission to roam the halls, you can be sure they won't be back soon. One writing team leaves the workshop with a stack of questionnaires and a hall pass from me. I don't see them again for three days. I suppose this verges on irresponsibility on my part. And I am to a degree abashed about comments from colleagues about my kids "roaming the halls." But only to a degree. Mostly, I'm proud of the kids. Sometimes the line between professionalism and irresponsibility is finer than people want to admit. It involves some risk but mostly it involves faith in kids. What is important for me is that after all the tomfoolery, the kids go home and write. They visit each other's homes, they confer on the telephone. Very little writing may be done at school, but school is the place that gives them the impetus to write. School is where they bring it all together. By God, school is the place where, the assistant superintendent in charge of curriculum be damned, they publish.

NOT EVERYBODY who comes to writer's workshop is lured in by the murder mystery. In the middle of this project, Joey shows up. Even though he is not one of my students, Joey is hard to miss in our student population of twelve hundred. It is difficult not to hear his cursing in the locker area. This kid earns his reputation as a roughneck. But when he comes to workshop, Joey announces his purpose. "I've heard about this place and I decided to come. I'm an uncle. My sister just had a baby. I want to make a card for the baby."

Not only does Joey want to make a card, he wants to write a poem on it. Joey could spend a dollar or two on a greeting card. He chooses instead to give up his lunch break and give the baby something of himself. Joey writes his poem. Then he comes back the next day to make it better. He comes the third day to type it. He continues to hang around a few days, watching the other kids. Finally he says, "I got an idea for a murder." With the help of the custodian, Joey introduces us to the possibility of hiding a body in the catwalks above the gym. I've been in the school five and a half years and this is the first time I've heard about catwalks above the gym. We take a workshop field trip to go look at the catwalks and agree that it is a dramatic site for a murder.

Yes, our writer's workshop is irregular: no pretest and posttest, no curriculum to cover, no standards to meet. All we have is a belief in kids and a belief in good words. I worry that too much of English instruction is preordained—that increasingly, English teachers feel constrained from sharing real writing with their students. They are too busy training kids to pass tests shipped in by the truckload. By "real writing" I don't mean filling out job application forms or writing resumes. I mean the words of real writers, words in real books, words about things that matter (like viscous oatmeal and police forms). And poetry. George Steiner reminds us that if we don't hear "words that sing" we will never become real readers. Or writers either. Too many teachers hand out those dull tomes carefully screened to carry only safe words, words written at the reader's assigned level, words that end up being dead to the possibility of ever touching the lives of children. Cindy is stunned to see that people who make their living writing sometimes write about stuff like oatmeal. Oatmeal, for Cindy, is an epiphany. Reading someone else's words about oatmeal convinces her she can write about veal parmigiana. Yesterday veal parmigiana, today murder during a grammar lesson, tomorrow the world.

Cindy flourishes in workshop because she is able to sustain herself, to write by herself. Deprived of any significant choices in her regular curriculum, she loves the choices she finds by nosing around in my file drawers. Probably for the first time since kindergarten she is being given choice time; she is being asked to be autonomous, to exercise judgment, to make decisions about her own education.

This is not a matter of getting rid of textbooks. The issue is much more complex than that. What schools must recognize is that different children learn differently. As David Hawkins points out in *The Informed Vision,* "There is an essential lack of predictability about what is going to happen in a good classroom." A good teacher isn't bound by the plans she hands in each week; a good teacher builds on what happens at the moment. If Hawkins is right, and surely he is, and "the best times in teaching have always been the consequence of some little accident that happened to direct attention in some new way," then we must have teachers who are smart enough and flexible enough to try new things. The sticking point is, of course, that for a teacher to be able to pull a funny line about oatmeal off her bookshelf, that teacher must herself be a reader. She has to be someone who loves words. And the sad truth of the matter is I am kicked off our district hiring committee when I insist on asking applicants, "Read any good books lately?" The superintendent chides me, "Such questions put people on the spot." Well, I sure hope so! When I write about the incident in an op-ed piece for a newspaper in a different city, English teachers write in, berating me. They, too, think the question is unfair.

IN MAY, I DISOBEY the assistant superintendent's rules and publish a limited edition of the students' eighty-page anthology, *Chronicles and Confessions of a Colossal Cat.* I photocopy enough illegal copies so that every contributor gets two. To produce that many copies, I learn to open up and unjam our continually malfunctioning machine. As I sweat and curse, I'm constantly looking over my shoulder for any of the administrators in our building who will happily report me to the assistant superintendent. I think how ironic it is that the least of my troubles is getting kids to write. My greatest worry now is that, despite my protests, they are writing too much. I keep declaring submissions closed, and they continue to hand me more cat stories with the plea, "Just one more." I have obtained permission from Kliban, Inc., to reproduce Hap Kliban's drawings, so stories accompanying his whimsical cats form the core of our book.

In an attempt to widen the audience of my young authors, I arrange for a group of them to visit several elementary schools and read their cat stories to primary children. The writers return as literary celebrities, reporting that their young listeners laughed in the right places and asked lots of questions about how they thought up the stories. Offering further evidence that publishing student work is an important part of their development as writers, Cindy points out that the primary graders were very impressed with the anthology. "They wanted to touch it," she said. "One boy even counted all the pages."

Working within the black-market system they have developed, writer's workshop participants somehow get more copies of the booklet made. They autograph each other's copies. Cindy gives a copy to her cousin for her birthday with the inscription, "Save this for when I'm famous."

Is this writing process? No. Neither is it writing by prescription. Not being one doesn't mean it has to be the other. Echoing Melville, I maintain that, like all true places, our writer's workshop is not down on anybody's map. I make no claims about knowing how to teach writing. I only know that if you don't recognize and accommodate and nourish uniqueness, you don't have any chance to educate the children in your care—not for writing, not for anything. And to recognize a student's uniqueness you have to offer him choices. Real choices. And to offer students choices, a teacher has to make choices herself. A teacher who makes choices is a teacher who is still alive.

6

Certifiably Crazy

Arnold is certifiably crazy. I note his condition not with malice but with regret and, I fear, resignation. I come to this resignation fighting all the way. It is not easy for a teacher to admit that a student is too bizarre for her to cope with, never mind teach. It is our duty, after all, to give students many chances, many options. For us, there must be no line in the chalk dust, no-high stakes checklist or exam or personality profile. Our motto must be: Send us your children and we will try. And try. And try.

When Arnold enters my classroom, I've been working for more than ten years with children school officials euphemistically label according to the fashions of the time. "Tough" and "incorrigible" segue into "remedial," "disadvantaged," "culturally deprived," "culturally different," "underachieving," "inner-city," "urban," "challenged," "opportunity," and "differently abled." As Jules Feiffer once pointed out in a poignant cartoon speaking from the point of view of the person labeled, "I'm still poor, but I've got a great vocabulary."

No matter how some kids are labeled or delabeled, they stand out in a crowd. William Bennett and his morality injunctions be damned; E. D. Hirsch and his list of cultural imperatives be damned; the U.S. and state departments of education and their sycophantic Standardistos and all their agendas and timetables and high-stakes tests be double damned. Arnold doesn't fit into the *Little House on the Prairie/The Little Engine That Could/Aesop's Fables* mold. Hey, for Arnold, Barney, Dr. Seuss, Curious George, and even Judy Blume are foreign territory. He does know about Stephen King—from the movies.

Many of my students are weighted down by achingly oppressive obstacles. Some learn to wear their troubles like a dare: Chip on the shoulder, they defy anybody to notice that they can't read, don't have decent clothes, come to school hungry. Others are secretive: Quiet, deceptively passive, they seem to will themselves invisible. Arnold joins neither camp. Scruffy and skinny, his pale skin has a green tinge. And he hears voices. He also loses track of time and space and seems unaware at times of where he is. But Arnold's most prominent characteristic is his belief that everybody is against him. At least once a week, Arnold launches into his litany of all the people who hate him: the principal, the school nurse, his gym teacher, his science teacher, his remedial math teacher, his regular math teacher, his social studies teacher, his art teacher, his PE teacher, and me. We all hate him, as do the thirteen other kids in Arnold's language arts tutorial classroom, the hall monitors, the bus driver, the cafeteria workers, the school secretary, the custodians, and the mail carrier. So do the 1,148 other seventh and eighth graders in our school. Arnold recites as many of these names as he can think of—all are engaged in a multitude of conspiracies to do him harm within the next fifteen minutes. The list is long. Arnold may not be so good at memorizing the geographic features of the Finger Lakes or the methods for figuring square roots, but he knows the names of lots of people in our school who despise him.

Some days Arnold refuses to enter my classroom because his voices tell him his persecutors are lying in wait for him (and I'm letting them hide there). But more often, Arnold refuses to *leave* my classroom—even for lunch. Make that *especially* for lunch. Arnold is terrified of the cafeteria, convinced that gangs of *those kids* are lurking both in the locker area through which he must walk to get to the cafeteria and in the cafeteria itself. "They're gonna jump me," he whines. "They have knives. Maybe even guns. They want to *kill* me." With the word *kill*, Arnold invariably grins broadly. I learn to dread that grin.

In his recitation of the names of everybody in the school who is out to get him, Arnold always starts with the principal, moving on to faculty and finally to students. Arnold desperately wants me to listen to him recite the whole list, the names of all the seventh and eighth graders who want to do him harm. "Alphonse." Arnold names the meanest, toughest kid in the building with dramatic pause, then gives the evidence he's collected against him: "He looks at me funny." He then moves on to more names, "Joey, Ramon, Sheila. . . " grinning as he catalogs their crimes against him.

Arnold's grin is disconcerting. He displays it all the time, whether he is being praised or cursed. His classmates try to avoid him, but when Arnold makes this impossible, when he pushes his way into their midst, they curse him—and he grins.

For a while, permitting Arnold to sit in my classroom during our twenty-seven-minute lunch break seems like the path of least resistance, certainly better than trying to drag him out. But Arnold won't shut up. When he isn't pointing the finger at others, I become the subject of his chant. "I bet you hate me. Yeah, you really hate me. I know you hate me, my mother knows you hate me . . . my sister . . ." On and on he drones and whines. And grins.

Okay, I tell myself. This is a thirteen-year-old kid. He needs attention, reassurance, and affection. I set myself the goal of never being negative around Arnold. I am determined to unearth and make visible to him and the world around him his positive qualities. About six weeks into this process, I realize that there simply isn't enough applause in the universe to reassure Arnold, who invariably turns praise into a negative. Any "recognition" throws him off balance. Actually, praise seems to make Arnold even more insecure. When a teacher yells at Arnold or a student mocks him, Arnold grins and even struts a little. When I praise him for a small accomplishment, such as completing an atlas assignment, he looks around with a "Who, me?" expression. Then he gathers himself up and begins whining, "I bet you thought I couldn't do it. Everybody thinks I'm dumb." This leads to his recital of the eleven hundred people (plus staff) who think that he is dumb.

And so finally I decide I'm not a saint. I admit that I cannot have Arnold in my classroom one hundred minutes a day *and* permit him to stay on during the lunch break as well. Before Arnold became a lunchtime tenant, I had used the break as a time to sit by myself. Sometimes I'd read. Six weeks of letting Arnold hang around has shown me how necessary it is to have twenty-seven minutes of quietude during a stress-filled day. If I don't get that quiet time back, I'll soon be loony too.

I talk to Arnold about the change and then, naively, I try to walk him to the cafeteria. This just starts a new game. Tall and gangly, Arnold jerks away from me and runs. But not too far. In the architectural marvel that is our junior high, Arnold is not the only thirteen-year-old who enjoys playing hide-and-seek among the locker clusters that fill the spaces between classrooms. Locker peekaboo is not an activity peculiar to remedial, disadvantaged, culturally deprived, culturally different, underachieving, inner-city, urban, challenged, differently abled youth. Few twelve- and thirteen-year-old males of any socioeconomic group can pass up such manifest opportunities for recreation.

If I return to my classroom after my aborted attempt to escort Arnold to the cafeteria, he soon appears in the doorway, taunting, "Can't catch me, can't catch me!" If I lock the door, he bangs on it. Finally, I give up trying to sit in my empty classroom. I reveal the depth of my desperation when I admit that I begin hiding from Arnold. In its own way, sitting in the faculty room would be worse than sitting with Arnold, so I begin looking for empty classrooms. But this proves futile. Forty-eight seconds after I find a classroom, Arnold appears in the doorway. The third time this happens, he boasts, "You can't escape me." Cold desperation chills my bones when I realize he's right.

Arnold and I have been playing a version of this game since early in the school year. He used to stand outside the classroom and yell, "I ain't comin' in and nobody's gonna make me." If I dragged him through one door, he'd bolt out the other one, laughing hysterically, "Can't catch me! Can't catch me!" Realizing finally that we must look like some bizarre reenactment of *The Gingerbread Man*, I give up chasing him. Usually it doesn't take more than ten minutes of my nonpursuit for Arnold to come slinking into the classroom on his own.

Once Arnold realizes that I won't chase him, he changes his tactics and tries to become a permanent classroom fixture. He wraps himself around his desk and refuses to move when the change-of-classes bell rings. I soon give up on physically removing him, and not just because he is five inches taller than I. What is the point of removing Arnold when there is no place else for him to go? There is no place in our school where people can cope with his behavior. Most teachers, faced with class sizes twice as large as mine (and no team teaching partner, as I have), as well as ridiculous college prep curriculum requirements, can't cope as well.

When Arnold refuses to move, I pick up the intraschool phone and notify the office. "Arnold is staying here this period." If I can't persuade him to move on the next period or the next, I pick up the phone and repeat the message. No teacher ever complains when Arnold doesn't show up. I'm sure more than a few pray he will be absent. In keeping with one of those immutable laws of education, Arnold has perfect attendance. I wonder if I should phone his mother and ask her what technique she uses to get him out of the house.

Of course I question whether I am doing the right thing by giving in to Arnold like this. But I don't see that I have much choice. The one time that I tried to bring up Arnold's behavior as a subject for discussion, the principal dragged Arnold into his office and gave him five hard whacks across the knuckles with a ruler for disobeying a teacher. The principal insisted that I watch—no doubt a very good strategy. I don't change my mind about the principal being a dim bulb, but now I acknowledge his cunning. It sure keeps me from sending Arnold to the office again. The first blow, delivered with the full force of a 220-pounder's swing, brought tears to Arnold's eyes. Nonetheless, he grinned. "Think it's funny, do you?" the principal raged, and landed another blow. Then three more. "Next time it will be ten," he warned. Arnold's grin widened.

Of course there can be no next time—not for Arnold, not for me. I can't be an accomplice to the principal's version of problem solving. Ironically, a couple of years later, this principal, who at the time hasn't spoken to me for five months because of my union activities, grudgingly admits to one of my colleagues that I am a "good teacher." He defines that. "She's a good disciplinarian." Of course I meet his sole criteria: A good teacher is one who keeps students out of the office. I guess that makes him a good principal. He does, after all, motivate me to keep my students out of his office.

Occasionally even the best of us needs to cry uncle. I once had a principal to whom I could send a kid with a note: "Please let _____ sit in the office for fifteen minutes. We both need it." That principal might ask the kid what had happened or just let him sit there with no comment. The kid would return to class and we'd both be better for that space.

So I "handle" Arnold, keeping him out of the office. Increasingly, he spends the day with me, so I am handling him for the whole school. Since he stays out of the office all day, the principal is convinced Arnold's behavior is improving. But I sit and stew about what Arnold and I are doing. I watch Arnold quack like a duck, lie down on the floor and roll up into a fetal position, sucking his thumb while humming; I watch him trip, poke, and spit on other kids; I listen to him sit at my elbow all day, whining, "How come you hate me? How come everybody hates me? How come my science teacher hates me? How come my social studies teacher hates me . . . ?" And on and on and on. I have to wonder how much my patient, forbearing attitude is helping Arnold and how much it is hurting him further. I am, I remind myself, an English teacher, not a drill sergeant. Not a psychiatrist.

ARNOLD'S EYES are with me forever. Some days these eyes are a vacant stare, fixating on some distant object for hours on end. My other students and I have an unspoken contract: On these days we just let Arnold be, accepting with gratitude that a fixated Arnold doesn't bother us. But more often, Arnold's eyes seem feral—darting here and there, daring anyone to make contact. Invariably on these days, a student glances at Arnold and then Arnold tries to provoke a fight. "Who you staring at, jerk?" After I break up the confrontation, Arnold grins his grin and starts complaining. "How come this always happens to me? How come everybody hates me?"

Arnold has one area of excellence. Not only is he the best speller of all my students, I would put him up against anybody in the school, student and faculty. But even this skill has its downside. When Arnold misses a word on a quiz it becomes an international incident. He stabs his paper and whines, "I spelled it right! Somebody changed this answer. Look here, somebody erased what I wrote and wrote something else. Look at this. Who changed my answer? Why don't you admit it?" He accuses kids one by one of changing his answer and then tries to pick a fight with me because I'm not rushing off to report this malfeasance to the principal.

Arnold and I muddle through the year as best we can. He is gleeful about passing seventh grade. "You thought I'd fail," he says. "You tried to get me held back, but I passed anyway." In a way, Arnold is right. Despite my long-held, deep-seated conviction that retention does more harm than good, I do give Arnold a failing mark in my class. My team teaching partner joins all the other teachers in awarding a passing grade, so I can't pretend that my position is anything but a minority view. Since kindergarten, Arnold has never failed a grade. In my mind's ear I can hear the yearly conversations about this student: "There's no point in holding this type of student back. Move him on." And part of me agrees. What *is* the point of holding Arnold back if the school fails to offer an alternative program? He certainly doesn't need an extra year of the same old same old.

What would the Standardistos, those calling for benchmark requirements from womb to tomb, have us do? Surely no one would argue that a fifteen year-old Arnold in third grade makes more sense than a fifteen-year-old Arnold in eighth grade. I agree that to hand Arnold a regular high school diploma is a sham and a shame, but I wonder why we don't offer him an alternative diploma that represents a significantly alternative educational path. Why do we insist on offering Arnold a college-prep curriculum (with a smattering of remedial reading)? It is democracy and all-men-are-created-equal run amok to pretend that Arnold isn't different, very different.

And so, as Arnold's seventh-grade teacher, I try to force the issue. I lobby for a report card mark of "ungradeable," a mark that acknowledges our teacherly perplexity, our admission that Arnold and more than a few other students do not in any way fit into a regular junior high precollege academic program. The principal vetoes my plan, insisting that the computer "requires a mark." So Arnold and the principal have something in common: They both hear voices from odd sources.

When a bureaucrat is backed into a corner, it's easier to blame the computer than try to justify his position. Another computer "requirement" presents other dilemmas. The computer insists that we teachers give marks that are precise percentages—an 86, a 72, or whatever. How do you pick a number for any child, let alone a child like Arnold? It may sound barbaric, but I give him a 50, the lowest mark "permitted by the computer." By school district regulations, if a student comes to class one day of the marking period, he is entitled to a 50 for that marking period. Authorities say that giving a grade below 50 "undermines a student's confidence," so that if he should ever decide to come to school more than one day, he will still have a chance to pass the course.

I give Arnold a grade of 50 because I feel obligated to send a message that this student is in deep trouble. But the kid who has spent three-fourths of the year sitting at my elbow instead of going to his other classes receives passing grades in all his academic subjects: biology, mathematics, social studies. And who can blame teachers for this? To fail a kid like Arnold is to run the risk of having him in your class for another year.

The truth of the matter is that Arnold's problems have been passed on for seven years. Every year in his permanent record his teachers have found euphemistic expressions to make note of his severe behavioral and learning issues. But officially, Arnold passes muster. Just get him—and kids like him—to high school, the thinking goes, where he can take a lot of shop classes. *Move them on, move them out. Rawhide.*

At the end of Arnold's year in seventh grade, even though I know the battle is already lost, I confront the principal. "Who's going to phone Arnold's mother and explain what this passing grade means? We're sending home a report card that testifies Arnold had a good year." The principal doesn't bother to answer. He knows as well as I do that nobody is going to come pounding on his desk demanding that he educate an underpriviliged white kid like Arnold. Middle-class kids, black and white, have advocates. Their parents fight for them, learning how to get special services out of a moribund system.

My goal is not to retain Arnold. By making Arnold repeat an unsuitable curriculum we'd only prove that we're as off center as he is. My real purpose is to cast doubt on the practice of mainstreaming, try to make school personnel admit that some children need and deserve a different curriculum. Hey, I'd like all children to have a different curriculum, but I focus on kids like Arnold because for them the issue is one of survival. There are things Arnold needs to learn, things he can learn, but because we insist on keeping him in the mainstream, there's nobody available to teach him these things.

My colleagues give Arnold passing grades because they know he could be in our school ninety-nine years and never learn the existing U.S. history curriculum any better than he's learning it now. I give Arnold a failing grade because I insist that we should develop a plan of curriculum reality. Both sides have a point. Neither does Arnold any good.

Mainstreaming, of course, is not a problem that pops up on the day late in June when we decide who passes and who fails. Obviously Arnold and his peers were with us all year, and they caused us a lot of distress. What amazes me is that in the six years I teach at the junior high and in the fifteen years I teach in the district, the faculty never sits down with the administration and talks seriously about how best we might help oddball children, never discusses what our options might be, never figures out what a good education might be for them. We just muddle along and wring our hands over kids like Arnold. And move them on.

The seventh-grade principal whom I confront on this sticky hot June day is frustrated with me. He mutters that I am the kind of person who is never satisfied, and that if we don't move along we will never get through all the kids on our list. "Getting through" is the mantra of the district. Some people use the saying *Live one day at a time* as a life-affirming beacon, but in schools like ours this is a dangerous practice. I am a teacher who lives her life in belief of the teachable moment, a teacher who is ever on the lookout for the bird in the window, a teacher who scorns the idea of seven-step lessons and reaching something called closure. But my faith in the moment is undergirded with a pedagogy. I may be reluctant to draw a road map for where the class is going tomorrow, but I carry a thick atlas of possibilities. I know a lot about the subject matter I'm teaching, and I know a lot about the kids too. Too often in schools the precept of Live one day at a time translates into Get through each day as best you can. Too often, everybody in the building lives from crisis to crisis. Everybody tries to cope with the antics of an Arnold, but they never sit down and figure out a better plan for him.

Over the years the principal and I have exchanged words about more than Arnold. He resents the fact that I produce the union newsletter. He complains that I give administrators a bad name when I reprint official memos as examples of faulty syntax, inflated language, and loony logic. But "Dirty Linen," the department in which they appear, is the most popular feature of the newsletter. Popular and widely quoted throughout the district. At one point the principal called me into his office. After insisting he never reads our "filthy rag" of a newsletter, he reprimanded my lack of civility. "After all," he complained, "it's only grammar."

The principal takes a similar jerry-built approach to pedagogy. He thinks it irresponsible of me to question his plan for getting Arnold out of our building in as speedy a manner as possible. Warts and all. The principal does not stand alone. Ours is a school where curriculum alternatives, mainstreaming, and the grading system are not matters for discussion. Administrators keep the faculty happy by not calling faculty meetings more than twice a year. And before we file into these assemblies, a few jocks act as ward organizers—"Look, no questions, no discussion. Cooperate and we're out of there in ten minutes." Not that the meeting could drag on anyway. The principal has to get to his second job. A district that pays its administrators nearly as much as the state pays the governor does not expect them to see the students off the property at the end of the day, never mind stick around and talk with teachers or meet with parents.

I state my case to the principal but nothing changes. The real irony is that, whether he passes or not, Arnold remains my student. As an eighth grader he gets a new principal and a new roster of teachers. And me.

WHEN SCHOOL STARTS in September, Arnold seems happy to be back. He is very proud of his set of new clothes. As we soon find out, it's a complete set, from inside out. Arnold struts around the room, showing off the special features of each item—logo on the pockets of his jeans, plaid flannel shirt with western cut, heavy lumberjack-style boots. "I even got new underwear," he announces, causing me a moment of panic. But he settles for whacking himself on the rear.

Despite the ninety-degree outside temperature (and the fact that the air-conditioning in our state-of-the-art new building with interior rooms and no windows is on the blink), Arnold removes his new padded parka only long enough to show off his new flannel shirt. Sweat pouring down his face, he refuses to take off the parka, insisting that somebody will steal it if he puts it in his locker. I offer to take it but he is doubtful of my abilities to keep it safe. Arnold announces the price of each item of clothing, describing how he and his mother made a special trip to K-Mart. He brags to the other students about the amount of money his mother spent on his clothes. Even the underwear. I mention this because it shows just how out of tune with the prevailing student ethos Arnold is. Ninety-eight percent of the students would die of embarrassment rather than admit they wear any item from K-Mart. As Orwell points out in *The Road to Wigan Pier*, poor people want the same thing rich people want. And so they waste their money cramming sugar into their tea and on other sweets and chips when they should be buying nutritional food. And Orwell is writing in pre-TV days. Television, of course, only exacerbates these shoddy desires. The values of our school are the values of every school culture—an exaggerated version of what kids see in TV La-La Land. Even the poorest kids wear one-hundred-dollar pumped-up sneakers and seventy-dollar designer jeans. The girls carry their expensive Aigner purses as they eat their free lunches in the cafeteria. But Arnold is oblivious to all this. He doesn't seem to realize that you can only brag about your clothes if they are Nikes or Calvin Kleins.

When other kids' moms shop at K-Mart, the kids cut off the labels. And this starts early. Once, when wearing what I thought to be an innocuous jeans skirt, a third grader asked me to lift my sweater so she could see the back pocket. "Ah, that's good," she grinned, recognizing the pocket stitching as Gloria Vanderbilt. She seemed relieved to see that her teacher didn't shop at K-Mart. Years later, I still worry about that incident. Knowing that a teacher teaches with her every breath, I worry that I unwittingly sent a terrible message about name brands to an eight-year-old who admired me.

Along with the clothes, Arnold starts the school year with a set of resolutions about how he is going to behave. "I'm gonna get all A's," he announces. "Just you wait and see." In case I missed it, Arnold repeats the "Just you wait and see."

Arnold wears his new clothes for three weeks straight. And his determination to fit in, to work hard and get all A's, seems to wilt right along with his flannel shirt. My partner and I do our best to help him find a structure within which to work. We zero in on social studies, talking with his teachers and helping Arnold set up a notebook with daily class assignments. Each day one of us talks with Arnold about what he needs to do for social studies. We give him time in our class to do homework and class assignments.

Arnold tries. He tries hard. But each day his deterioration is more visible. Each day Arnold loses a bit more control, becomes a bit more scattered, more bizarre. I try hard too. I try to ignore the goofy grin, try not to see it as an omen. Then, during the third week of school, Arnold launches into one of his paranoid routines about kids trying to kill him. I take a deep breath and brace myself for pandemonium.

But this time it's different. As Arnold begins his familiar litany, I glance at Cathy. She looks terrified—and sick. I look around the room. Michael and Jeff and Laurel and the eight other students also look scared and miserable. I have one of those flashes of insight, actually a thunderbolt of awful awareness. Arnold is nuts. And I have a roomful of children who are scared. I have a room filled with children who, in the best of circumstances, also have a lot of trouble with school, children who don't deserve Arnold. None of these children are without serious, even severe, problems, but for the most part they are within the normal range of problems that afflict kids in school. For a whole year I have looked at Arnold as a difficult student but one with whom I am supposed to cope. This is, after all, what teachers do. I take very seriously the credo that a teacher must deal with the students she has rather than to wish for better students. This sentiment is actually much more practical than pious; one of the axiomatic truths of education is that if one difficult student moves away, a new difficult student emerges to replace him. It's odd: We don't realize how difficult student number two is until student number one moves away. I guess this is the Nuttiness in the Wings theory of education.

Seeing Arnold through his classmates' eyes forces me to question my long-held forbearance. I have to ask myself: Where is the rule that Arnold's classmates must endure his bizarre behavior day after day, year after year? Most of these classmates are obstreperous themselves; many of them are fairly tough. Some are sneaky; some are mean. But they aren't nuts. Their socioeconomic circumstances range from welfare to solid middle class, their academic abilities from "developmentally challenged" to above average; I can see a range of Gardner's multiple intelligences among them. The one thing they all have in common is that they don't read well. They all have histories of tough times in school, but most of them are learning to compensate for their reading difficulties; some are even learning to cope with the curriculum demands. I have to ask myself if struggling directly with their reading troubles two periods a day isn't torture enough: Why do they have to put up with Arnold too?

As Arnold continues his tirade, I dash off a note to the principal:

Arnold's going around the bend again—and I think I'm soon to follow.

The eighth-grade principal is no pedagogical prince, but he doesn't hit kids every time a teacher complains either. And since I'm not a complainer (not about my students, anyway), he takes my note quite literally, appearing in my doorway five minutes after I send it to the office. He takes Arnold away. I learn later that he has put in an emergency call to the district psychologist, requesting an immediate referral.

Even some years later and with the dispassion that comes with distance, it's hard for me to talk about the what happens next. Ordinarily, a psychological referral takes months, requiring the teacher to fill out numerous forms, supplying all kinds of arcane statistics and justifications. Usually prereferral meetings are required. To assure fairness, to document the range of a student's behavior, every teacher the referred student comes in contact with is interrogated at these meetings.

Not this time. I don't even know the referral has been made until a few days later when Arnold bursts into the room, panicked, "I gotta talk to you," he says. "The doctor's gonna put me into the class with the retards." He clings to my arm in a panic. "Don't make me go. I'll behave. I promise. I'll behave. I really will. I promise."

The referral that I don't even know about has catapulted Arnold all to way to the top of the chain of command, bypassing the school psychologist. The "doctor," the district psychologist, has told Arnold that since he hasn't adjusted well to the change of classes at our school, it will be better for him to be placed in a self-contained class, one where he can stay in the same room all day. According to what the principal tells me later, Arnold insists that he has to stay in my class because I am his "only friend in the whole school, in the whole world."

Funny thing. I referred Arnold for psychological and intelligence testing when he was in seventh grade. Knowing it was an act of cynicism, I did it anyway. I did it for self-protection, not because I harbored any hope that it could benefit Arnold. I'd been in the district too many years, been on the psychological testing treadmill too many times, to think testing Arnold would provide any clues about helping him. But I feel the need to go on record that Arnold is weird. In his official evaluation, the psychologist repeated (without attribution) my comments from the referral form, stating he gained this insight about Arnold's behavior from "extensive interviews." The psychologist did not observe Arnold in my classroom or in any other classroom. His report concludes:

I discussed some possible recommendations with Arnold's mother based on her history of him and our clinical impressions in school—namely that referral to Family Services for a complete CAS might certainly be of value at this time. This interviewer advised Arnold's mother to have a good medical examination before we proceeded with any further recommendations or changes with respect to his school situation. Also recommended was contact with the Big Brothers program so that Arnold could experience a positive relationship with a male role model.

A formal testing evaluation was not done inasmuch as the main problem appeared to this examiner to be one extending from his emotional-behavioral adjustment difficulties. We already have him in modified classes recognizing that his intellectual endowment is only borderline level and certainly no pressure is being put on him in terms of class work. Perhaps some help in calming him down should be given before any changes are made in his school program.

This is the classic pass-the-buck psychological report that teachers know to expect from the psychological team. In every evaluation that I read in my fifteen years in the district, every child is referred to Family Services; the families of problem boys are advised to get him a Big Brother. The result is that, whenever a teacher then asks about a child's status, the principal can reply, "We are waiting to hear from Family Services." In fifteen years, nobody from Family Services ever comes knocking on my door asking about a student. I am sure that Family Services is located at the same address as Kafka's Castle.

Modified program? No pressure being put on him? Arnold has a modified language arts class. Everything else is regular. For starters, this means Arnold has to mingle with and adjust to about 175 classmates in seven different classes, meeting the demands of seven different teachers. No pressure? Arnold's biology, mathematics, and health courses are heavily academic. Even gym and art have essay requirements and written exams. And the classes are large.

Based on my brief note of exasperation, the principal and the psychologist show up to remove Arnold from my classroom and transfer him to the self-contained class for emotionally disturbed children. They appear, without warning, in my doorway and announce that they are taking Arnold away.

It is one of those moments you hear about: My pedagogical life flashes before me. In our school the curriculum in the self-contained classroom, where four students stay with one teacher all day, is popcorn and movies. The smell of their class's daily popcorn production wafts through the building about twenty minutes after school starts and lingers after the buses depart at the end of the day. I can't speak with authority about the faculty room assertion that soap operas are heavily represented in the curriculum, but I do know that no other teacher has a movie projector and a television as part of the permanent classroom equipment.

So when the principal and the psychologist appear, confirming what Arnold has already told me, that he is going into the self-contained classroom, I stand in the doorway and announce, "Over my dead body!" These are my words. Knowing that I'd move out of the state before I'd let any relative of mine be stuck in such a classroom, how can I sign over one of my students to that fate? Even Arnold.

The principal is startled and upset. "Your note said he was driving you crazy."

"Yes," I agree. "Arnold has a way of doing that. But is that how the system works? A teacher gets frazzled and then you come to cart the kid off?"

The psychologist, oozing his terminology, interjects. "Arnold has serious dysfunctional—"

I interrupt, gesturing them out of the room, shutting the door. "This is hardly the time or place to deliver a report on Arnold. Not with him and his classmates sitting there, all ears. I really wonder how a transfer can be made when his teachers weren't consulted formally. How do his other teachers feel? I thought there was supposed to be a hearing with the Committee on the Handicapped and his mother and his teachers. I wouldn't even know you'd seen Arnold if he hadn't told me. There's nothing official in his folder. I looked."

After assuring me I would receive a copy of the psychologist's evaluation, they leave. Arnold is ecstatic. "Wow! Miz O, you sure told them off. And you're gonna let me stay, right?"

The next day I receive a two-page report labeled Psychological Consultation. Here's an excerpt.

> This interviewer conducted an extensive interview with Arnold today. Before talking to Arnold the interviewer had a long, detailed interview with Principal, who stated that Arnold has been sent down on numerous occasions—all for essentially the same thing—constantly disrupting influence in the classroom, bizarre actions, making noises, etc., not having work done properly, and not obeying rules and regulations. Principal also states that of late Arnold has taken on a tough-guy attitude toward teachers. "He wants kids to see him as a tough guy."
>
> Before talking with Arnold the interviewer reviewed a letter sent by his language arts teacher who apparently has "had it" with him. Both language arts teachers feel that he does not belong in their program but would be open to something in respect to suggestions as to how they might help him if he must remain with them.

INTERVIEW WITH ARNOLD: Throughout the extensive interview Arnold was a very pleasant and cooperative person who related well. He recalled our visits in the past and stated that he had made attempts to improve his behavior but "they just don't seem to stay." He seemed to have some insight regarding the fact that he becomes very easily distracted, cannot remember material being taught him for any length of time. During the interview he was extremely anxious regarding what might be happening to him because of so many reprimands—to the point that he stated, "Are you going to send me away?" He also had a fear of being sent out of Mrs. O'Hanion's room because he stated the two teachers there really seem to like him and he knows they do help him. This interviewer explained that another type of program might be more beneficial to him inasmuch as he had trouble changing classes.

This interviewer discussed at length with Arnold the possibility of recommending a contained classroom setup and he was not too receptive to this—primarily because he did not want to leave his class with Mrs. O'Hanion. This interviewer explained that the final decision would be made by the Committee on the Handicapped.

This interviewer went upstairs to talk with Mrs. O'Hanion after the interview with Arnold and apparently he had already gotten to her—telling her of the thinking regarding a different placement for him. Discussion with Mrs. O'Hanion indicates that she would not mind keeping Arnold in the class as long as something could be done to control his disruptive behavior.

The interviewer's recommendations for Arnold at this point would be:

1. To have a conference with his counselor at Family Services in order to see if some help might be given Arnold in terms of his hyperactive or uncontrollable type disruptive behavior.

2. That Arnold continue in his present program—rather than be transferred to a more contained type classroom—inasmuch as his teachers indicate he has the potential to benefit by their setup as long as he can be controlled.

3. If he gets the outside help which we are requesting and if his behavior does not improve in his present class setup then certainly he should be removed to a self-contained classroom—the type which would benefit children with behavioral adjustment problems as well as having a program geared to his needs and abilities.

I read this report, which goes on for three more pages filled with excruciating prose and total disregard for Arnold's needs. Mostly the report repeats statements I've made on the previous year's referral. I want to spit on Mr. Ph.D.

Psychologist. The report was written only after I complained that the psychological services department had neglected to follow their own procedures. The report has little to do with Arnold and everything to do with covering the Ph.D.'s ass. But even taken at face value, it's pathetic. I complain about Arnold and he is jerked from my room. I complain about his removal and he's put back. I wonder why lower-class kids have no advocates looking out for their best interests. I haven't a clue what Arnold's best interests might be. All this mumbo jumbo about the "extensive interviews" with the principal and with Arnold and with me is just so much hot air. I know how much time he spent with me—about two minutes. I doubt that he spent much more than that with Arnold. In two years of testing, the good psychologist has never bothered to give Arnold an IQ test. As controversial and ill-used as the tests are, they would at least give us an indication. Is Arnold's erratic behavior concealing a normal IQ? Or is limited intellectual capacity causing him to act so aberrantly?

I take the report along with my anger to the guidance counselor's office. "Isn't it illegal to make placements on a student without doing the full psychological workup, including IQ test?" I ask. She agrees it is illegal and expresses the same concern I have about the needs of a poor, lower-class kid, one lacking any savvy advocate, being summarily dismissed. "They wouldn't dare treat a middle-class student this way," she says. She asks if her husband, a newly elected member of the school board, can call me at home.

The school board member calls that night and we talk for two hours, as I walk him through my fourteen-month relationship with Arnold—and my longer relationship with psychological services. I air my bitterness and frustration over years of witnessing the neglect and abuse of lower-class children. I point out that although I teach students with a very high rate of referrals, no psychologist has ever observed a student in my classroom. "How can they make declarations about Arnold's best learning environment when they've never looked at any of the environments available? They make these grand statements that are meant to flatter and cajole me, but what if a smart observer could spot twelve ways I set Arnold off? What if Arnold needs a neat and tidy, highly structured environment but instead spends half the day in my clutter? Why is the only choice offered that of Arnold trying to cope with seven different teachers or his being dumped into a self-contained classroom? Why couldn't Arnold come to my class, say, three times a day, attend one more class—and then go home early? Or come in late? Why don't we find out if he does better in the morning or in the afternoon and then offer him half a day accordingly? Any of Arnold's teachers could offer twenty-five more academic alternatives. Why haven't any of us ever been asked?" I point out that I'd taught in an alternative high school program where we let disaffected students choose any three hours of the day for their required in-school time, and the school district did not collapse as a result. Many students did, in fact, turn their disastrous school careers around, graduate, and get jobs.

The next day I learn that the board member has expressed his concern about the psychological services program in general and Arnold in particular to the school district superintendent. I gather he expressed himself rather strongly, because at 11:00 A.M. the Ph.D. and his boss, the assistant superintendent in charge of psychological services, and the assistant superintendent's aide, all appear in my doorway. They start to complain about my talking to a school board member about a "mentally defective student." I cut them off, saying, "I'm teaching. I will not talk about matters affecting any of my students or my own professional behavior during class time. If you have anything to say to me, I'll meet with you during my lunch break, my planning period, or after school. You can find my schedule in the office." I shut the door.

Arnold is again present when I shut the door on administrators and again he is very impressed. "Wow! Did you see that?" he asks the world at large. I wonder how so many adults, people paid to be knowledgeable about kids, can walk into a classroom and assume that the students there are blind, deaf, and dumb.

Arnold is not the only one who is impressed. The superintendent is so impressed, he wants to see me. I receive a summons to his office the next day. Although he had been assistant superintendent in charge of personnel when I was selected as the district's first Teacher of the Year three years previously, I have never talked to him, have never received any communication from him other than official, district-wide memos. In the ten years that I have been teaching in the district, I have never seen him in any of the school buildings.

I ask the building union representative to accompany me to my appointment. Because of my own allegations and because of the official attempt to intimidate me, I decide I don't want to talk any more about Arnold's case without witnesses. The superintendent questions the rep's presence. "Does she need to be here?"

I counter, "I don't know. Does she? All I know is that three administrators interrupted my class yesterday and accused me of improprieties. I have no idea why I'm here."

"I want to talk with you about your conversation with a member of the school board," he says.

"I'd like to ask just one question before the union rep leaves," I say. "Did you know that the three administrators were coming to my classroom yesterday?"

"No."

"Then I agree that my union rep may leave," I concede.

First the superintendent asks me if I had initiated the conversation with the school board member. When I reply in the negative, he starts feeding me his best public relations line, telling me that although he knows the school board member in question has the children's best interests in mind, we professional educators must be careful that a layman doesn't get a distorted view of the very complex options offered by the psychological services team. In the future, he advises me, I should direct any concerns I may have about psychological services to that department.

I make an intemperate remark about psychological services and its failure, in its two purported examinations of my student issued one year apart, to do something so basic as to administer an IQ test. The superintendent ignores my remarks and so I ask a direct question. "Are you telling me not to talk to a school board member?"

"Certainly not," he insists. "I'm just advising you that information about students must be treated in a highly confidential manner."

"Are you telling me not to answer direct questions from a school board member about my students?"

"Yes, I am—for the protection of the students and for your protection, too."

I don't ask from whom Arnold and I need protection.

That seems to be the end of the matter. In my five additional years in the district I never again speak to the psychologist. I speak to the superintendent only once more—on the phone.

Three weeks after my meeting with the superintendent, I go to the seventh-grade guidance office to look in another student's permanent record folder. I ask the counselor why there is no psychological report in the folder. "I'm sure she's been tested," I say.

"Maybe so," he tells me. "But we no longer have those records. All psychological reports have been removed to the District Office of Psychological Services—due to concern that teachers browse in these folders and then repeat information of a confidential nature in inappropriate places." He adds that "teachers don't always understand how to interpret test results."

I don't bother to argue. I have to admit that it's a tough call and in different hours of the same day I'd probably argue different sides of the coin. When I'm not involved in the heat of the moment of dealing with a kid with problems, I come down on the side of teachers not knowing a lot of the information in those folders. The information rarely helps the teacher and it often harms the kid. On the other hand, if you can't trust a teacher with the folder, how on earth can you trust her with the kid?

Ignoring the news about the folders, I zero in on the existence of this Office of Psychological Services. I consider myself an in-the-know teacher, but this is my first inkling of the existence of such an office. And it is in our building. I go knocking on the door.

The secretary confides it is her first week on the job. Maybe that's why she gives me the run of the files—and the copy machine. On impulse, I look for Arnold's file. And I discover a new report. Titled Psychological Report, it is dated two days previous to the form titled Psychological Consultation, the form that caused me to damn the Ph.D. for not giving Arnold an IQ test.

This new report, the third one issued on Arnold within one year, contains several pieces of information that I find nothing short of amazing. First of all, Arnold is listed as a fifteen-and-five-months-old adolescent male. Fifteen years old? Other school records tell us Arnold is fourteen, a kid who has never failed. I am not a conspiracy theorist but I begin to wonder if Arnold is being set up to achieve his "leaving school" age a year early. But that's another issue. For me, the issue of the moment is the very duplicity of the report itself.

Arnold is a fifteen-and-five-months-old adolescent male, presently in eighth grade, who is in a modified type education program—getting help from the language arts teachers but having an extremely difficult time adjusting in that room with Mrs. O'Hanion and her partner. At this point Mrs. O'Hanion is claiming that she feels very strongly that her program, which is a language arts class and not a special education room, "does seem inappropriate" for him.

Arnold was tested today by this examiner on the WISC-R, Verbal Scale, on which he scored a VIQ of 72. He had a low of 5 on the information subtest to a high of 9 on the comprehension, with the other subtests scattered in between. He impressed this examiner on testing as having difficulty with the arithmetical reasoning as well as difficulty in being able to understand what was being asked of him on many of the verbal type questions.

On the Raven's test which is a nonverbal test of abstract reasoning and logical thinking ability he scored an IQ of 75. Both these scores would place him in the diagnostic classification of "borderline range of intelligence" according to the recent APA IQ classification scale.

A review of his referral sent in [one year previously] indicates under the school history section that Achievement Test results on the SRA Form F test given while in Grade 7 he scored Grade Equivalents of: Reading 2.2; Arithmetic 3.7; Language 2.7. On the same date in terms of mental ability tests (STEA) he scored an IQ of 70. Under daily level of achievement, also filled out by his teacher, he was reading on a third-grade level but there was no indication of what he was doing in arithmetic, spelling, or other areas.

The rest of the report on Arnold is specifically regarding his interview with this examiner and some of the personality aspects gathered from the interview (reader should refer to other reports on Arnold dated [two days later]) which was written immediately afterwards in order to have some rec- ommendation for him which this examiner could present to the teacher as well as Family Services personnel in order that the school and outside agen- cies might coordinate whatever efforts could be done for Arnold's best interests.

SUMMARY: In view of the present test results, clinical impressions and observations and a review of the records provided plus conference with his guidance person, teacher, and principal this examiner would go on record as recommending the following.

1. That we have another conference with Arnold's parent(s), Family Ser- vices personnel working with the family, teachers, guidance person, principals, and anyone else concerned with Arnold's welfare—in order to coordinate our efforts to afford Arnold the best possible academic program in the city system.

2. After reviewing the records, talking with him, and testing him this ex- aminer feels that he should be in a more self-contained type of class- room setup geared primarily towards remediation, and management of the behavioral adjustment difficulties would be an appropriate move at this time.

3. It appears to this examiner that restating my recommendations of last year—that he be seen for a complete medical evaluation—might be good in terms of helping us deal with his uncontrollable type disruptive type behavior in the classroom, much of which appears to be of a "hyperactive" nature.

4. That the teacher(s) deal somewhat firmly with Arnold in order to bring his behavior more to a conforming type manner—but yet recognizing from an academic standpoint that he does have limitations and proba- bly will need to be worked with slowly but consistently because of this. He is very inconsistent in his academic abilities and it would be up to the judgment of the teacher as to how much pressure she could put on him both from an academic type as well as behavioral type adjustment standpoint (keeping in mind the intellectual level mentioned earlier in this report and noted throughout the permanent record file).

Whew! What a performance, not the least of which is the remarkable ef- fort made, by removing all psychological folders from all teacher access, to en- sure that I would never see it. I do see it—and even obtain a copy—only by a fluke. In her seven-day tenure in the office, the new secretary has not yet been engulfed by tales of teacher ineptitude and malice. She probably thinks teachers are highly trained professionals who need to be well-informed in order to make the best decisions possible for their students. My experience is that school secretaries maintain this attitude of respect toward teachers for about ten days. In any case, when I ask if I can use her Xerox machine to copy Arnold's new report, she says, "Sure."

I don't believe in coincidence. A week later all teachers receive an official memo from the Department of Psychological Services, informing us that all psychological folders are held in confidence by the department. Should a teacher wish to consult a psychologist about a student, a request must be made in writing.

My teaching partner and I do an intense deconstruction of the psychological text we have in hand, tracing the Ph.D.'s careful attempt to dissemble and distract. We can attribute every word in this third report to a note I sent the principal or a conversation I had with the principal or the Ph.D. For one, that statement at the end, that Arnold is "very inconsistent in his academic abilities"—implying that the report writer has intimate knowledge of Arnold's academic functioning—causes us loud hoots of derision. Prior to report number two, the Ph.D. had caught me in the hallway—his usual practice—and said that "Arnold's extremely low language arts skills are evidence that he is mentally deficient."

I objected. "Arnold failed my class because he is so erratic in his willingness to do work, but he is one of the best spellers in the school." This news, of course, surprised the good doctor, and he accommodated this information on his report: "inconsistent in his academic abilities." Every other bit of information that he claims comes from his astute, in-depth conversations with Arnold and his teachers, comes, of course, from notes I wrote to the principals.

Before I cause the flap over the psychologist's duplicity, Arnold's seventh- and eighth-grade principals are frank about the use they make of the psychological services department. One principal says flat out, "We use psychological services to give us what we want." Getting a troublemaker labeled and into special class simplifies day-to-day school operations. The other principal chides me for even suggesting that a psychologist should make any sort of recommendations to teachers. "He's too busy for that sort of thing. His job is to cover us in case a parent complains when we put a kid in special class."

I like to think I caused the good Ph.D. and his cronies a few restless hours waiting for me to drop the other shoe, waiting to see what trouble I would cause over Arnold's third report. I fantasize about calling the crew up before some grand inquisitor of student welfare, but I have to face the fact that my district has no such person.

In the end I don't do a thing with the third report. I don't even tell the concerned school board member or his guidance counselor wife. In the end I ask myself, Am I trying to find a good place for Arnold, anywhere in the district? Or am I just trying to wreak vengeance on the Ph.D.? I have to face my own lack of power. Whatever I might conceivably do to annoy the psychologist won't help Arnold.

I have to admit I am confused about what *is* good for Arnold. Few issues in education are black and white, and this one seems particularly murky. I can see that the Ph.D. and the principals have plenty of evidence that I am causing trouble just to be causing trouble. After all, I don't want Arnold in my class, but I won't let him go to the self-contained class either. I want us to radically change the curriculum and the mainstreaming policy. My school wants to preserve the status quo, to continue to put out small fires. I want a revolution.

ARNOLD STAYS in my class and he passes eighth grade for the same reason he passed seventh: Nobody wants him around for another year. The eighth-grade principal repeats the bromide about getting Arnold into an industrial arts program at the high school. It doesn't matter that nobody believes that enrolling Arnold in industrial arts classes two, four, or seven periods a day constitutes a legitimate curriculum. The truth of the matter is that such a program doesn't even exist in our district. In any case, I wonder who could be foolhardy enough to put Arnold near electric saws and power drills or even plain old hammers.

This time I offer no resistance to passing Arnold on. I even award him a passing mark in my course. Better than passing, actually. After the flap with the psychologist, I strike a deal with Arnold: for my part, I will become his spelling teacher, grading him on nothing else. For his part, he will make an effort to contain his obnoxious behavior. I help him do this by supplying a physical boundary: I drag a refrigerator carton into the room. When Arnold feels the need—or I indicate that it is time—he goes into the carton. I am not proud of the fact that Arnold spends a lot of eighth grade in his cardboard compartment, but he loves it, and it gives the rest of us the space we need to get on with our work. If a teacher learns early on that there's no justice in the world, she also learns how to pace herself so she can try to perform the greatest good for the greatest number. So Arnold retreats to his "office," as we come to call the cardboard box, and I get on with teaching forty-four other students.

Year after year, I seem to come to the same conclusion: Teaching something is better than teaching nothing. Teaching spelling can certainly be a whole lot better than chasing a kid around the locker area. Through spelling, I introduce Arnold to word roots and origins, and we find other ways to widen his horizons. His spelling tests include the names of all the presidents and all the state capitals. On his report card I cross out English / Language Arts and write in Spelling. At the end of the term I give Arnold a 95. No, that's not right: Arnold earns a 95. He doesn't say anything when I hand him the card. He just stares. He bites his lip and blows his nose, complaining that something is in his eye. Actually, I have something in my eye too.

Nobody ever says a word about the mark on Arnold's card. Not even the computer.

Once Arnold gets to high school, he doesn't take industrial arts. He is required to take the same traditional English, math, and history courses that everybody else takes. After all, we have rigorous standards to uphold, and there are no exceptions. The buck finally stops, and after the first marking period Arnold appears in my doorway. He seems to have grown an additional five inches over the summer, and now he is sporting a scraggly moustache and goatee. He has the old wild-eyed look, and he is grinning his big goofy grin as he stands in the doorway. "I failed all the classes," he announces. "Every one." Two weeks later Arnold turns sixteen and drops out of school.

7

Jean's Story and Other Tales

"I feel really tired today," Jean sighs as she walks into the classroom. She flops into a chair and sighs again. "We were up all night waiting for my sister's babies to be born."

"Babies with an *s*?" I ask.

"Yep. Twins." Jean smiles. "Two girls."

"That must be exciting." Being as intrigued as the next person by multiple births, I sit down across the table from Jean, inviting her to tell me more.

"My mother is really excited. They are her first grandchildren." Jean pauses and then adds, matter-of-factly, "My sister isn't married, but she has a boyfriend and they're gonna get married when he gets a job." She straightens up, seeming to gain a burst of energy. "All of us went to the hospital and waited. My father bought us cokes and hamburgers in the coffee shop. We had to wait until four o'clock in the morning for those babies to get born."

"No wonder you're tired," I say. I ask about the babies' names, weight, hair color, and so on.

Over the next few months I hear a lot more about the babies. Jean usually has an anecdote as she comes into the classroom, and I arrange for her to do a research project on twins for across-the-curriculum credit in social studies, science, and language arts. Jean becomes very knowledgeable about twins in fact and fiction; so does everybody else in the class.

In our daily note exchange, Jean tells me all about the twins: how much they sleep, what they eat, which one is cranky, and so on. She writes a funny note about how much trouble she has getting food into their mouths and not all over them—and her. Jean writes about rushing home from school to take the babies for walks, about staying up very late babysitting. After a few months, the twins become a frequent excuse for missing homework, for poor spelling test scores, for inability to concentrate on class assignments. I begin to worry that Jean is being worn down by too much responsibility. She is, after all, just twelve years old.

The day Jean comes back to school from a four-day absence and tells me she's been out because she had to take care of the twins, I make no comment to her but know I have to act. Over several months I've been listening to Jean tell me about the babies' mother's failure to assume responsibility. "My mom is kind of mad 'cause my sister never stays home to take care of the babies. She wants to party. My sister says she's only sixteen and she's too young to be an old lady yet. Her friends party and she wants to party too." Jean shrugs and ads, "So I have to help out sometimes when my sister is gone. My mom is afraid she'll get fired if she misses any more work. And my dad just isn't any good with babies."

During my planning period I rush to the guidance office. "I know people have their problems," I announce to the counselor, not bothering with pre-liminaries, "But Jean is a child. She needs to be in school. She has the *right* to be in school. I don't know what her parents can be thinking. Jean has ability. If the adults in that family could exert a little responsibility, she wouldn't be failing half her subjects. She wouldn't even need our tutorial class. But if her mother continues to keep her out of school to babysit the twins, Jean will end up being a dropout and an unwed mother. Just like her sister."

When I finally pause to take a breath, the guidance counselor manages to get in two words. "What twins?"

Okay, I admit it; I feel just a bit smug, learning that the counselor is in the dark. Our school is like all the others I've ever known or heard about, op-erating with a structure that ensures friction between guidance counselors and teachers. We teachers, after all, have the hard work; we have these hordes of restless, turned-off adolescents over whom we are expected to exercise every manner of beneficent moral, health, consumer, and citizenship influence, while at the same time teaching them to read, write, divide fractions, and memorize General Washington's battle plans. Guidance counselors are set up to become pals with individual students who wander into their offices.

Now there's a major inequity right there: Where are the offices for teach-ers? A counselor has an office, a telephone, and ready access to a secretary. A counselor can get someone to file her papers and she can go to the bathroom when she wants. A seventh-grade teacher tends to the needs of twenty-five adolescents at a time; a counselor lends a sympathetic ear to individual chil-dren—by appointment. A teacher assigns homework; a counselor hands out jelly beans. If a student complains, the counselor appears at the teacher's door asking with a smile, "What seems to be your problem with Johnny?" It's always the teacher's problem, not the student's. Every teacher is convinced that graduate courses for guidance counselors consist of specific techniques for putting teachers on the defensive. Teachers are convinced that counselors learn the obligatory snotty intonation for that what-seems-to-be-your-problem question in a required course called Have You Stopped Beating Your Students?

I know these judgments are unfair; I know that just thinking about counselors turns me into a whiner. Nonetheless, at this very moment I savor the knowledge that Jean has favored me with inside information, information the guidance counselor who long ago crowned herself Princess Pal isn't privy to. I enjoy letting this woman know that a regular old language arts teacher is Jean's confidante. And so I lay on the detail. "They must be about eight months old by now—Jane and Joan. They all live with Jean's parents—the mother and the babies. And it sounds as though all the kids stay up half the night, with Jean in charge. Jean's sister seems to be out partying most of the time."

The counselor looks at me for a moment. "Jean doesn't have a sister," she says. Her calm, confident voice unsettles me. "She's an only child."

"She can't be!" I insist.

"She's in here a lot," the counselor says with conviction. "I'm sure I'd know if she had siblings." She is very sure—both of herself and her information. She undoubtedly aced another one of those required courses: How To Avoid Revealing Any Smidgeon of Insecurity in Front of Teachers. Otherwise known as Omniscience 301.

I keep repeating, "I don't believe it." Not only do I know all about Sherry, Jean's older sister and mother of the twins, but there are also the three younger siblings. Jean is lackadaisical and sloppy about most school work—starting many assignments but finishing few, losing the ones she does complete—but she is a devoted letter-writer. Every day she writes me a long, detailed note, and most days this note is about her family. Even before the twins were born, Jean wrote funny family stories, describing the antics of her three younger siblings. Jean doesn't generalize in her notes: She describes trips to the country to pick apples, painting the fence at their grandparents' house, her brother getting himself locked in the bathroom. Jean writes about card games, skating and sledding mishaps, birthday parties, trips to the mall. I can recall a long, detailed list of the activities and adventures of Jean and her siblings.

The counselor pulls Jean's permanent record file from the cabinet, and there it is: Jean is an only child. Right then and there, the counselor phones Jean's mother, a homemaker who does not have a job outside the home. The counselor explains that the school is updating files and verifying information. Mom confirms that Jean is an only child. An imaginative only child, I suddenly realize, and one who must know more about twins than anybody else in the school.

I am fascinated by what Jean has pulled off. I am especially fascinated by the fact that nobody squealed on her. Kids who live on her street—right next door, in fact—haven't even hinted that there might be anything amiss in the stories she has been spinning about the babies. As I look back, I now realize that other students had paid little attention to Jean's and my enthusiasm for the twins. But in seventh grade much communication with a teacher is individual. Seventh graders interact with each other in packs—in the hallways and the cafeteria. Those who choose to talk to a teacher usually do it one on one.

I wonder if race has anything to do with it. Most of the class is black. Jean is white. Are the twins Jean's way of making sure she gets noticed? Black kids squeal on each other all the time—accusing each other of cheating, of exaggerating, of being full of it. Is there some sort of reverse code that prevents them from squealing on a white kid?

I've never known seventh graders to be particularly loyal to each other simply on the grounds that they are all of an age and banding together against adults. If seventh graders don't snitch as readily as third graders, they do, nonetheless, snitch. So why do they choose to keep silent about Jean's tall tales? Jean is an ordinary sort of child—neither particularly popular nor an outcast. She isn't a good student, but neither is anybody else in the class. By helping her with her projects on twins, I'd helped her raise her marks in science and social studies, but that kind of help is available to any student in my class. Besides, neither Jean nor her classmates sustain any long-term interest in grades.

Every student in our language arts tutorial class, as well as most students in Jean's other classes, must have known there were no siblings, no twins. Students see Jean getting all that special attention from the teacher—all those "How are the twins?" remarks—and they let it happen. They let it happen for eight months. And who knows? Maybe they'd have let Jean's tales go on forever had I not stumbled across the truth. Maybe Jean's classmates figured she needed the fantasy. Live and let live; lie and let lie. And maybe I am a coward, but I never confront her with the lie. I just stop asking about the twins, and Jean just stops talking about them.

I guess, instead of confronting Jean, I confront myself. I pride myself on being so savvy, someone with such a good feel for kids and their talk, so tuned in to their hopes, dreams, fears, and longings, that it never occurs to me a student might be lying. No teacher wants to think she actually sets herself up to being conned, or, even worse, that she might actually encourage students to lie. But faced with Jean's stories, I have to ask myself, "Why me?" Of her seven teachers, two principals, two guidance counselors, numerous librarians, aides, nurses, secretaries, custodians, hall monitors, why does Jean choose me?

Is it my ever enthusiastic ear? My willing heart? My alacrity for dropping formal lessons and capitalizing on one child's particular interest of the moment? Or am I just more gullible than most? And more energetic, perhaps? I mean, I don't just listen to Jean's stories; I become an active participant, organizing all those grand, across-the-curriculum study units. I prod and push other teachers, the librarian, and the nurse to get involved. The science teacher, for one, does not know of the twins' existence until I suggest that I might guide Jean in producing a research report worthy of science credit. The science teacher readily agrees, but does not become involved in listening to twin stories as an excuse for missed homework.

There is more to this puzzle. I teach on a team. There are two of us in the classroom. Although I am officially the seventh-grade teacher and my partner the eighth, we both teach everybody. But I am the one Jean tells about the twins. After the fact, I realize that my partner has never expressed more than a casual sort of interest. Yes, I am the twin enthusiast.

Certainly Jean's tall tales are not the first I've heard. Nor are they the last I fall for. Jean is not the only one of my students to lead me down that garden path of fantasy, wishful thinking, and just plain lies. Long before she enters my classroom, I have stopped worrying about whether what a child tells me is 100 percent factual or not. Although I don't like to think that I encourage lies, I do know that they are important. I suspect that for many children, lies express real needs more than the truth ever can. In stamping out lies I wonder if we might not be trampling on some important truths.

I AM THE ONE Steve chooses to show his elaborate, precisely scaled drawings of the rattlesnake trap he invented. With the drawings, of course, comes the explanation. Steve recounts how he has built several such traps and caught lots of rattlesnakes. Sixteen, as a matter of fact.

How should a teacher deal with such a claim? I have no idea what a moralist would say or even a psychologist or a cop. My principal once gave Steve ten hard whacks across the knuckles with a ruler and told him to write a five-hundred-word composition on the evils of lying. That lie and subsequent trips to the principal's office didn't occur in my class. In two decades of teaching, complaining to the principal about a child's lies has never occurred to me. The cynic might say that's because I rarely know a lie when I trip over one, but the truth is I would have to be ready to charge a kid with a felony before I'd considering sending him to this principal.

When I do recognize a lie, it interests me. As I look at this undersized, sickly kid who, according to the social service worker, has a father who abused the mother and terrorized the children before abandoning them, I have to wonder about the significance of snakes. Steve is a boy whose mother has recurring episodes of unspecified origin that put her in the mental wing of the local hospital. When she is in the hospital, Steve and three younger siblings are left in charge of a sixteen-year-old brother who apparently terrorizes them worse than their father did.

I don't hear about either reign of terror from Steve, who I don't recall ever breathing a word of truth about his family. I hear about his mother's illness and his terrorist brother from a colleague whose husband works at the hospital. I decry faculty room gossip; I worry that teachers know too much about students' private lives, worry that salacious information taints our responses as we go about our daily classroom rounds. But I also feel that knowing something of Steve's erratic and terror-filled home life helps me figure out how to be his teacher.

Not that I count myself successful in this role. Over and over I ask myself how a child like Steve survives. I have never been able to answer the question, but I do know that if a teacher is to survive, she must be a pragmatist. Unlike ivory tower generalists or sociopolitico pundits, a teacher doesn't have some easy adages to proclaim, some preconceived presumptions on which to base a knee-jerk reaction. Each day truly is a new day; each day a teacher is faced with real kids, not the ones politicians invent. Sure there are universals in education, as in life. But idiosyncratic kids, unique circumstances, and aberrant behavior require individualistic solutions, which is why behavior checklists and schoolwide discipline policies, matched with steel-encased consequences to match every student misdeed, are a terrible mistake. We must never forget that when we pass a rule, we have to live with it.

A teacher has to learn to pick her own peas, to deal with each day as it comes. When Steve tells me about trapping rattlesnakes, I have neither pedagogy nor moral compass on which to draw. When faced with Steve's tall tale, I do what I always try to do: avoid direct confrontation. I send Steve to the library with this assignment: "Find out what kinds of snakes live in New York State." Steve spends two days in the library. Every time I look in on him, he has his head buried in a book. The librarian tells me she has never seen anyone as engrossed as Steve. All around him students come to the library to socialize, to relax, to fool around, just to get out of class. Steve keeps his head buried in snake books. For two days. When he returns to class he tells me he caught the rattlesnakes not in New York but the last time he was in Arizona.

You have to admire such a kid. I'd sent Steve to the library for mostly ignoble reasons. I am annoyed by his outrageous stories and his refusal to do regular school work. I am as reluctant to let some snotty kid think he can bamboozle me as I am to call him a liar face-to-face. So I decide that he should figure out, indirectly, that I know he is lying. But after he has camped out in the library for two days, I am forced to let him have the last word. For me, "Arizona" becomes a private icon of one kid's wonderful tenacity, ingenuity, inventiveness. "Arizona" becomes emblematic of a child's will to survive.

In retrospect, I can see that I did act on pedagogy after all: I encouraged Steve to find a way out of his story. I don't know if it's better to let a child keep hold of his stories or to let him know that his teacher has command of the world. So I do what I usually do: ignore provocation and proceed with a variation on whatever work is at hand.

WHEN OBVIOUS fabrications appear in the daily notes my students and I write back and forth, I have several options. I can treat these whoppers as literary devices, written to entertain me. In my written reply I can let the student know I appreciate the humor, imagination, and effort he has taken to write a good note. If his fabrication makes me nervous but I don't think his mixture of fantasy and reality does any harm, then I just ignore it. I simply change the subject in my reply. I accept the fact that I am not a therapist: I can't confront the circumstances of their lives which provoke the lies.

And I must admit that I do encourage some of the tales. When I write Dennis that my cat ate pea soup for dinner, he responds, "My cat ate two chickens and a turkey last night." Dennis knows that I enjoy such hyperbole. Denise, however, gets a little carried away with her cat tales, and I am never quite sure how much she believes herself. I write her a note about how much my cat hates to be given a bath, how he yowls and scratches and then, when it is all over, mopes in a corner for hours. Denise writes back that her cat loves baths, that he swims laps in the tub. "My dad gets mad. He can't get a bath because my cat is in there swimming laps." I laugh when I read this and turn to Denise, "Laps in the tub? That is very funny. You have a good imagination."

Denise insists that it isn't imagination but 100 percent fact. She claims her cat dives in the tub every night and swims laps. I think I can trace the origin of this story to a tablet of Kliban cat pictures my students sometimes use as a prompt for writing stories. They enjoy creating funny stories to go with the zany pictures. Kliban cats, of course, hula hoop, rollerskate, perform gymnastics, and float on their backs in the bathtub with a rubber mousie. When writing about these cats for a class project, Denise seems to understand that these are imaginary cats and that we are just writing stories for the fun of it. "I know cats don't really wear hula skirts," she agrees. But in her private notes she insists that her father gets annoyed because there is that cat in the tub. Swimming laps. Denise adds a P.S. to one note: "My cat is a very good swimmer, but he's not so good at diving yet. Sometimes he belly flops."

The cat tales are unique for Denise. In all the time I have known her she has shown me only a single-minded literalness. Certainly I would never describe her as a creative child. My colleagues have a lot of names for Denise. "Stubborn as a mule" is one of the nicer descriptions. Certainly we have plenty of time to try to figure her out. Despite my insistence that retention is cruel and unusual punishment for any child and particularly for this one, the principal, in cahoots with a few teachers, doom Denise to repeat seventh grade twice. She is a stubborn, defiant, single-minded child-woman who, twenty years ago, probably would have been labeled as mildly retarded.

Now that the word is banished from schools, Denise muddles along without a label, which means she receives no special help other than being enrolled in our language arts tutorial class. She doesn't cooperate in social studies, math, and science. If she would smile and copy her pages from the encyclopedia, she would pass her courses. But because the work makes no sense to her, Denise is belligerent and disruptive. And so she is made to repeat the work she doesn't understand. When she refuses to cooperate the second year, she is made to repeat it for the third time. The same curriculum. Where Arnold seemed beyond anybody's control, including his, Denise's obstinacy seems deliberate, so a few teachers try to get even.

When Denise decides not to do something, she is awesome. Nobody can move her. She treats threats, entreaties, rewards, punishments, and silence all the same. Every minute of the school day has to be on her terms. As her teacher for two periods a day for four years, I never see her yield an inch.

And so when Denise shows this interest in writing cat stories, I am delighted. The pleasure both she and I get from these stories seems to provide a breakthrough. She asks if she can join the writing workshop I sponsor during students' lunch break. What an extraordinary request coming from this child who is legendary for her refusal to do school assignments. Attending writer's workshop does not transform Denise's attitude about work in our classroom. It is not unusual for her to staunchly reject a writing assignment in class and then give up her lunch break to attend a workshop session.

Denise does not talk to me or to other students in writer's workshop. She is too engrossed in her own work to bother with anybody else. Other students write plays, mysteries, biographical sketches, poetry, and love ballads, sharing them with each other. Denise writes cat stories and talks to no one.

When I suggest that everyone attending the workshop submit a cat story for an anthology, Denise submits two. When the anthology is published, she tells me she is going to give it to her mother for her birthday. "It will be the best present she ever had."

Denise eventually makes it into high school—more, I think, because she wears out her junior high teachers than because she ever toes the line in terms of curriculum or behavior. She finally convinces teachers and administrators that they can't wreak justice on her. They give her a diploma by default because she refuses to earn it. Denise drops out of school in tenth grade. She continues to write me letters. And she mentions the cats. "Do you remember those cat stories? They were the best thing I ever did in school. Maybe I'll write some more some time."

SOME STUDENTS' TALL TALES are better classified as yearnings. These stories reveal such a hunger for identity and affection, such an aching to be part of the American mainstream as pictured in television commercials, that I can't bear the responsibility of insisting that the teller face up to reality. Besides, I'm not at all confident that I know the reality. When I teach third grade, Bobby shows me that. Annoyed by his exaggerations because they seem unnecessary, I set out to pin him down to reality. I am used to working with deprived children—children with pinched, peaked, pained faces, faces sometimes starved for emotional as well as for material support. And so when I am confronted with a third grader in his Irish wool sweaters, his Nike sneakers, carrying his computer games and his miniature cars, I wonder why he has to exaggerate. Bobby has all the possessions, the opportunities, the parents and grandparents that go with the storybook middle-class life. His parents and grandparents are educated, caring people who dote on this only child. What's more, they aren't part of the sterile, possession-grabbing middle class that is so easily criticized for its lack of values. Bobby's family are decent people whose values I respect. So how come Bobby feels it's necessary to spin such whoppers to me?

I know I am prejudiced: If a kid whose mother cleans toilets at Howard Johnson's to support six fatherless children exaggerates about how much money he spends every weekend, I "understand his needs"; if Bobby does this, I inwardly fume and outwardly try everything I can think of to get him to stop. I try to bring up the subject of Bobby's exaggerations with his mother, but she chooses to interpret the examples I give as further evidence of his wonderful creative potential. I admit I give her only vague hints and then chicken out, not being able to bring myself to state baldly, "Bobby lies." After all, who am I to draw a line in the sand between lying and creative potential? Besides, I adore this kid too.

Bobby's lies are never malicious or even sneaky. They might be classified as part of the tall tale tradition except they lack any smidgen of humor. At least I think they do. If humor is there, it is too artfully concealed for me to detect. Bobby's lies are patently obvious, I think, and I worry that Bobby, who is pretty much of a loner by disposition, will completely alienate his peers by his exaggerated claims. If Carol mentions that her mom has just bought a microwave oven, Bobby announces that they have three microwave ovens at his house. The day he responds to Eric's declaration that his mother has bought an electric typewriter by announcing that at his house, they have twenty-six electric typewriters, I just can't take it. I move in on the story.

"What do you *do* with twenty-six typewriters?" I ask.

Bobby rolls his eyes, giving an exaggerated sigh. "I don't really know. You'll have to ask my dad." He shrugs, adding, "I guess he just likes type-writers."

I let the matter drop. Instead of encouraging Bobby to tell the truth, I seem to be serving as straight man for his budding comedy routine. And I had thought he didn't have a sense of humor.

Another time, when a student mentions what a good time her family had skiing over the weekend, Bobby claims his family went mountain climbing, sightseeing in New York City, and skiing in Canada—all in the same weekend. I turn my back on him, studiously ignoring his contribution to the class discussion. The next day Bobby brings me a brochure from a mountain resort near the Canadian border. "My mom thought you might like to go there sometime," he says.

When we are studying parts of the body, I bring out a disarticulated rabbit skeleton to show the class. Bobby announces, "Well, we have two human skeletons at home." I refrain from rolling my eyes, but I know my skepticism and my irritation are palpable. "Want me to bring them in?" Bobby asks.

"Sure," I answer, "if it's okay with your mom." I am weary of these outrageous claims, but I still feel obliged to give him a way to save face when the other children begin to pester and taunt him about bringing in those human skeletons. They don't much care about his twenty-six typewriters, but I feel sure they will pounce on this skeleton claim if he doesn't produce. After all, I remind myself, Bobby is only eight years old. He deserves an escape hatch from his own tall tales.

The next morning Bobby walks into the classroom carrying a brown paper bag. Inside is a human skull. It is plastic but it is life-size, a medical specimen. "I couldn't carry the whole body," he explains. "It's kind of big."

So just when I think I can pin this boy down to reality, he has the last word. I don't ask why his mother can't drive him to school with the rest of the skeleton. I figure she is climbing the Matterhorn. His father is, of course, busy typing. The appearance of the skull makes me wonder if maybe Bobby really is, as he claims, depending on the religious holiday at hand, both Jewish and Catholic.

ONE OF THE MOST AMAZING examples of student lying to come my way probably would never have been revealed if the seventh grader hadn't also been a thief. In my more than twenty years in classrooms, I have never had my purse stolen. But I am also vigilant about never leaving it readily available. My purse stays in a locked drawer in my desk, and, even so, other than my driver's license, it contains nothing of value. On the rare occasions when I need to carry money to school, I carry it in my pocket. When my team teaching partner is out sick, the substitute's purse is large and won't fit in my drawer that locks. I advise her to take it to the office so they can lock it up. "Oh no," she insists. "It'll be okay. When I subbed for you, I just stuck it here in the file drawer." This sub likes the kids and she works very well with them. I know that part of her reluctance to lock up her purse stems from her wish to believe that kids who like her won't steal from her. I again urge her to lock it up, but the bell rings, bringing in the students, and I forget about it.

During fourth period the sub goes to the file drawer to get something from her purse, and there is no purse. The purse that contains her driver's license, innumerable credit cards, her spare four-hundred-dollar prescription glasses, and her eighty dollars for groceries.

I grill every kid, even telling the "usual suspects," "Look, those glasses are important. If we get them back—plus the wallet with the driver's license and the credit cards—we won't ask any more questions about the cash." Every one of these kids swears he doesn't know anything about the purse's disappearance.

Two weeks later that sub appears again. She has replaced the driver's license, credit cards, and prescription glasses. And her purse is stolen again. "I know I should have put it in the office safe," she says with a forlorn smile. "I did put it behind a whole lot of papers in the cabinet." Even though I find it more difficult to be sympathetic the second time around, I again grill the students.

The third time this sub's purse is stolen, we are giddy. "Don't worry; it was an old purse and I didn't even bring my driver's license this time. I just felt I have to prove I can teach here without losing my purse," she says. "I guess I can't." Exasperated, I try to explain that a teacher's popularity has nothing to do with whether or not she gets ripped off. Being ripped off is a function of how vulnerable you make your possessions, not a revelation of your personality profile.

This time I don't grill anyone. Instead, I enlist the principal's help in violating students' constitutional rights. During my planning period and while students are in other classes, we search lockers of likely suspects. I find lots of my personal book collection in Tiffany's locker and lots of overdue library books in other lockers. But there's no purse. Not finding it makes me feel terrible for invading students' privacy. I wonder if I'd feel so guilty if I'd found the purse?

I suppose when something like this happens, a teacher always has a mental list of suspects. Clarice's name was not on my list. If I had rank-ordered every student in my classes according to my suspicion of their criminal tendencies, Clarice's name would have been at the bottom. Clarice is matronly in appearance, a big girl who dresses in dark, serviceable skirts, blouses without ornamentation, and an oversized cardigan sweater that she wears every day, regardless of the weather. Clarice appoints herself teacher's helper: she passes out paper, collects notebooks, and straightens the bookshelves. If papers need to be collated and stapled, Clarice is at my elbow to do it. When we run out of paper clips, Clarice volunteers to beg more from the dragon of a secretary who grudgingly metes out school supplies. If Clarice doesn't seem to have any special friends, she doesn't have any enemies either. Students know that if they need a pencil, Clarice has one to lend. If they need to copy math homework, Clarice has it there to copy. If someone needs a quarter for lunch, Clarice has one to spare—within reason. If anybody tries to take advantage and begs too often, Clarice tosses her head and turns her back with an imperious, "Get your own. I ain't no charity."

Then one day Clarice's grandmother comes to school, accompanied by the police. They take Clarice out of the building, and I never see her again. The principal asks me to come look in her locker to see if I can identify anything. The locker is jammed full of more items than anyone could imagine possible, a Dickensian jumble of school materials. There is a huge stack of grammar exercises: twenty-five copies each of enough grammar skills to satisfy any Warriner devotee. Worksheets on irregular verbs, noun-verb agreement, contractions, homonyms, and proper nouns. In Clarice's locker are dozens of sets of the grammar exercises I haven't inflicted on students for ten years or more. She also has squirreled away old ditto master books on holidays, famous Americans, and fire safety. Here we have the relics of education past: Not only are these items that I will never use again, they are things I cringe to admit I ever used. And yet, being a teacher, I don't throw them away.

In a school where teachers come close to shedding blood for copier paper, Clarice's locker contains four unopened reams. In a box in the locker are some trinkets that had gone missing from the top of my desk: a multicolored glass paperweight, a small china cat, a fountain pen. There are books of poetry whose disappearance I have bewailed for months. Going through Clarice's locker is rather like conducting an archaeological dig of objects that had once adorned my desk and cupboards. At the bottom of the pile are one cloth and two leather handbags, all belonging to the hapless substitute teacher. We find two driver's licenses, two pairs of prescription glasses, and a stack of credit cards. We don't find money.

Clarice's locker is not why the police are in the school. They were called because Clarice had stolen an Aigner purse in the girls' locker room. A number of these purses—ever popular among students—had disappeared over a period of several weeks.

It is not unusual for student possessions to go missing in a school. What's unusual in our school is for the police to be called in. As it happens, this is the second Aigner purse lost by the same girl within two weeks. Her socially prominent parents are steaming, and the theft is so audacious, the authorities pounce. Clarice had gone to the custodian, telling him she's lost the key to the lock on her gym locker. "The teacher told me if I miss dressing for gym one more time, I'm going to fail this marking period. Could you use your shears?"

Like every adult in the school, the custodian likes Clarice. "One of the few polite kids in this whole place," he tells me. So he takes his heavy metal clippers and snips off the lock. Clarice thanks him for saving her hide and he leaves. The only problem is that the snipped lock is not on Clarice's locker but on the locker holding the Aigner purse. Clarice lifts the purse, stuffs it into her book bag, and goes to the office, requesting a late pass to get into her next class.

The sheer audacity of Clarice's caper has the faculty and staff buzzing for days. What I want to know is where she got all those class sets of grammar exercises. "I ran them off for her," volunteers the secretary. "Clarice said you needed them and would I please run off twenty-five copies. She'd appear about once a week with exercises for me to run off. It was never all that much—maybe two or three exercises. And she was also so courteous with her pleases and thank yous."

The secretary adds that Clarice is the one student in the school who she trusted to sit behind her desk and answer the phone when she needed to run an errand elsewhere in the building. "And I always left my purse right here in the bottom drawer," she adds. "That child is trustworthy."

"She just doesn't like your brand," offers the principal.

Students tell me that Clarice has "piles of school papers" at home. She likes to play school. Kids gather on her stoop and she leads them through their grammar drills. I wish she'd taught me the secret of her success with the secretary. In my six years in the building, I have never had the nerve to ask her to run off any papers for me.

The school, the police, and Clarice's grandmother strike a deal. She is sent south to live with an aunt, never to darken our doorstep again. The aunt must have struck a deal of her own, as one of Clarice's cousins comes from Alabama to live with Clarice's grandmother.

IF CLARICE BECOMES the stuff of legends, Laurie is the kind of child who slips between the schoolhouse cracks. Her academic skills are poor but she is quiet, hands in her homework, and never causes any trouble. I confess that it isn't until I go to California on spring break that Laurie causes me to sit up and take notice. From California, I mail each of my students a postcard: pictures of the Golden Gate Bridge, Fisherman's Wharf, sea lions along the rocky coast, Lake Tahoe, Sutter's Fort. About a week after school resumes, Laurie writes me a note. "I liked that postcard. I was in California when you were. My dad took me to dinner there. It is nice in California."

I acknowledge Laurie's note and at the same time try to give her a hint that I don't believe it. I write, "It's a long way to California." Then I change the subject.

But Laurie does not want to change the subject. In her next note she writes, "My dad wanted to take me someplace nice." As I look at her note years later, I can see a sort of funny, off-the-wall humor in it. Want to go somewhere nice for dinner? How about traveling twenty-five hundred miles across the country to California? But the reality of the matter has no humor. Because I have taught three of Laurie's older siblings and am more familiar than I want to be with her family circumstances, Laurie's note is one of the saddest tall tales I have ever read.

Again, I try to change the topic in our note exchange, introducing all sorts of subjects. But Laurie keeps coming back to the California theme, writing about all the nice things her father did for her there, all the things he is continuing to do for her now that she is back in New York. One week he buys her new clothes (which are too good to wear to school); another week he tries to persuade her to go to Texas to live with him and his new family. "I told him I want to finish the school year first," writes Laurie. "Then I'll go."

Laurie's correspondence reveals years of yearnings—hopes, fears, deprivations. I can trace every item in her notes to the desperate circumstances of her family. Her father buys her pretty new clothes? In truth, Laurie's one new outfit each year comes from Clothe-a-Child, a community charity that supplies practical clothes to needy children each Christmas.

Laurie's older brother once spoke bitterly of his father's desertion when he was small. "I don't even remember what my father looks like, but I hate him." He told me, "My mom is okay. Who can blame her if she gets lonely sometimes? We all have the same name and the little kids think we all have the same father. And what difference does it make anyway?"

Obviously it makes a difference to Laurie. But I don't have any help to offer her. In our notes I keep changing the subject away from her dad in California but she persists. Then, after eight days, she doesn't mention California or her father again. I wonder if this is progress. I believe that the language of school is a public discourse and that teachers should not encourage students to write in a confessional style. Our TVs and newspapers are filled with people who pimp their privacy. I don't want to add to it. Still, I wonder and I worry that Laurie does not get what she needs from me. It is hard for a teacher to face up to the fact that she can't provide what a student needs. But there it is.

I TRY TO KEEP QUIET about children's vulnerabilities, their hopes and dreams. Seared in my memory is what happened once when I "went public." Although many students stay in our tutorial class for both seventh and eighth grades, Tiffany had tested out at the end of seventh grade. So she isn't even one of my students when, as an eighth grader, she comes up to me in the hall and says, "Mrs. O, I thought you would want to know. My grandmother died yesterday."

I am heart-stricken for Tiffany. I have heard various tales recounted in the faculty room and the guidance office, tales about how Tiffany came to be living with an elderly woman who apparently is not a blood relation. I don't care to probe for the ins and outs of Tiffany's parentage or why she isn't living with a parent. All I know is that all through seventh grade, Tiffany, one of the most obnoxious students I have ever encountered, expresses her love for her grandmother in our daily note exchange. Her grandmother is, in her words, "the only real friend I have ever had."

One of the most poignant letters I have ever read is one Tiffany's quasi grandmother wrote to the principal and he put in her permanent record file. Crippled by arthritis and unable to come to school as required after one of Tiffany's many infractions, this woman writes, "I know Tiffany lies and steals and gets in fights, but she is very helpful to me. She loves me and I love her." I am relieved to know that Tiffany has this woman to love and be loved by. At school, on her good days—and ours—we try to tolerate Tiffany. Nobody at our school can find the way to love this child.

After Tiffany gives me this terrible news about her grandmother, I hug her and try to give her some comforting words. I send her to another teacher who is working hard at getting her involved in a special language arts project. Then I go back to my classroom and write Tiffany a long letter. She enjoyed our correspondence and I want to send her home with words that might be a comfort.

Then I go to the guidance office to make sure they have the news. Tiffany is the kind of kid who makes a home-away-from home out of the guidance office and the nurse's office and any other place where, when you knock, they have to let you in. Tiffany overlays her very real problems with a never-ending string of petty gripes. She is such a perpetual whiner that it is hard to feel real sympathy for her for more than about three minutes at a time. Tiffany tattles on students when they copy each other's homework and then whines that nobody likes her. Tiffany steals things from kids' lockers in gym and then whines that nobody likes her. Every adult and every student in the building knows that trouble travels in Tiffany's wake.

But the counselor's reaction is the same as mine: "My God, what will Tiffany do without Grandma?" The counselor starts making phone calls, trying to make sure that someone is willing to be responsible for this thirteen-year-old. A number of relatives indicate they know nothing and don't want to know anything. Then the counselor reaches one of Tiffany's aunts, who is stunned. "Grandma's dead? I was at the hospital yesterday and they said she's going to come home in a few days."

Meanwhile, a hall monitor who lives near Tiffany hears the news and starts calling neighbors, arranging for food to be taken to the family, a funeral wreath to be delivered to the house, and so on. Later in the day an irate family members calls the principal, wanting to know if everybody at our school has gone mad. We'd put the whole family along with everybody on their street into an uproar. Grandma, the caller informs the principal, is not dead; she is recovering nicely from heart bypass surgery and is coming home from the hospital in a few days. The caller wonders what kind of sick practical jokes we play at our school—and what are they supposed to do with all the flowers people keep leaving at the house?

I try to talk with Tiffany, but she is so shook up and scared about the havoc her tale has wrought that she can't listen. She just keeps saying, "Well, she's in the hospital. She could die. She still might die." My heart cracks for this desperate child, sick with worry about the only person in the world who loves her. I could wish she had come up with a less dramatic way to deal with her fears. Instead, I try to understand.

I AM SURE plenty of school board members, politicians, media big shots, and members of august commissions setting school standards will express righteous wrath over my insistence that teachers had better tread carefully around kids' lies. But I'll say it again: A child's lie is a fragile thing. When all the self-proclaimed education experts hint that everything from a rising crime rate to an unfavorable balance of trade is a result of the schools' laxness in inculcating moral values, it will do us no good to buy another behavior modification system. Or read from someone's book of virtues. Or nail the Ten Commandments on the schoolhouse wall. Or require students to recite passages from the Declaration of Independence. Or make them wear uniforms. The same politicians who implore teachers to bring school back to some good old traditional American values, kick children off the minimum sustenance provided by welfare, post their individual scores on standardized tests on classroom walls, deny children recess, art, music, and gym so that they can get filled up with more skills, and assign lockers based on how they do on those tests. These fellows live in a simple universe: Right and wrong. Black and white. Sex and abstinence. Hard work and welfare. Skills and ignorance. Mom and apple pie. The only trouble is, Mom is out working three jobs to make ends meet, apple pie was long ago supplanted by Twinkies and potato chips, and presidents and members of Congress are fending off charges of sexual improprieties. And worse.

All I know is that even when I do recognize a lie when it stares me in the face, I hope I have room to back off fast. I just don't feel fit to cope with lies. Byron, quite a scoundrel himself, once pointed out that a lie is truth in masquerade. *The truth will set you free* is a slogan that should freeze any teacher's soul. As often as not, all truth does is complicate your life. Every day a teacher works with difficult children in difficult circumstances. Every day she must decide if she has any business trying to peel away any of those layers of protective coating that wounded children wear. I, for one, never found that Omniscience 301 course in the catalog. All I can do is try to deal with each day as it comes. I can't pretend I have ever believed in a master plan—not in the classroom, not in life.

As I sit here looking back at events, I can recognize two patterns: I rarely smelled a lie right under my nose, but when I did, I tried to deal with it sideways, never directly. When you teach, you have to rely on your instincts, because you have no time to think. None. Kids are in your face, not sitting at your feet waiting patiently while you contemplate your navel. Or your options. I don't confront lies directly because I know in my teacherly bones that it is better to do nothing than to do something bad. When I go home at night, the first impulse is to thank my lucky stars that I did not behave badly that day. Later I may think about what I tried to teach, but first is that injunction we must share with doctors: First, do no harm.

More than two decades in classrooms has shown me that even when we do recognize Dame Truth, she doesn't set us free. For teachers, anyway, the truth is often unbearable to live with. In the end, what counts more than truth is working with the children we have, helping them to cope with the difficult lives they live.

Jean does well academically and tests out of our program and into regular eighth-grade English. Steve isn't with us for eighth grade, either. His mother commits suicide and he is sent away to a group home for disturbed children. The following September, I am too busy with new students to contemplate my relative success or failure with either Jean or Steve. Now, a decade later, I realize that if I take credit for Jean, I also have to accept failure for Steven. And that would seem to mean that aiding and abetting a lie leads to success and halfway confronting a lie leads to failure. Such conclusions come as no surprise: To be a teacher means to confront the dark ambiguity of not having clear landmarks of success and failure. To be a teacher means to do what you can.

8

Who's On First?

News! From the G*U*I*D*A*N*C*E Office

9/12
To: 7th Grade Faculty
From: R. J. Rankin
Re: Jerome Johnson

Please be advised that if Jerome Johnson is in your class, he needs to be excused from class six minutes early so that he can negotiate the locker area unimpeded. Please send another student with Jerome to carry his books.

Memorandum from the Office of the Vice Principal Marcella E. White, Ed.D.

BULLETIN #35
9/12
To: Faculty
From: Marcella White, Ed.D.
Re: Traffic in the hallways

As we get off to a fresh new start in our marvelous new building, we need to remember the discipline policy adopted 2/10/69 and revised 2/9/70, 1/11/71, 1/10/72, 3/12/73, 10/23/73, 11/10/75, 11/14/77,

139

1/14/80, 11/6/81, 9/9/87, 1/4/88, 6/25/90, 5/27/91, 2/16/92, 10/14/92, 11/13/93, 4/18/94, 3/19/95, 5/27/96, 3/27/97, 11/10/97, 3/23/98, 12/3/98, 5/11/99. This policy so states that no student shall be in the halls without a pass—except during the passing period.

From the desk of . . . Susan Ohanian

9/12
Dear R. J.,

Not to be difficult, but do I have to write a pass for Jerome and his hall buddy every day? (See Office Bulletin 35, which arrived in my mailbox at the same time as your memo.)
Thanks.

News! From the G*U*I*D*A*N*C*E Office

9/14
To: 7th Grade Faculty
From: R. J. Rankin
Re: Jerome Johnson

At the beginning of each school day Jerome will pick up a wooden pass in the guidance office, which entitles him and one companion to be in the hallway six minutes before the end of each period. Jerome will return this pass to the guidance office six minutes before the end of seventh period.

Thank you for your assistance.

FROM THE DESK OF. . . LEONARD WILSON

9/15
TO: GUIDANCE

YOU MAY CALL IT A PASS. I CALL IT A WEAPON. I DO NOT FIND IT APPROPRIATE FOR ANY THIRTEEN-YEAR-OLD HOODLUM TO HAVE IN HIS POSSESSION A FOUR-BY-ELEVEN-INCH HUNK OF WOOD, EVEN IF HE IS A HOODLUM WITH CEREBRAL PALSY.

From the desk of ... Susan Ohanian

9/15
Thanks, R. J.,

Now, what can you do about getting my clock fixed so I'll know when it's time to launch Jerome? Kind of strange, isn't it, that none of the clocks on the second floor of a brand-new multimillion-dollar building work?

By the way, have you noticed that Jerome doesn't use that six minutes to travel through empty halls and get safely to his next class? What would be the fun of that? Let's not forget that he IS a seventh grader: he hangs around the locker area until the bell rings so that he can horse around with his pals when they get out of class.

Any word about when Jerome's records will get here? Is it reasonable for us to expect him to hold a pencil? Am I a dreamer to hope that the records might include some specific information about the dos and don'ts of working with this kid?

From the desk of . . . Joe Piaggi

9/16
R. J.,

I want to be in compliance with regards to having Jerome John-son in class, but he claims he can't change for gym. He says his mother does his buttons for him. In other regards, he is a terror—probably wants to prove he can be as macho as the other boys. I'd sure like some information about how much I need to protect the kid and how much I can insist that he toe the line.

From the desk of ... Susan Ohanian

9/16
Dear R. J.,

Jerome knows how to form letters, so obviously at some time in his school career he has held a pencil. But when I ask him to write (or print), he often cries. When he does try to write, I can't read it. And I've always bragged I could read anything! Any chance of getting him an electric typewriter? How has he gotten this far in school without one? What did his previous teachers do?

News! From the G*U*I*D*A*N*C*E Office

9/22
To: 7th Grade Faculty
From: R. J. Rankin
Re: Jerome Johnson

Members of the Cerebral Palsy Awareness Society will meet with teachers at 7:30 A.M. on Oct. 3 to provide an overview of Jerome's status. All concerned faculty are urged to attend.

Teachers Association Alert

9/23
To: 7th Grade Faculty
From: Ann Burke, Building Rep
Re: Contractual Obligations

Please be advised that we are working without a contract and under these conditions we recommend that teachers work to rule. Meetings should be scheduled during the hours in which we are obliged to be in the building, not before or after our specified work hours.

cc: regional field rep

Memorandum from the Office of the Vice Principal
Marcella E. White, Ed.D.

BULLETIN #62
9/26
To: 7th Grade Faculty
From: Marcella White, Ed.D.
Re: Professionalism

I am sure I do not need to remind a community of concerned professionals that our students must always be our top priority. Occasionally it is necessary to schedule meetings outside the confines of the contractual school day. I feel assured that every faculty member will want to cooperate in every way with professionals from the outside community who come to share their expertise with us.

FROM THE DESK OF. . . LEONARD WILSON

10/4
TO: 7TH GRADE FACULTY
RE: LOONY TUNES 7:30 A.M. MEETING

AM I THE ONLY ONE WONDERING WHY WE WERE CALLED TO A MEETING WITH THREE NICE LADIES WHO HAVE NEVER SEEN JEROME BUT WHO WANTED TO MAKE US AWARE OF DISCRIMINATION AGAINST PERSONS WITH CEREBRAL PALSY? IF THESE WOMEN HAD EVER SEEN JEROME IN OUR CLASSROOMS, SURELY THEY WOULD KNOW HOW LUDICROUS THE IDEA OF DISCRIMINATION IS. IF EVER THERE WAS A KID WHO IS *NOT* DISCRIMINATED AGAINST, IT'S JEROME. MORE TO THE POINT, I HAVE SOME SPECIFIC QUESTIONS REGARDING JEROME'S EDUCATION THAT NOBODY AT THE MEETING COULD ANSWER.

- HOW CAN I BE EXPECTED TO TEACH SOMEONE WHO CANNOT TAKE NOTES, WHO CANNOT RESPOND IN WRITING, WHOSE SPEECH I CANNOT UNDERSTAND?
- WHO IS RESPONSIBLE FOR MAKING THE DECISION THAT JEROME BELONGS IN A MAINSTREAM CLASSROOM?
- WHO IS RESPONSIBLE FOR HELPING ME HELP JEROME BE SUCCESSFUL IN MY CLASSROOM?

From the desk of . . . Joe Piaggi

10/4
R. J.,

I'm a practical guy. I admit I'm not into the history of cerebral palsy. Can you please find the answer to the question that nobody in our meeting could answer?

QUESTION: Can Jerome be required to dress for gym?

Check One:

Yes   No

Date _____

Signature _____

News! From the G*U*I*D*A*N*C*E Office

10/5
To: Joe Piaggi
From: R. J. Rankin
Re: Jerome Johnson

I am sending Jerome's mother a copy of his class schedule, high-lighting the days he has gym, and asking her to be sure he wears clothes that do not require buttoning on those days. I will remind him the day before he has a gym class about appropriate clothing.

Thanks for your help Joe. I realize this isn't easy.

From the desk of . . . Joe Piaggi

10/6
R. J.,

Have you thought about how insane our class schedule must look to people in the real world? How many regular people could cope with going to class (or work) three times in a revolving six-day cycle which operates in a five-day week?

News! From the G*U*I*D*A*N*C*E Office

10/6
Dear Mrs. Johnson,

As we discussed in our phone conversation, Jerome's teachers would like to help him participate in school activities to the fullest extent possible. With this in mind, we would like him to adhere to the dress code for PE. Please make sure he wears clothes without buttons or other complications so that he can change his clothes for PE.

Please note that our school operates on a six-day cycle and that Jerome has PE on days two, three, and six during that cycle. For next week, for example, Monday is day six, so that's a PE day for Jerome, as are Wednesday and Thursday. Then, in the following week his PE days are Tuesday, Thursday, and Friday. In the next week his PE days are Wednesday and Friday. And so on.

If you have any questions, don't hesitate to call me. All of Jerome's teachers join me in thanking you for your cooperation.

Sincerely,
R. J. Rankin

News! From the G*U*I*D*A*N*C*E Office

10/17
To: 7th Grade Faculty
From: R. J. Rankin
Re: Jerome Johnson

Attached please find a copy of Jerome's evaluation.

Office of Vocational Training/
Occupational Rehabilitation
EDUCATIONAL SERVICES

To: Guidance Office
From: Judith P. Melrose, OTR
Re: Occupational Therapy Update

NAME: Jerome Johnson
DIAGNOSIS: Cerebral Palsy, athetoid quadriplegia
I. General Information
Jerome is a thirteen-year-old boy in the seventh grade. He is being seen in Occupational Therapy one time weekly for assistance in maintaining range of motion, attempting to normalize tone, assisting in teacher education and planning.

Consultation with teachers has shown improvement in Jerome's behavior through use of consistent firm approach toward undesirable behavior.

Meeting with mother and phone conversations have provided Jerome with a consistent approach to self care, homework, and behavior.

II. Physical Functioning
Fine Motor Skills: It has become evident that although Jerome can demonstrate the ability to write for short periods of time with limited accuracy, his writing ability is not now nor will ever be adequate for school requirements. Therefore, an electric

typewriter with self-correcting feature is necessary for full participation in academic work. A typewriter may be adapted for Jerome by providing a face guard to facilitate accuracy in typing.

RECOMMENDATIONS

1. Occupational Therapy in school setting 1 time weekly.
2. Consultation with teachers as needed to adapt conventional school program for Jerome's physical needs.
3. Continue to provide adapted equipment for increasing independence in activities of daily living.

FROM THE DESK OF. . . LEONARD WILSON

10/18
TO: 7TH GRADE FACULTY
RE: LOONY TUNES REDUX: JEROME JOHNSON
    EVALUATION

PARDON ME, BUT AM I THE ONLY ONE WHO SEES SOME INCONGRUITY IN GETTING A REPORT ON A THIRTEEN-YEAR-OLD FROM AN *OCCUPATIONAL* THERAPIST?

MIGHT NOT JEROME BE BETTER SERVED HAVING A THERAPIST WHO WILL HELP HIM PASS HIS COURSES? DOES IT MAKE SENSE TO TAKE HIM OUT OF CLASSES (HE IS FAILING) SO THAT HE CAN READ THE CLASSIFIED ADS? AND ROLE-PLAY JOB INTERVIEWS? HAS EVERYONE GONE MAD?

AT LEAST THE OCCUPATIONAL THERAPIST SEEMS TO HAVE LAID EYES ON JEROME. HOWEVER, SHE ALSO SEEMS GIVEN TO GRAND GENERALIZATIONS. HOW ABOUT A FEW SPECIFICS?

· IF JEROME CAN TYPE, WHERE IS THE TYPEWRITER?
· WHEN AND WHERE DID THIS "CONSULTATION WITH TEACHERS" OCCUR?
· WHEN AND WHERE HAS THE "IMPROVED BEHAVIOR" OCCURRED? PLEASE TELL ME IMMEDIATELY SO I CAN OBSERVE IT!

News! From the G*U*I*D*A*N*C*E Office

10/18
To: 7th Grade Faculty
From: R. J. Rankin
Re: Jerome Johnson

Pursuant to the recommendations of the occupational therapist, our office has sent a request for an electric typewriter to the Office of Special Services. I'll keep you updated on this matter.

From the desk of . . . Susan Ohanian

10/19
Dear R. J.,

Not wanting to be a whiner, but I, as a teacher responsible for Jerome's academic program, requested an electric typewriter over a month ago. It is disheartening, not to mention not in the best interests of the student, to learn that this request was ignored.

When teachers' judgments aren't respected, they get cynical . . . and restless.

News! From the G*U*I*D*A*N*C*E Office

10/25
To: 7th Grade Faculty
From: R. J. Rankin
Re: Jerome Johnson

Please excuse Jerome Johnson from his fourth-period class on Tuesdays so that he can participate in occupational therapy.

News! From the G*U*I*D*A*N*C*E Office

10/26
To: 7th Grade Faculty
From: R. J. Rankin
Re: Jerome Johnson

Please excuse Jerome Johnson from his fourth-period class on Fridays so that he can participate in group counseling.

FROM THE DESK OF. . . LEONARD WILSON

11/1
TO: ASSISTANT SUPERINTENDENT COCHRANE,
    DR. WHITE, R. J. RANKIN
FROM: LEONARD WILSON
RE: JEROME JOHNSON'S EDUCATIONAL PROGRAM

PLEASE BE ADVISED: I CANNOT ACCEPT RESPONSIBILITY
FOR THE ACADEMIC PROGRESS OF A STUDENT WHO, FOR
WHATEVER REASON, ALREADY DOES NOT TURN IN ANY
WORK AND WHO NOW WILL MISS 40 PERCENT OF CLASS
TIME IN ORDER TO ATTEND VARIOUS THERAPY SESSIONS.

Office of Special Services

1/6
To: 7th Grade Faculty
From: Office of Special Services
Re: Typewriter for the Use of Jerome Johnson

An IBM Selectric Typewriter has been purchased for
the classroom use of Jerome Johnson. The typewriter
is on a stand that can be rolled. If Jerome will need
this typewriter for a given class period, send a
request before 4:00 P.M. the previous day. Authorization will be in the teacher's mailbox. A student
may be sent, with the authorization, to pick up the
typewriter at the beginning of the period for which
the machine is required. The typewriter should be
returned before the end of the period. It is the
responsibility of each teacher to make certain that
no other student uses this typewriter, which is
provided for the sole use of Jerome Johnson.

From the desk of . . . Susan Ohanian

1/9
Dear R. J.,

Can you intercede on this typewriter comedy of errors? We've waited four
months to get the machine, and now we're supposed to waste all this time

writing out requisitions and rolling it back and forth? Every period? Since Jerome is in my class two periods a day, and since I am helping him do the work for his other classes, I will assume responsibility for the machine. When other teachers want it, they can get it from me. At least I'm on the same floor! It's a wonder that they didn't decide to store it one and a half miles away at Central Office.

Please alert me if there will be a typewriter patrol, investigating as to the machine's sole use by Jerome. These people should get real.

Rowena Rawlins
Coordinator Business and Business Studies

2/4
To: Junior High Administration and Faculty

It has come to my attention that a junior high student has been given access to a typewriter to use in facilitating the satisfactory completion of his or her school work. Please be advised that typing studies classes are available to all students grades 9-12. It is imperative that students who wish to type learn proper keyboarding techniques. Moreover, research shows that it is difficult for students who have been allowed to type in a nonconventional manner to break old habits and learn these proper keyboarding techniques at the appropriate time. This office would not wish to see a precedent set in allowing a student unsupervised access to a typewriter without proper instruction.

My office appreciates your consideration of this matter.

cc: Office of Special Services
    Assistant Superintendent in Charge of
    Curriculum

**Memorandum from the Office of the Vice Principal
Marcella E. White, Ed.D**

BULLETIN #218
5/18
To: 7th Grade Faculty
From: Marcella White, Ed.D.
RE: Shared Decision Making in the Matter
    of Jerome Johnson

I am sure I do not need to remind a community of concerned professionals that our students must always be our top priority and that, according to our school's statement of goals, we will endeavor at all times to honor a philosophy of shared decision-making. With that in mind I have asked the guidance department to facilitate a meeting of all of Jerome Johnson's teachers with the goal of deciding on the program schedule that will be most appropriate to his needs. This meeting will take place in Conference Room A at 3:30 on May 18.

Jerome's case is fairly straightforward. Excepting the onetime appearance of representatives from the Cerebral Palsy Awareness Society, we teachers are all too familiar with all the specialists who evaluate Jerome, pulling him out of our classes in the name of better meeting his educational needs. Typically, the professional services system can become quite complex for any student who deviates from the norm. Every teacher has her horror stories about how the system, well-meaning as is its intent, frustrates teachers and seems to work against the well-being of the children it is set up to serve. Most teachers don't even try to differentiate among workers in the health, welfare, and juvenile justice systems. Psychologists or parole officers, they're all the same to teachers: They all seem indifferent to and oblivious of what goes on in classrooms.

Students who don't fit the norm are tested and retested, labeled and relabeled; nothing seems to change in the reality of their lives. In *Stuck in Time*, Lee Gutkind documents in excruciating detail how putting an adolescent in the juvenile health care system for four years can cost $2 million dollars for basic care, psychiatric and other health treatment, and education. And after four years the child involved still can't read or write or in any way function acceptably. I frequently wonder what would happen if, say, one-tenth of that money were given outright to the family. Would dramatically changing their economic circumstances change the children's lives in a way that our baroque social/penal/education systems cannot manage?

Teachers share their horror stories. I sometimes wonder if social service people have similar gatherings, where they sit around trading tales about the lousy teachers they have known. After all, we have these kids with us all these years, but they still hate school, have no manners, and still can't read. When kids don't fit in with group norms, every adult who has contact with them seems intent on finding somebody else to blame. If only they had parents who cared; if only our religious institutions were effective; if only big business weren't so greedy; if only politicians weren't so corrupt; if only teachers unions didn't protect incompetent teachers; if only the curriculum were better. The litany of the "if onlys" is long and predictable; it is also futile.

Every school I have ever taught in or heard about has a predictable pattern of pretending to deal with kids who don't measure up: test and retest them, label and relabel, as though an unlabeled child were an affront to some great pencil pusher in the heavens, as though getting a label on a child puts that child into some sort of state of grace. Children who are physically handicapped are often helped by labels: the label can provide money to buy "stuff" the student needs—glasses, large-print books, hearing aids, fancy wheelchairs, electric typewriters, and computers. Sometimes the label buys special services of the human kind. When blind students were assigned to my classes in my first year of teaching, I found the braille transcriber to be an invaluable resource, enabling those students to have a copy of everything I wrote on the board, every piece of paper I handed out. It also caused me to be very organized as long as those students were in my care: I had to think ahead about what I'd want to write on the board. With blind students in my classrooms, my desk was neat. So were my lesson plans. That transcriber never needed to set foot in my classroom, but with his rather minimal assistance, blind students could be a part of the mainstream.

Jerome's occupational therapist has her uses. Once she issues her report, his teachers and guidance counselor can push the office of special education to provide him with an electric typewriter. The machinery is Jerome's federally declared right, but this doesn't mean that getting it is easy. It takes four months and a barrage of complaints and threats. Never mind asking why and how he has already been in school seven years without this essential equipment. Maybe junior high teachers deserve their reputation for being aggressive: We got Jerome that electric typewriter.

Mostly, we are frustrated by our failure to move the system, our failure to get practical advice that we can use in the classroom. For starters, Jerome's therapists never come to see him in the hallways during the passing bell, in the classroom, in the cafeteria. He functions very differently in these different sites. Among his peers out in the hallways, Jerome is an active, assertive, popular boy. In the classrooms he assumes the role of whining victim: his favorite phrase is "I can't do this." Funny thing: I never see him whine "I can't" in the locker area. When, after the forty-five-minute historical and social overview of cerebral palsy, teachers are invited to ask questions, no expert can tell us whether or not it is advisable to ask Jerome to hold a pencil. That's pretty basic, isn't it? Seven years in school and nobody knows if he can or should hold a pencil?

Bureaucrats think their job is over once a problem is defined. Labels for emotionally disturbed and learning disabled students are helpful to the school, bringing in more monies from state and federal sources. But those labels rarely change much in terms of what those students are taught—or what they are expected to learn. Trailing behind the school district labeling specialist (some people call them psychologists) come the social service case workers, university reading clinicians, speech therapists, occupational therapists, and people who hang up shingles as learning disability specialists. Not once have I seen any of these people, these experts whose stated purpose indicates an effort to keep the child in school, even help the child perform better in school, express any interest in observing a child in my classroom. Nor do these people want to hear my opinion of how a child performs in my classroom. The experts never come to watch how a child might interact with his peers or with me; they never see how a child might organize his time and materials, work under pressure, stick to a task, daydream, fall asleep, hassle people, help people, get frustrated, find pleasure. They never see him bully, tease, hoodwink, charm, hide, confront. Not once has any of the professionals asked me how I run my class, never offered me any specific advice on how I might help a child; nor have they solicited my opinion on how I think they might help a child. Specialist is specialist and generalist is generalist. And never the twain shall meet.

Instead, twice a year the experts gather up their number two pencils and give the child yet another battery of tests. They get entry data in the fall and outcome data in the spring. And then they file it. They collect their data and write their reports on a child's social and academic functioning—without ever leaving their nice, quiet offices. Without ever seeing the child in action, they make their decisions on where the child will best function in the school. They pronounce on "where," never venturing into the territory of "how."

I THINK OF JOLENE. This seventh grader's wild tales and suggestive smirks indicate that she is sexually promiscuous, but she tells me she hopes she'll get a doll for Christmas, a collector Barbie with an extravagant wardrobe. At age fourteen, Jolene is pretty much of a nonreader. She recognizes a dozen sight words but cannot distinguish sounds. For her, clap, cup, and cake sound the same. Jolene knows her phone number but can't seem to remember her address. She "learns" it one day but forgets it by the next. Like many of my seventh graders, distinguishing between rivers and oceans and cities and states is impossible for Jolene. She finds it very confusing that we live in the United States and also in New York State. She isn't the only one. Asked on a daily geography quiz to name five rivers, 30 percent of the class don't even mention the Hudson, which flows a few blocks from our school.

When Jolene, who is already on probation, is arrested for shoplifting, her probation officer increases their meeting time from once a month to once a week, but I never meet the probation officer. Nor do I meet Jolene's occupational therapist, who does appear in our building once a week. All I can get out of Jolene about these sessions is that she sometimes rolls back and forth on a big beach ball. Jolene describes this activity as "weird." Nor does my path cross that of Jolene's group therapist, who meets with her and four similarly antisocial adolescents twice a week. I don't know who makes the decision that Jolene should be sent "away." Suddenly she is simply gone.

ON ONE OCCASION an outside professional does enter my classroom. An aide from the social service department is sent to watch over Tommy. "Guard duty" describes her function.

Tommy is short and skinny, with the pasty look of a child whose diet consists of Twinkies washed down by Coke. But appearances can be deceptive: Tommy is also a bundle of energy. He is an active, tough little kid with a depressingly long arrest record for petty theft, breaking and entering, malicious mischief. And truancy. It's anybody's guess which is thicker—his police record or his truancy file. They may seal the records, but that doesn't stop the gossip: News travels quickly in a school district.

Tommy's name appears on my official class list the first day of school. When I ask where he is, the other students inform me, "Oh, Tommy never comes to school. Not even in first grade." Students are often a teacher's best, if not only, source of practical information, but I check the official files anyway. I discover that my students haven't exaggerated. It isn't unusual for a child to gain a truancy record in fifth or sixth grade, but Tommy is a legend: He quit school before he even started. He didn't even attend kindergarten with any regularity.

According to official school records, Tommy showed up eight times in sixth grade. He was passed on to seventh grade because he had already been held back three times, and teachers think it's disruptive to have tough, streetwise sixteen- and seventeen-year-olds in the same class with naïve and more childlike eleven- and twelve-year-olds. Parents aren't crazy about this mix either. Hardliners who insist on the elimination of social promotion don't seem to be stepping forward with advice on how to protect the little girl who keeps a teddy bear in her locker from the randy hulk who should keep condoms in his.

According to the official records, twice during Tommy's elementary school career the school psychologist had caught up with him long enough to give him a battery of tests. Both times Tommy had been diagnosed as having a "severe reading problem" and was referred to remedial reading. I wonder how many graduate courses in psychology one needs to sit through to figure out that most kids who go to school just eight days a year aren't going to read very well. The psychologist did his job as he saw it. He gave a test and stuck on a label. Neither he nor anybody else offered any advice on how the remedial reading teacher might locate Tommy so that she could teach him to read.

But since Tommy is on my seventh-grade list, I start looking for him. I complain to the vice principal that I have a kid on my list who hasn't shown up. The counselor warns me, "Count your blessings. Tommy's reputation precedes him. We hear he's a real terror."

Nevertheless, I persist. When casual complaint gets me nowhere, I ask to file an official complaint. "The school district should take his mother to court," I insist. The vice principal informs me that such matters are difficult, even impossible. According to the rules, a school can't take a child's parents to court until he's been absent thirty days. That's thirty days in a row. Whenever a student makes an appearance in school, his truancy record rolls back to zero. The court does not look at how many times a child has attended school in one year; it looks at how many days he's missed in a row: thirty is bad, but twenty-nine is acceptable, even when it's a twenty-nine-day absentee pattern repeated six times a year.

At the same time I am hounding the guidance office and the vice principal's office about Tommy, the student I've never seen, somebody in the juvenile probation department and/or social service agency decides that if Tommy can be kept in school, maybe he won't be able to spend so much time on the streets, time spent committing crimes. It makes sense: If we can keep Tommy in school six hours a day, then that's six fewer hours he'll have available for breaking into parking meters, vending machines, parked cars, convenience stores, and churches. According to the story circulating in our hallways, Tommy has not only broken into several churches, he's also robbed the priory. The fact that the nuns were in residence when he climbed through a window is what got him into his current legal situation. According to faculty room scuttlebutt, he broke two fingers of the nun who tried to stop him. I have not heard kids mention this detail, however, and when it comes to gossip about students, I put my money on what their classmates tell me.

I don't know who came up with the plan. After all, I am only Tommy's English teacher. And strange as it may seem, as much as administrators in our district love to send memos, Tommy's stay in our building has left no paper trail. At least none that teachers are privy to. Tommy appears and disappears with no written notification, at least none that I can find. Any teacher in our building could have told the well-meaning official in the juvenile probation department and/or the social service agency that their plan was doomed to failure. That is putting it kindly. Their plan is whacko. A kindergartner could have advised them that it wouldn't be of much use to pick Tommy up at his front door every morning and escort him to the front door of our school. But that's what they did. A caseworker would take the elevator to the sixth floor of the public housing building where Tommy lives, escort him from his apartment to her car, drive him to our school, and escort him to the front door. She would watch Tommy enter the building, and then she would return to her car and drive off. Tommy would enter the front door, race through the building, and disappear out the back door.

My students would tell me, "Tommy came to school today."

"Where is he?" I ask, revealing curiosity and even a little excitement at the prospect of meeting the legend at long last.

"Tommy doesn't stay long!" the kids laugh. They enjoy telling me about the caseworker picking Tommy up and dropping him off. "He has his own private chauffeur." They drag out the last word with obvious relish. "Tommy comes to school. He just doesn't come to class." This information is followed by gales of laughter.

Had we teachers been informed of this plan, we could at least have blocked the back door. As it is, we don't know what Tommy looks like, so how can we be expected to keep him in the building?

Once this scheme for getting Tommy into school goes haywire for a few weeks, the juvenile probation department/social service agency personnel actually contact the school principal, asking for cooperation. The plan then is that Tommy's caseworker will escort him to the front door of the school, where he will be met by a guidance counselor. The guidance counselor will then escort him to his first-period class. So Tommy attends his first-period class for a week. Every day, when the bell rings ending first period, he scoots out the nearest exit.

Undaunted, the public agency folks come up with a new plan. They send a department aide to school with Tommy. Her job is to sit with Tommy in all his classes, to walk with him from one class to another, to make sure he doesn't sneak out of the building. Of course Tommy's teachers are not informed of this plan either. One day a young woman just appears in my doorway with an unhappy looking, scruffy kid, nods her head toward the kid and announces, "I'm with him." I never learn her name or exactly what agency she works for.

From this first day, Tommy's escort isolates herself from what is going on in the classroom. She pulls a chair into a corner and reads from a thick text-book she carries with her. It is a text on adolescent psychology, no less. When the bell rings sounding the end of the period, Tommy dashes out of the room and his escort runs after him.

I phone the principal's office and ask what is going on. I am informed that this is Tommy and that he now has an aide, sent out from a public agency—welfare or probation or some such place. The office isn't sure from whence the young woman comes, but they assure me her presence is both le-gitimate and necessary. The implication is that nobody would attach herself to Tommy unless she were paid to do so.

After I work with Tommy for a few days, I realize his escort could be a godsend. What Tommy needs is one-on-one tutoring. He is a very poor reader, but he cooperates when I give him my undivided attention. Obviously, I can't devote whole class periods just to him. I have a room full of students, all of whom have serious difficulties, all of whom need a lot of help, encourage-ment, and individual attention.

Since I try to help my students figure out the books and the assignments and the tests in all their classes, and since Tommy's personal escort attends all his classes with him, it makes sense that she can help him begin to come to grips with the academics in those classes. I am convinced that he has ability; he just needs to get used to school. I figure that Tommy may be a prisoner of the court system and in the school building under duress, but maybe if he finds some academic success right away, he might decide school isn't so bad. My idea is to organize a plan with his other teachers so that the aide can help him one-on-one.

All of Tommy's teachers report similar behavior. He is a likable kid— one-on-one. Whenever a teacher can steal a few minutes to sit with him, he responds positively. He even works hard. But whenever a teacher turns away to work with other students, whenever she isn't giving him her undivided at-tention, Tommy stops working. For all practical purposes, Tommy has never been to school; he has never learned any of the school rituals that are so neces-sary for survival. He doesn't know how to work by himself or how to wait his turn. So when he doesn't get the teacher's immediate and total attention, he shoves the work aside. He becomes hostile and destructive. First he pesters other students. If they ignore him, he finds something destructive to do to get their attention. He takes apart a tape recorder, tears pages out of a book—anything to cause a stir. He has a small child's need for instant and constant gratification.

I hope I can engage Tommy's escort in a plan that will help us teachers help Tommy get used to school, to help him learn how to accept delay, to work independently, and even to find some satisfaction and pride in school work. She is, after all, reading a book on adolescent psychology. How about psychology in action?

Tommy's escort quickly lets me know how mistaken I am. When I try to present a plan for us working together with other teachers to help Tommy learn how school works, she informs me that her job is to escort Tommy to each of his classes and to see that he stays in each class. Period. Her job, she insists, is not to teach Tommy, not to listen to Tommy, not to respond to Tommy once he is inside a classroom. That, she insists, is my job and the job of his other teachers. She lets me know that she is taking graduate courses at night school; she has her own books to worry about. She certainly does not plan on bothering with Tommy's books. "He's just a piece of garbage, anyway," she comments. "Any effort on him is a complete waste of time." I don't have the heart to ask her what profession she is training for.

I protest to the principal, but he just shrugs his shoulders and tells me we can't fight city hall. Or in this case, probation and/or social services. "They make their own rules," he insists. His attitude is that Tommy is trouble and his escort is a dingbat and that the sooner we are rid of both of them, the better off we'll be. He certainly is not going to get involved in any attempts to get a social service agency involved in an integrated educational program for Tommy. "The kid is no good. He's been no good since kindergarten. He'll be at Elmira as soon as he's old enough to qualify. And then Sing Sing. The sooner he's out of here, the better. That kid will rob us blind if he stays here."

So Tommy's escort continues to sit all day in Tommy's classes, reading her textbook on adolescent psychology. She makes a point of sitting on the opposite side of the classroom from Tommy. And Tommy gets frustrated at waiting his turn for help from his teachers. He becomes increasingly restless, increasingly disruptive. He begins racing out of his classes faster and faster. When the bell rings, Tommy jumps out of his chair and whips out the door. For a few days he just runs around the locker area, gleefully eluding his escort. Other kids stand and watch, cheering him on. I suspect a few teachers are cheering too. Certainly none of us intervenes. His escort has, after all, set the ground rules: Our job is to teach, hers to chase.

For a while, Tommy lets himself be caught after a few minutes, and he even goes on to his next class. But that game soon loses its charm, and Tommy begins dashing out of the building as soon as the bell rings ending his first-period class. He quickly loses his escort in the city streets. Before long, he returns to his life of petty crime.

And thus the new project for keeping Tommy in school is dropped after just a few weeks—with no more notification of its demise than there had been notice of its commencement. Two months later, one of my students tells me Tommy has been to court and then sent away. When I check in the office I am told he's been declared incorrigible and sent off to a residential facility.

The principal feels vindicated. He likes to remind me that I am a bleeding heart and that exerting any special effort or shedding any tears for the likes of Tommy is both futile and foolish. I've been hearing this same refrain for years—ever since this fellow and I taught in the same school. Maybe he becomes a principal and I stay a teacher because I find it difficult to give up on seventh graders—even when they're nearly fifteen years old.

I don't shed any tears for Tommy. I have too little invested in him to cry. But I remain angry that he wasn't given a better chance. Where were the psychologists, the caseworkers, the probation officers, and the judges when Tommy started skipping school in first grade? In third? In kindergarten? Where was his mother? Did any one of them ever think to go look at the school, to talk to his teachers, to sit down and come up with a cooperative plan for helping him give school a try? And where were his teachers? I think of an Italian proverb: She who is silent consents. Why did I stand by, a passive observer and watch all this happen? Why do we teachers so eagerly don the mantle proclaiming our own victimization when it is Tommy —and kids like him—who is the real victim? Lots of questions. No answers.

9

The Boy with No Past

In some twenty years of teaching students acknowledged to be difficult, Jackson is the only student who ever scares me, really scares me. Jackson Lincoln Johnson is intimidating from the first moment he swaggers into the classroom, sneering, "This the English class?" Somehow, he manages to draw out the word *English* into five syllables. Although he says he is thirteen years old, Jackson can easily pass for eighteen — or thirty-four. He is a superb physical specimen — six foot, 175 pounds, all muscle. He sits in my classroom alongside little kids not even five feet tall. And it isn't just his physicality that sets Jackson apart from many of the other students. Other kids talk about the cartoons they watch on TV; Jackson talks about the pictures in *Hustler*.

Jackson's intellectual development does not match his physical prowess. As far as I can tell, he is one of the least able readers in a class of extremely poor readers. He tries to prevent me from getting close enough to him to tell for sure, refusing to cooperate when I attempt to administer an informal reading inventory, refusing to read aloud, refusing to read silently. The truth of the matter is that when Jackson is around, nobody is thinking much about reading. After one day in his company, I think of veteran seventh grade teacher James Herndon's observation, "He was a mean son of a bitch, no matter how he got that way."

People who set up what they like to call curriculum standards for seventh and eighth graders, or for any other grade, seem to think that kids in the same grade are like identical vessels on a conveyor belt, moving along to receive an identical infusion of skills. Any kindergarten teacher can describe the great diversity of development among the children in her care — physical, emotional, social, intellectual. Of course this diversity just gets wider as children get older, so that by the time they are seventh graders, a Grand Canyon–size chasm of skills exists in any classroom. But this is a truism the people pushing the standards refuse to acknowledge. They cannot afford to admit that within any classroom, children are more different than they are alike.

Jackson isn't in my classroom fifteen minutes before he announces that he doesn't like the reading materials. He sneers that he'd rather read *Hustler*. Of course I stop him from elaborating, but not before he gets out enough details to convince me and everybody else that he knows what he's talking about. From that day on, Jackson lives to prove his ability to dominate students and teachers. He uses his size, his snarl, and his smutty remarks to make everybody uncomfortable.

I'm no stranger to classroom bullies, but I figure I learned from the best. I am not of a size that would allow me to get physical with kids, even if I wanted to, and although I choose not to notice all sorts of high jinks, what the jargonists call time off-task, bullying gets my attention every time. When faced with bluster and bombast, a teacher needs to take a step forward, psychologically as well as physically. Otherwise, she might as well walk out the door. And keep walking. Usually I try to touch the kid who is mouthing off. Just a light touch, a way of making contact.

I touch Jackson only once. On the second day, when he launches into a menacing, threatening speech. I take a step forward, lightly touch his arm, saying quietly, "Oh, come on, Jackson, knock it off and let's get to work."

Jackson jerks back as though I've stuck him with a hot poker and says slowly, "People don't touch me." Instantly, the room becomes very quiet. I feel that we are playing that old game of statues, and suddenly Jackson and I are frozen in place. Jackson breaks the silence by repeating very slowly, as though explaining an important rule to a young child. "People don't touch me."

I believe him. Even if the kid is 80 percent bluff, as bullies frequently are, I don't want to mess with the other 20 percent. Although Jackson keeps mostly a low profile in our class, I hear rumors that he dominates the hallways, confiscating students' pencils, lunch money, and anything else that takes his fancy. From what I can tell, he chooses his victims carefully—kids who will be afraid to squeal on him, kids who live on his block, who he continues to terrorize after school. He chooses kids who are already pretty much down and out. He doesn't steal from tough black kids who will fight back. He steals from "easy victims," kids whose mothers aren't likely to come to school and lodge a complaint even if their kids do tell them what is happening.

The principal doesn't exactly look the other way or shrug it off, but he doesn't do anything effective. Maybe the principal is right in saying that he can't do anything if the victims won't testify against Jackson, but he isn't offering them any witness protection program either. I point out that since Jackson doesn't have any friends, "If we see him in close conversation with another student, we can bet he's shaking that kid down."

When I talk with a few of my students, I hear complaints about Jackson's thievery. They are scared and evasive, certain that if they squeal, Jackson will find out. Find out and get even. I can't pretend they aren't right. Anyone with a smidgen of school savvy knows that whether you're a child or an adult, if you want to keep a secret, you don't blab about it in school. To anybody. Since it is neither fair nor realistic to expect any student to squeal on Jackson, I do the only thing I can think of: I begin tailing him to lunch. When he stops near students, I stand at his elbow. All the way to the cafeteria. I'm sure my tactic merely results in forcing Jackson to move his shakedowns to other parts of the school and to the streets, but a teacher can only do what she can do.

After Jackson has been in my class for a week or so, I find out that he's been silently terrorizing the girls. In the classroom, there are tables for group work as well as some individual desks. One day, when Jackson sits at a table with girls, he surreptitiously reaches out his foot and runs his shoe up and down their legs. The girls are so terrified they sit still the whole period without saying a word. And I don't notice. They come to me after school, elicit my promise "not to tell," and explain what's going on. So I get rid of the tables and bring in more individual desks and chairs. Then Jackson tries to further torment the girls by deliberately brushing against them as he walks by their chairs, but by now I'm onto him and bird-dog his every move.

I'm a teacher who prides herself on not looking at a student's cumulative folder until I've had time to make my own judgment. But at the end of Jackson's second day in my class, I want information. I go to the guidance office and ask to see his file. I am told that as a new transfer student, Jackson "has no records." I protest. "We must know where he went to school before he came here. Why not phone and ask if there is anything we should know?"

Although I do not know it at the time, this is a significant question. At the moment I ask it, the guidance staff and the principal know exactly where Jackson has been to school for the previous two and a half years. But they feel they have good reasons for not telling teachers.

I accept their unwillingness to call Jackson's previous school because in our district this is the canon: Neither a borrower nor a lender be, info-wise. You know what you know and there's no use asking anybody else to interpret for you. And, since you don't get anything from anybody, you don't share what you know with anybody. Years later, when I visit schools around the country, I learn that my school isn't unique after all. From Maine to Alaska, "lack of information" is a common teacher complaint. Most schools are set up so that teachers can't even learn anything from other teachers in the same building, never mind from teachers in other buildings in the district. And with Jackson, we're talking about communicating with an educational facility seventeen miles away, an unfathomable distance in schoolspeak. In terms of my finding out something about Jackson, his previous school might as well be on another continent.

I can best illustrate this point by telling how Elizabeth Berger and I met a continent away from the school district where we both taught in upstate New York. Elizabeth and I met in Los Angeles, where we were both attending a convention of the National Council of Teachers of English (NCTE). What is singularly remarkable about this encounter is that Lib and I taught in the same district—about one mile apart—for more than ten years. For a number of those years we were both public high school teachers assigned to an alternative program for difficult students who had been excluded from the regular high school. Lib taught students in a residential detention/treatment facility. I taught in a storefront school. Some of my students lived at the detention facility but were allowed to travel to the storefront school. So Lib and I taught the same type of student, we had the same pro forma school principal (the man who entered our school once a year to make his official observation), and we were given the same charge of coming up with innovative curricula and methods to captivate hard-to-reach students. But no one thought that it might be helpful for teachers undertaking the same difficult task to meet.

I didn't even know there were teachers at the detention hall. At the urging of students who wanted me to see their place, I sometimes went there to lunch. Each time I went I hoped to meet their counselors, house parents, and other staff. I accepted the fact that these people were never available, because that's just the way it was in our district: Nobody ever wanted to talk to a teacher. I just never dreamed there was another English teacher in the building. I had to leave teaching and travel to a conference in Los Angeles to find a colleague with whom I could discuss common educational concerns. We have been friends and confidantes ever since.

Here's the kicker: Most teachers to whom I tell this story don't find it surprising or even out of the ordinary. The fact that Lib and I met three thousand miles from our teaching sites is typical of most school districts' inability to foster professional collegiality or communication. For teachers, the only unusual element in the story is that we did manage to meet.

This failure to foster communication is not just a sign of omission in my district; they actually work at preventing teacher collaboration. One year I decide to take advantage of the fact that the provisions in our union contract allow us two "school visitation days." There is no record of any teacher ever exercising this option, but after teaching in the district for ten years I decide to test it. In the spirit of Henry David Thoreau, I try to examine my own backyard, to travel widely in my own district. I file an application to take one school visitation day in my own school and one in another school in the district. To this application, I append details about the programs I want to observe and the reasons I want to observe them. Without discussion, the assistant superintendent in charge of curriculum vetoes my plan, stating that the district will never pay for a substitute teacher so that I "can go gossip with friends." Not that the assistant superintendent wants me to observe strangers either. When I receive invitations to speak at NCTE and IRA conferences, the assistant superintendent decrees that a teacher cannot travel out of state on school time. Then, when I am invited by the New York State Education Department to present a program at a conference in Albany, fewer than twenty miles away, she vetoes that too. In frustration, I go over her head to the superintendent, who reluctantly grants me permission to go to Albany—provided that I pay for my substitute. I have never been able to figure out what administrators fear about us teachers getting out of the district once in a while: What we might hear? Or what we might say?

LACKING SCHOOL RECORDS or other information about Jackson, I muddle along as best I can for two months. It is hard to be absolutely certain, because Jackson has ways of avoiding most work and diverting most observation, but the best I can figure is that he has a sight vocabulary of about twenty words. He makes a big production of printing his name, but in two months I don't see him write more than a dozen other words. I suspect a lot of his bluff and bluster in class is to cover up the fact that he can't read. Everyone in the class has severe reading problems, but all the other students can read to some degree, and everybody writes me a note every day, responding to my notes to them. Everybody but Jackson. He tries to tell dirty stories and tries to touch the girls; every day he struts his muscled masculinity. But he doesn't read and he doesn't write. In contrast to most students who jostle for my individual attention, Jackson rebuffs my efforts to engage him in one-on-one conversation, never mind instruction. In these two months I don't see other students horsing around with Jackson, initiating conversations with him, or even listening to his ramblings. We all keep our distance. And we wish he weren't there. But in keeping with one of the great laws of education, during these two months Jackson is never absent. Not once.

At the time, I tried not to put too much emphasis on one incident, but years later it stands out as an emblem of my experience with Jackson. I show the classic film *The Red Balloon*, and at the end, when the balloons rescue the boy and carry him off to balloon heaven, or wherever, the students gasp, laugh, and clap. A few kids even cheer. Everyone but Jackson. Jackson pulls out an imaginary gun and sits there grinning while he shoots down the balloons:

Bam! Bam! Bam! In the half a dozen or more years I have shown this film, even the toughest, meanest, most streetwise student reacts with awe and smiles as the balloon rescues that winsome little boy. But there is Jackson aiming his two fingers at the images on the screen, shooting down those balloons. *Bam! Bam! Bam!*

Two months after Jackson's arrival, I happen to mention his name to a friend who teaches in an elementary school across town. "Is he still around?" she asks, her rising intonation revealing shock. She says Jackson attended public school in our district until fourth grade. Throughout his first four years, he was uncontrollable, frequently flying into rages against teachers and children. In fourth grade, when Jackson was nine years old and the principal tried to remove him from his classroom for fighting, he went berserk, attacking the principal. The police were called, and it took three officers to restrain him. They strapped him to a cot brought in by paramedics, but the nine-year-old Jackson broke the restraining straps. My friend said Jackson's mother went to family court and told officials she couldn't cope with him at home any more than educators could cope with him at school. Jackson was sent "away" to a custodial care institution.

I return to my principal's office, armed with what I suspect might be the name of Jackson's previous school, the custodial institution. The principal reluctantly concedes that I am right. He claims he's "just learned" this information himself, that he's called the institution, and that Jackson's school records, are "in the mail." Some coincidence.

"Why not phone and find out if there is anything we should know about Jackson? I mean, shouldn't we be alerted if he's a firebug or something?"

Admittedly, this is dirty pool on my part. Suggest that a student is loony or learning disabled or a bully or a sex maniac, and administrators and the guidance staff will shrug their collective shoulders, tell you that you can file a psychological referral if you want, remind you of the federal "least restrictive environment" statutes, which they hold up as the Eleventh Commandment, and say they know you'll do your best. Hint that there's a pyromaniac in the school and everyone jumps into action, setting in motion bureaucratic wheels to get the kid out of the building.

I am standing in the guidance counselor's office when the principal asks her to make the phone call. Jackson's counselor at the custodial facility is reluctant to reveal what he insists is "privileged information," but presents the institutional position: According to expert opinion, after nearly three years in custodial care, it is in Jackson's best interest that he return to a normal school setting. The counselor states that Jackson's performance indicates he is capable of carrying a regular seventh-grade academic program "with a little help in reading." The counselor offers one bit of personal information about Jackson: "Don't ever touch him. Jackson can't stand to be touched."

To be sure, Jackson is not exactly the kind of kid who invites touching. But, like most schools not intimidated by the media's love of salacious headlines, we are a faculty of touchers. You can't walk down a hallway without seeing a teacher with an arm slung over a kid's shoulder, calming, listening. It hasn't taken us two months to figure out Jackson's aversion on our own. But it seems bizarre that the custodial institution would not have alerted us before now.

My relationship with Jackson is brought to a state of crisis because of my participation in a National Endowment for the Humanities teacher teaching project. For a lesson on ambiguity, I collect images of the cat in the art of various cultures to teach a few basic concepts. I try to liven up these concepts and make them more personal by interspersing some funny stories about my own cat, MacDuff. The lesson—and student reaction—is videotaped for use in the course.

Students in my classes usually work on individual assignments, so this lesson on art is the only time in six years that I deliver a lecture to a whole class. Students in the designated class are so enthusiastic about the material that I decide to repeat the lecture for my other classes. These classes are equally enthusiastic, really getting into the quiz on artistic terms. They seem to revel in the new terminology as well as in the art itself.

Everybody, that is, but Jackson. He makes a few rude gestures and remarks throughout the lesson but stays reasonably quiet for about the first half. Toward the end, he starts in. "You know what I'll do to your cat when I see him? I'll grab him by the neck and twist and twist until that ole' cat is strangled dead. Dead. I'll just twist that ole' MacDuff's neck right off." He grins. "That's what I do to cats." Jackson's words are accompanied by a vivid pantomime of strangling. He looks around the room and widens his grin. "That's what I like doing to cats when I see them." He continues twisting his hands, and graphically details what my cat MacDuff will look like when he has finished.

My students, many of whom could be described as tough urban-youth, are shocked. Some, both boys and girls, have tears running down their cheeks. I am sorry the videotape isn't running. I figure there is no way my retelling of this incident can carry the horrific authority of the real thing. Nonetheless, as soon as the class ends, I rush to the principal's office, where I relate Jackson's graphic description of violence and sadism.

Even as I speak I am halfway convinced that the principal will think I'm overreacting—filing a discipline referral because Jackson threatens my cat, who is safe in my house fifteen miles away. I am wrong. The principal acts

immediately. By now, records from Jackson's institutional placement have arrived, and apparently they contain information that makes the principal reluctant to keep Jackson around. But the principal decides to bypass a disciplinary
referral from me and to run his own little test to prove that Jackson is capable
of violence. He asks a big, strong male teacher to join him and Jackson in a
small, vacant office. They call Jackson a "dirty nigger." Then the principal uses
Jackson's "violent reaction" as evidence that his placement in our school is inappropriate. Jackson's angry reaction to the racial epithet becomes part of the
psychological profile assembled by the district psychologist.

Of course I am outraged. For one thing, what business do two educational professionals have betting their physical prowess will outmatch that of
a student? More seriously, what business do they have deliberately provoking
any student, never mind one who is mentally ill? I don't like Jackson, but more
than that, he scares me. I don't like this feeling. I don't think Jackson belongs in
our school. But we have plenty of evidence to document our inability to deal
with his inappropriate behavior. Why is it necessary to construct this bizarre
scenario of entrapment? Wouldn't anybody who is called a racial epithet get
angry? I wonder why, in two months time, our administrators haven't noticed
that Jackson is angry all the time, that he doesn't need provocation to do mean
and nasty things. I am outraged that in the end my educational leader resorts
to a macho shootout to force a twelve-year-old boy out of the building.

I have never talked to the district psychologist about Jackson's behavior
in my classroom, but nonetheless I am summoned as "the referring teacher"
to testify at the hearing of the Committee on the Handicapped. Since the district is attempting to expel Jackson, that is, not just kick him out temporarily
but exclude him permanently, law requires that the Committee on the Handicapped must meet. Such a committee is formed, ostensibly, to act on a student's behalf, to protect a student's interests. Because my students are often
the subject of the committee's business and because I share classroom duties
with another teacher and can leave the room, I end up attending a fair number of these meetings. I have never seen an advocate for students at these meetings. I have never seen the committee do anything but rubber-stamp the psychologist's recommendation, which turns out to be an echo of what the school
principal requests. I have to admit that it is usually what teachers want too.
Nonetheless, I think the student should have an advocate. In my more than
ten years of attending such meetings I have never heard anyone question the
system, never mind challenge it.

The committee always assumes that something is wrong with the kid.
Liberals like me can wring our hands that social and environmental stresses
have produced his defects, but we agree the defects are there, within him. And

we turn our backs on the fact that those social and environmental inequities will continue to exist, continue to deform kids like Jackson. If such kids don't fit into our system, we find ways to exclude them. We never change the system: not the housing system, not the social services system, not the school system. We judge Jackson a failure because he didn't adapt to The System. I wonder if there will be a judgment day for the system that failed to make any adaptation to Jackson's needs when he was in kindergarten or first grade, or second, third, or fourth. But that's a rhetorical question, of course. The school system was not designed for the Jacksons among us. The overt curriculum, with its emphasis on students meeting standards, is designed to train students to jump the hurdles of high-stakes tests. It's called equal educational opportunity for all. The hidden curriculum enforces the ideological and practical distinctions demanded by the marketplace. Purely and simply, schools are mechanisms for the reproduction of a hierarchical, compliant workforce, the division of labor.

Jackson's mother is at the meeting, accompanied by a social service worker. She is a small, shriveled woman who looks old enough to be his grandmother. I find out later that she is twenty-eight years old. Twenty-eight going on fifty-eight. She sits directly across the table from me, huddled in her chair, staring at her hands. The psychologist tries to ingratiate himself by making a few jokes. No one laughs. The psychologist then intimates that he has observed Jackson in my classroom. He doesn't quite say that he's been there, so his remarks skirt just on the edge of a lie. I marvel that he can do this while I'm sitting there. His remarks are just another indication of his contempt for teachers; he doesn't give a fig about what I hear him say, because the district has shown him he doesn't have to.

The hearing becomes an institutional version of Alice's tea party, though more off center even than Carroll. The psychologist assumes the role of host at a friendly social gathering. Smiling his wide grin, he introduces Jackson's mother to each person around the large table, telling her what function each of us plays in Jackson's school life. The effect has to be overwhelming: eight of us, just one of her, unless one counts the social worker as being her ally, which I don't. The social worker is a governmental office worker, pushing paper, on nobody's side. Jackson's mother does not look up or acknowledge any of the introductions, but sits in her chair bending over her clutched hands.

Intermittently, the psychologist asks if she understands this or that report. She nods her head slightly when asked a direct question, but she never looks up. The psychologist tries to be kind, warm, chatty, even jocular. His gentle humor is singularly out of place, brushing up against this woman's inability to react or respond. Hey, the rest of us aren't amused either. This is a sad, glum, necessary, if pro forma, ritual, not a tea party.

The psychologist explains that Jackson's IQ of 67, his violent temper, and his emotional instability indicate that he cannot handle a conventional school setting. The psychologist recommends home tutoring. This is the cue for the social service caseworker to speak. In a prepared, legalistic statement that is delivered more like a ritualized Miranda warning than a genuine communication about a particular preteen boy about to be abandoned by his family as well as his school, she intones that Jackson's family feels they can no longer handle his antisocial behavior. She states that Jackson is uncooperative at home and in constant trouble on the streets. "The family requests that Jackson be returned to custodial care," she says.

At that moment, for the first time, Jackson's mother speaks. At first her mumbled words are so soft we cannot catch them. The psychologist asks her to repeat what she has said. She doesn't raise her head but, huddled over her hands, she says, "He should of took his pills." Then, as if exhausted by this spate of words, she sinks further into her chair.

Pills? This is the first mention I've heard of medication. No one around the table chooses to pick up on this remark. Probably it is more accurate to say that we choose to ignore this piece of information. At that particular moment, none of us wants to rock the boat; we are desperate for someone else to step in and accept responsibility for Jackson.

Still, I wonder why the personnel at the custodial institution that sends Jackson to a regular school don't send the advice, "Be sure he takes his medication." I wonder what pedagogical/psychological/political principle impels them to send Jackson as a tabula rasa, even without pills. I wonder how they dare pretend that this boy has no past but only a future, how they dare to pretend that a boy with a 67 IQ and serious emotional problems can find a rosy future enrolled in a regular academic program.

I applaud giving kids a second—or a fourteenth—chance, a fresh start. If students in inner-city schools have taught me anything, it is that tomorrow *is* a new day. A student can call a teacher a white "mother f—er" one day and come in the next cheerfully ready to work hard. My students have taught me not to bear grudges, not against students, anyway. I understand and applaud the laudable intentions of not tainting teachers' perceptions or fueling their fears with lurid stories of a student's past. But it is worse than inconsistent to assume the best of students and the worst of teachers. As a group, we teachers are not the moral pariahs this refusal to share student data implies. Although it is unlikely, Jackson's teachers might have been able to help him had we been given even a modest amount of information or advice. We were never given a chance, and as a result neither was Jackson.

Even as I sit in that conference room wanting Jackson to be someone else's responsibility, I can't help feeling pain for that nine-year-old boy cast out by his family as incorrigible. Is his violence a way of trying to get even with his mother? Of trying to get that vacant woman to notice him? Or has this uncontrollable child ground down this poor woman's sensibilities to the point of numbness? If Jackson had been a middle-class nine-year-old, he would have been declared autistic or suffering from Apsberger's and had his own personal aide by his side throughout the school day. But because he was a welfare case, he was sent off to an institution for incorrigibles.

The hearing is a formality. Before we ever walk into the room, the key players have agreed that Jackson will be returned to custodial care. Nonetheless, as we are leaving the room, I ask the social worker, "Is Jackson taking medication?

"He is supposed to," she sighs, "but he doesn't like it. He complains it slows him down. He needs it though. Desperately. He's dangerous without it."

So the social service worker knows about the medication, but social service workers don't talk to teachers. They ply their trade outside school walls, entering a school only if a parent requests them to do so. A teacher can't request a meeting; everything has to be initiated by the parent. Even when just plain common sense would dictate a simple phone call to the school to confirm that Jackson is taking his medication, social workers don't do it. And their excuse is, "The mother didn't request it."

Every year I teach a handful of children who are "cases," as they say in social service lingo. Not once has a caseworker contacted me to suggest we might work together for a child's benefit. When I try initiating the relationship, I am made to feel like a snoop just trying to pry some privileged information out of them. They inform me that it is not appropriate for schools to initiate such contact.

I am worried about my own culpability. Why have I never talked with Jackson's mother? Why haven't I met more than 20 percent of the parents of my students? When I first started teaching I tried being proactive about such contacts. I remember parking in front of a tenement building one morning in late August, addresses of my prospective students in hand. The week before I had sent postcards announcing that their new English teacher was eager to meet them and would be visiting. I confess I felt a certain relief when nobody answered my timid knocks in the dark, narrow hallways of the tenement or at the front doors of nearby brownstones. Later I ask myself, "Why would anybody answer the door to a white woman carrying a briefcase?" They probably thought I was a bill collector, social service investigator, or worse.

Later in that first year I renew my efforts for parent contact, making an appointment to visit Lurene's family after school. Her mother and two aunts are watching a soap opera when I arrive. They do not turn down the television—or take their eyes from the screen—during my agonized fifteen-minute appearance. I try to initiate a conversation, but the three women seem to regard my presence as an intrusion. They chat among themselves about the doings of the soap opera characters and respond to my direct questions with a perfunctory, monosyllabic answer or a shrug. After a couple of attempts at conversation, I shut up and watch the soap opera too.

So much for parent contact. I find it difficult to assert myself among strangers, and so I am derelict about initiating face-to-face meetings with parents. I'm good at writing notes and describing the work children are engaged in. I am not good at phoning parents or appearing on their doorsteps. I feel guilty about this. I am sure people who teach troubled children could do better jobs if we met with people where they—and we—live. But asking us to live where we teach is asking too much of most of us. Jonathan Kozol once wrote that a teacher who went home to the suburbs and listened to Vivaldi could never be effective. I disagree. We cannot deny teachers the right to lives outside the classroom. We have as much right to a rich, full life—to privacy and Vivaldi—as anyone else. I don't think I can fight the good fight twenty-four hours a day. I need Vivaldi. And maybe it's just a little arrogant to assume that the families of the children we teach want us in their backyards twenty-four hours a day. Maybe they need and deserve some space from school too.

Nonetheless, I feel guilt, and I know that my school bears guilt in just about every direction I look. Although Jackson's is a special and dramatic case, it does bring up my perennial complaint. I regularly storm the office demanding to know why the school places kids with serious learning difficulties in a regular academic program. "What is the measure of success for these children?" I ask. Every year I ask. Every year the principal intones that these children are in academic classes for "social reasons." It is all so futile. I'm not looking for a scientific fix for these children. Nor am I looking for a room in which to isolate them. What I'm looking for is a way we can spend our time and energy helping children learn things they can understand, things they need to know.

STUDENTS WITH learning difficulties don't ask me to help them make friends. Every year these students ask me to help them pass science and social studies tests. Take Lucille. After PL 94–142, the Education for All Handicapped Children Act, becomes law, my school district uses it as an excuse to delabel all kids coming into seventh grade—except those with Down's syndrome. A cruel take on equity. All seventh graders are declared equal, and placed in full academic programs. Those with the lowest reading scores are given language arts tutorial instruction three days out of every six. Yes, although there are five days in a school week, we operate on a six-day curriculum cycle. Only the kids figure it out. Three days in tutorial English, three days in academic English. Not only are kids with low skills put in a class they can't cope with, they must miss half the sessions.

None of Lucille's teachers know that she spent her entire elementary career in special class. Lucille isn't with me for a week before I ask to see her records. I learn she is the youngest of six siblings in special education. She has never been in "regular" class but the district insists that "the least restrictive environment" means Lucille must take our school's version of college prep: biology, social studies, math, and English.

When I ask why we teachers haven't been alerted to Lucille's special difficulties, I am told that such information is confidential. "Such information might prejudice certain teachers and prevent them from treating educable children equally with other children in the class." So educable children like Lucille are dumped willy-nilly into the mainstream and under the name of "socialization" made to suffer embarrassment and humiliation in front of their peers when they can't read Dickens, locate rivers on a map, or solve math problems at the board.

Lucille is kind, cheerful, cooperative, and terribly anxious to please her teachers. She is very proud of her high marks in spelling. In my class there is no stigma in working on third-grade-level spelling words. Lucille has good decoding skills but she seems to comprehend and recall little of what she reads. She likes writing notes to me and reading my replies. She likes listening to tapes of poetry. The smallness of our classes—fourteen students and two teachers—and the individualization of the curriculum provide a haven in her rigorous academic schedule. But all this isn't good enough for Lucille. Like most tutorial students, she doesn't regard this remedial class as quite legitimate. Operating on the school-induced theory that if they can do the work, the work must not be legitimate, every year tutorial students tell me, "Miz O, we wish you wuz a real teacher."

Lucille decides that, having been placed in academic classes, she has to do the academic work. When she first tells me she is having a terrible time in science, I try to avoid the issue. I have heard her science teacher talk about the importance of maintaining standards. She is proud to have designed a course that is rigorous and comprehensive, a course modeled on her own college biology course. I want to stay as far away from that course and that teacher as I can. But I can't ignore Lucille's pleas. Lucille is so anxious to pass a test—any test—that I go to the teacher, get the syllabus for the course as well as the questions for an upcoming exam. I begin to coach Lucille. I read the text on tape so that Lucille and other students in the course can listen to it. I prepare study guides to help students through the material.

Other students make a halfhearted pass at the material. Lucille is determined, if not obsessed, and I guess I become a little obsessed too. She and I work during the lunch break for three weeks, laboring over the structure of cells. Lucille draws cells on the chalkboard and cuts cells out of construction paper; she makes flash cards of definitions. We drill; we invent acronyms to help her remember terms. Lucille learns the material one day and forgets it by the next. And so every day we seem to be starting from scratch. Every day I try to figure out a new approach. Lucille never gives up. She desperately wants to pass that test.

Lucille appears in my doorway right after the biology test. "I didn't do too good," she confides, adding in a whisper, "I think I'm going to be sick."

I try to rush her to the lavatory, but we don't make it, and evidence of Lucille's "failure" lies visible in the hallway. She tells me she is sorry she has let me down. I know she's got it backwards; I'm the one who let her down. After all, I am the adult, the professional. I am certainly the one who knows better than to subject this child to this kind of torture. As I clean up the vomit, I vow never again to drill children on such inappropriate curricula.

Unfortunately, it is a vow I can't keep. Every year there are mainstreamed students who, being declared equal, are determined to live up to the declaration. When a student asks for help in science or social studies, I can't refuse. But after Lucille, never again do I conspire with a child to lay so much hope on a single test. I try to negotiate with teachers for special projects, and I try to convince the students that these are legitimate alternatives. But every year some students won't accept this way out. Kids like Lucille don't want a watered-down test or a special project. They want to pass the *real* test.

Kids want to pass the tests not so much for academic achievement as for social acceptance. There are a lot of official proclamations about socialization, but nobody addresses what happens when kids hit seventh and eighth grade. Kids have a great need to be part of the pack, but the pack is very cruel about differences. Lumping everybody into an academic twilight zone doesn't mean that socialization follows.

SCHOOLS HAVE A WAY of making everything seem abstract and unrelated to the lives of children, even sex education. But kids talk about sex all the time.

"Gonna show us some pussy, Nessa?" asks Dwight.

"I'm a fox," announced Vanessa. "Want to see my bush tail?"

"Yeah! Show us your tail!"

Whereupon Vanessa walks to the front of the room, pulls her skirt up to six inches below her navel, and starts undulating while she announces, "I've got hips . . . just let me show you my hips."

"Did her brother really beat her baby out of her?" goes another conversation.

"He kicked her in the stomach. The baby didn't come right away, but in a little while she started bleedin' and hollerin.' The neighbors called the cops. They took her to the hospital but the baby was dead. My sister saw it. She said it was all yellow, like a dried out lemon."

"Do you know Shayna, who was in eighth grade last year? She lost her baby down the toilet. She took Ex-Lax."

Most of my students fail the health test asking them to "name any seven parts of the male reproductive system" and to fill in the blanks on sentences like this:

- Sperm are contained in a fluid called _____.
- Sperm are stored in the _____.
- Sperm are produced in the _____.
- When the penis becomes filled with blood and is stiff and sticks out from the body it is said to be____.

Students are asked to write an essay question on this topic: "Explain why the testes are located outside the body instead of inside the body like many other organs." I read the questions and wonder if the teacher has suffered a mental breakdown.

One of the teachers finds a group of girls giggling over a notebook being passed around the room. The teacher confiscates the book and soon it is being passed around the faculty room. I have seen "slam" books before but this is the first with a sexual theme. Each page contains a question of an intimate nature and respondents are invited to describe themselves or a classmate. The topics include the size of boys' organs, how many times can you jerk off in a night, how many times do you do it in a week, and so on. I suspect, or maybe it's a vain hope, that more than a few respondents are bluffing, but I can't pretend to be blasé about the book. Virgil may not know a scrotum from a uretha on the textbook diagram, but he seems to know the street meaning of "butter the popcorn," an expression that is stumping everyone in the faculty room. The book is filled with similarly mysterious phrases of obvious sexual content. The health teacher would do better to help students deconstruct the slam book rather than memorize the health text, which conceals sex under the cloak of anatomy. According to the slam book, my perception of Jason as school stud is correct.

It is sadly emblematic of school folks' refusal to recognize the sexual identity of their students that for the one question on the test dealing with matters we could hope would matter to a fourteen-year-old boy, the true/false statement "Teenage boys are not able to become fathers because they are too young," Jason answers "True." Jason and plenty of his peers probably can't decipher most of the other true/false statements, such as:

• The penis can ejaculate semen when it is flaccid.

• Circumcision is of assistance in maintaining the cleanliness of the penis.

Sally is one of the girls passing around the slam book. She is thirteen, has a sight vocabulary of about twenty-five words, and loves *Where the Wild Things Are.* She remembers her first-grade teacher reading it to the class. Clearly no book since had ever come close in capturing her imagination. Sally shows us what we need: sex education that can cope with the nubile body and the emotionally starved psyche.

Jackson and Jason and Sally are in the same health class. I can only say I'm glad I am not teaching it. School personnel don't want to talk about the issue of just what would be normal behavior for an adolescent boy of, if you'll excuse the expression, 67 IQ, as he sits through an academic science class or an exam on the male reproductive system. I know we're not supposed to use That Word any more. But banning the term or the test doesn't do away with the fact that some kids are slower than others. Some kids really aren't going to "catch up." How does one judge normal in such abnormal circumstances? What does being in that class for "social reasons" mean? How sociable is it to be the class dummy in every class all day long? For every day of your school life? I don't want to shove slower learners or retarded children—there it is— into an isolated room and throw the key away, but by placing them in a situation that they can't possibly cope with, by forcing them to confront certain and absolute failure day after day, we ensure not only that failure but also an erosion of their confidence and dignity. In some cases, like Jackson's, we may actually drive them to violence. Certainly such placement, masquerading under the language of *mainstreaming children*—in the words of federal law, "to the maximum extent appropriate to their needs"—cannot be termed an act of kindness. I have trouble seeing it as an act of sanity. Instead of teaching these children things they can learn, things they need to know, we dump them into the mainstream and wring our hands while they drown. Even the survivors learn only one thing: they learn they are no good.

The authorities intone over and over that "these kids" aren't expected to master the academics, that they are in regular classes "for purposes of socialization." I wonder if anybody explained that to Jackson when he was in first grade, second grade, or seventh grade. I wonder if anybody ever stopped to ask him how he felt about his socialization experience. The dumbest kid in every class every year. How sociable can it be to feel the need to invent bizarre new schemes for directing attention away from the fact that you can't read the book—or even understand it when it is read to you? In 1992, K. L. Ruhl and D. H. Berlinghoff researched the literature for studies designed to improve the academic skills of troubled children, children labeled emotionally disturbed.

They found only ten articles published between 1976 and 1990. Researchers design studies to teach behavior control, not academic achievement.

In recent years I have written newspaper op-ed pieces about the pitfalls of mainstreaming, about how painful it can be for seventh and eighth graders. I have received the same reaction from parents whose children attend small country schools as from parents whose children attend large urban schools. Parents of preadolescent mainstreamed children proclaim a resounding "Thank you!" Then they ask for a shoulder to cry on. After years in the system, these parents feel they have no advocate against mainstreaming mandates that decree their children must sit in regular academic classes. These parents recount that the mainstreaming that seemed to work in primary grades becomes a nightmare for pubescent children. I'll never forget the question Jerry, a boy with uneven gait and speech slurred by cerebral palsy, a boy whose reading and writing skills were very poor, asked me, "Will it always be like this? Will people always hate me? Will it get any better when I'm out of school and get a job?" I had to think that over. I told Jerry I thought so. I told him that what he had going for him was a willingness to dig into certain topics and learn a lot about them. Even though his reading skills were not excellent, when he cared about a topic, he persevered, he used the Internet, he sought out knowledgeable people, he made himself an expert. Since the topics Jerry cared about were trains and baseball, these skills didn't help him much in school, but I told Jerry that I thought one day his bosses and coworkers would appreciate his talents and interests—if he could just hang in there until then.

This may be true for Jerry, but I know that for Jackson, the world will be even harsher than were the schools. It is hard to see how anything less than a miracle can save a boy who has been institutionalized since the age of nine. We can condem the social service agencies, but that does not mean the schools did any better. I know that my frightened reaction to Jackson's threats precipitated his removal from our school. I didn't cause him to exhibit his menacing behavior, but certainly my response affected how his behavior was perceived by authorities. For the two months before his outburst, I let Jackson drift in my classroom. That is my style: I believe in letting a student find his space. This should not be interpreted as refusal to teach, a refusal to confront the challenge of an angry, turned-off student. I am not saying that if a teacher waits long enough, students will learn what they need to know—on their own.

I am a teacher. I care passionately about being a teacher. I prod; I challenge; I try to inspire. I provide a stimulating environment. I think I have a knack for knowing when to notice a student and when to look away, when to move in and teach and when to stay on the fringes of a student's territory. A time to behold and a time to ignore, or pretend to ignore. I don't believe students learn what teachers teach, not directly anyway. A teacher cannot make a student learn; she can only provide a setting in which he may want to learn.

And the result of all this is that Jackson probably didn't learn anything in my classroom—except that he could scare me. Years later, I still ask myself if things might have gone differently. If I'd set up one of those behavior-mod deals, giving Jackson programmed and sequenced worksheets to fill out, rewarding and punishing his output every three minutes, would it have made a difference? Of course this is a rhetorical question. The hardest part of being a teacher is that we don't get a second chance with a kid.

I don't really believe that such a scheme would have worked. I've based my career on the belief that a student must have autonomy, that his work must have meaning. I can't hope to teach kids unless and until they do find meaning. If, like my other students, Jackson had been in my class for two years, we might have had a chance. But I sure wasn't stepping forward to suggest I could endure his presence for that long.

When school critics descry the failure of American education, they're not talking about Jackson. For school critics, the Jacksons of the world are invisible. School critics are talking about everybody taking algebra in seventh or eighth grade and whether the kids in Larchmont score as well on high-stakes tests as the kids in Palo Alto, not to mention Singapore and Kyoto. But when I talk about the failure of American education, I'm talking about Jackson, who stands forever as my failure as a teacher. He isn't the only student I disliked, but he is the only one I feared. He is the only student for whom I can't recall even one small moment of a teaching/learning bond. Not one positive moment.

Garrison Keillor says he doesn't believe people learn from punishment. He believes they learn from being happy. When the Jacksons in our world commit atrocious crimes, newspaper headlines scream about their low reading scores, proof positive that the schools have failed. I wonder about the larger failure of a society that does not nurture its children, a society that defaults on giving even its youngest members a chance to be happy.

10

Better Read Than Dead

When I ask seventh and eighth graders to fill in the blank in the following sentence: I would rather read than____; I would rather write than ____, Michael writes "I would rather read than write; I would rather write than DIE." Of course I am distressed to see Michael's raw feelings expressed so starkly, but I can't say I am surprised. For Michael, reading and writing have been a kind of slow death for his eight years in school. Michael is one of the few students who doesn't lie and claim that he likes to read. Most students play the school game: they lug books home from school; they check books out of the library; they claim they spend the weekend reading. Every June I study the overdue list sent out from the library. The prime offenders are my non-readers. I wonder if they check out—and lose—more books than anybody else in school because they're trying to cut down on the number of books in the world.

Many of my students go so far as to try to convince me they *love* to read. A few even decorate their folders Hyman Kaplan style: I L*O*V*E R*E*A*D*I*N*G. They develop strategies for avoiding reading while at the same time simulating reading. The library is a favorite spot to practice these strategies because, besides being a social gathering point, if you're in the library you can't be called upon to read in class. The library is a place where everybody can act like a student. I see my students there copying long passages out of their textbooks, copying out of dictionaries, copying out of encyclopedias. They don't understand what they are copying—they can't read it—but some days they are anxious to please their teachers and producing a pile of copied papers is easy enough. Copying out long, incomprehensible passages is the remedial reading strategy for coping.

177

But I'm not a remedial reading teacher. When I applied for a transfer to this new junior high, I announced that I wouldn't take the job if it had a remedial reading label. Names are important and, for a variety of reasons, I want to avoid that one. Remedial reading still exists in our school. Kids who score between the twentieth and forty-fifth percentiles on standardized tests go to remedial reading. Those below the twentieth percentile come to my class, language arts tutorial. Listed as LAT on the report card, the first semester one parent phoned wanting to know how come her daughter, who has always had so much difficulty in school, is now taking Latin. Mom says she asked her daughter, who insists she is indeed taking Latin. Admittedly, our class probably doesn't look like any English class the kid has ever had; Latin is a logical conclusion.

When our school opens, LAT has the craziest schedule imaginable. The administrators got together over the summer and decided our school should run on a six-day schedule. So my students come to LAT three days in a row; then they go to regular academic English class for three days. The students have a much easier time figuring out who goes where on which days than do the teachers. On any day, this schedule is a disaster for subject-area teachers. They're in the middle of a unit on, say, *The Old Man and the Sea*. And then the kids who have the most difficultly understanding the material disappear for three days.

After one term of this insanity my team teaching partner and I ask the authorities to reconsider: We suggest that instead of giving the students with the greatest difficulties half-time help, why not give them double-time help? Why not send them to LAT for two periods a day instead of one period three days out of six? After recovering from being dumbfounded, the principals warm to the idea of somebody volunteering to take those kids for an *extra* period a day. Then they begin to figure where the extra period can come from. They decide on shop, art, or music. I protest, "Why cut the students out of the one class where they don't have to read? The one class they might enjoy? Why not let them choose which class they want to drop?"

The idea of giving any junior high students, let alone those in the bottom twentieth percentile, an academic choice is revolutionary. The principals can't fathom it. But my partner and I do some research. We discover that although PE is state mandated, social studies and science aren't. So we suggest that the kids choose which one of these to eliminate in seventh grade, and then in eighth they can switch these subjects. My partner and I make the proposal for a double dose of LAT in the hopes that double periods of small, intensive classes for two years will give students a last best chance to become readers and writers before they move on to high school. I'm not sure the principals had exactly the same thing in mind. I don't mean to sound overly cynical, but the simple truth of the matter finally dawns on the principals: On any given day, that bottom twentieth percentile occupy something like 93.6 percent of the office space. Remove them from the classes in which they are acting up and you remove a whole lot of congestion in the office.

Kids end up in LAT for a variety of reasons. Some, like Michael, are bright, verbal, and curious. If such a thing as dyslexia exists, then Michael could be its poster child. Other kids, like Debbie, are sullen, withdrawn, uncommunicative. She shows up at school about one day out of four. Fred, fifteen and in the seventh grade, would have been labeled retarded two decades ago, but now, for good and for bad, that's a term no longer used. We have mainstreaming and least restrictive environment, so Fred is in language arts tutorial. If a child has cerebral palsy and his regular English teacher complains that he can't write, he comes to LAT; if he is profoundly hard of hearing or just off the boat from Cambodia or just out of juvenile hall with no records available, he comes to LAT.

Many of our students score in the third-grade range on standardized reading tests, but that doesn't mean much. Certainly any third grader scoring at grade level is a far better reader than our students. And all our students who score at this mythical third-grade level are more dissimilar than similar. Take Billy, a very angry seventh grader. He gets suspended for fighting fairly frequently, and then his poor mother has to give up half a day's wages, changing buses three times to get to school for the official interview that will allow his reinstatement. She wrings her hands and apologizes, explaining that Billy is just like his dad in his reading difficulty and his temper. It would be just as fair to dock Billy's teachers' pay. After all, it's our failure to help him unlock the key to reading that makes him so angry and belligerent. The sad fact of the matter is we don't know any more about why he can't read than does his mother. When I need someone to assemble a new cart, or get my desk drawer unstuck, I call for Billy, who is clever at anything mechanical. But school gives him few minutes in which to exercise his talents. Mostly we just send him to classes that reveal how ignorant he is.

I spend a lot of time complaining that these kids shouldn't be struggling with the skills-intensive elementary school version of the skills-intensive high school college prep science and social studies courses. Nonetheless, we keep right on telling all students that they must memorize the Preamble to the Constitution and "learn"—i.e., memorize—the three parts of government, find the theme, the climax, and so on. Now, in the name of standards, people are pushing formal algebra for younger and younger students, and across the country, social studies standards are so out there they don't bear repeating.

The nonsense keeps extending to lower grades. I think of the chapter in my third graders' social studies text that includes a flowchart of decision makers for the New York City budget. Despite the warnings of my colleagues that I could be fired for insubordination, I scrapped the social studies curriculum and read aloud E. B. White's *Trumpet of the Swan* instead. I am sure my students are better for it. I wonder why we elementary teachers continue to buy into the notion that having standards means teaching from a syllabus that looks like something out of a Harvard catalog.

I read *The Acorn People* by Ron Jones aloud to Michael's class, a group of rough, tough, turned-off seventh graders. I read it because it's a good story and because many of Michael's classmates have disabilities, are poor, are living in single-parent homes, are involved with petty crime and drugs. They need to know about climbing mountains, overcoming odds, being decent to one another and to unknown strangers. For this group, *The Acorn People* delivers this message better than, say, Shakespeare, Mark Twain, Dickens, or even Aesop, authors frequently extolled on the official best-books lists.

The Acorn People becomes an instant classic in our classroom. Tough, obnoxious kids see themselves in its pages, and they are moved and challenged by the reading. Kids like Michael, who are neither tough nor obnoxious but who face formidable struggles, also see themselves in its pages. Long after the last page, kids are still talking about the characters as though they live next door. The book inspires Michael and his classmates to reach out to a class of Down's syndrome children in our building, becoming the unofficial mentors for these children. Seventh graders aren't universally known for their tact and sensitivity, but my seventh and eighth graders, some of the toughest and most emotionally vulnerable kids in the school, are proud to be depended on by students much more vulnerable than they. We become regular guests at programs and other special events put on by the Down's syndrome class because we can be depended upon to be a good, supportive audience. Keith, one of the most whacked-out kids in my classes, is the biggest pal of the Down's syndrome kids, exchanging enthusiastic high-fives in the hallways.

Keith finds triumph in my class when, as a fifteen-year-old eighth grader, he reads his first book from cover to cover: Dr. Seuss's *Hop on Pop*. Not on most peoples' recommended reading list, reading it astounds Keith. Whenever things get tough, he pulls up a chair and reads it aloud to me. And whatever happens to Keith in the rest of his life, at least he's found a book that knocks his socks off.

A teacher never knows what messages stay with students when she's no longer around to reinforce them, so when *The Acorn People* appears on television three years later, I am both surprised and delighted to see Michael, now a tenth grader, appear in my doorway. "I made my whole family watch," he tells me. "The TV show was good. But the book was a lot better." We both grin. "I bet you never thought you'd hear me say that about a book," he says.

No, I never did.

When I first tell Michael's class that we are going to exchange daily notes, he is not shy about telling me his opinion of the idea. "Why would we write to you when you're right here to talk to?" Michael has been told since first grade that he has a severe reading dysfunction, and I have to agree that he does. He labors over the sounding-out rules that he's learned all too well in six years of remedial reading drill. He makes the "standard" reversals; he can't spell; he has illegible penmanship.

Once he recognizes my intransigence, recognizes that his charming wheedling won't move me, Michael gradually becomes an avid note-writer, and wonderful things begin to happen. His mother regards our note exchange as nothing short of miraculous. At parent conference night she says, "He just may write you from the Senate one day." Michael's notes are messy and horribly spelled, but they reveal a humor and wit and compassion that is lovely to behold. In January, when I complain about the snow, Michael advises, "I just take the months as thae come."

We write a lot of notes about the trip his family is planning to Florida. He writes, "I'm getting excited about florada coming so soon. I herd that thae are cansuling flits to save on gass. I don't know fi thye wod cnsul our flit. I hoep thay don't." When, because of illness, the family has to cancel the trip, Michael writes, "Now I'm not going to florada I can onle wish you the best of luk of your trip to Calafrna and hop the wethur is gud."

As spring approaches, I begin to ask students for the first signs of spring. I confess that for me, the asparagus ads in the paper are a sure sign that winter is loosing its strong grip. The kids, of course, think that this is a hoot, surely a teacher thing, paying attention to asparagus. But they begin to watch the paper, competing for who can find the best asparagus bargain for Mrs. O. They leave ads on my desk. Michael wins the contest. One day he walks in and tells me he's going to type his note:

Dear Mrs. O,

As you no I want to Boston firday. It was a lot fo fun. Wen I first got to Boston we drov aron looking for a parking plas. We fon one and then we got out of the car. We walkt to a fance market and had a bite to aet.

Than we went to the aquarium and that was eciting. There was a shoe with dolphins and seals. Wan we got out we want by a fruit markt. I thogt of you and chekt the pric of asprgus. It is $1.00 a lb in Boston and 3 heds of letis for $1.00. Boston is a long way to go for asprgus tho.

Your frend,

Michael

At the time Michael writes me this letter I'm enrolled in a course funded by the National Endowment for the Humanities. New York University professors have been coming to our school for four years—trying to retrain us. I love the intellectualism of the course—erudite and elegant lectures on art, philosophy, and Asian culture, as well as literary theory. But increasingly I am bothered by the fact that the professors insist that this model curriculum is not appropriate for rotten readers. I have been attending this fellow's lectures for four years. He has never entered my classroom. As a matter of fact, when I teach the demonstration lessons required by the course, I have to go over to the high school and present them to an honors class, because lessons on ambiguity in art are not deemed appropriate for my students. Or maybe the good professors can't stand the idea of being in the same room as my students.

I am convinced that Michael's note will show the professor that what I am doing is worthwhile, will force him to acknowledge that my students have merit. My plan backfires. The good professor looks at Michael's note, shakes his head, and says, "Sue, when are you going to stop wasting your life? When are you going to join our doctoral program and pursue something worthy of your talents?" Ironic as it may seem, this fellow leads a team of professors under the banner of bringing the humanities into the public schools. I am so disgusted that I quit the program. I miss the erudite lessons but I can't stand the hypocrisy and the downright stupidity about what's important. In the end, kids are more important than art. Or core knowledge. Or standards. Or politics. I don't want Michael forced into algebra or Shakespeare by political edict. But I insist that every esoteric art theory or other possibility be ever available to me and to Michael. If teachers are to be responsible for children, then we must be allowed to exercise our informed judgment.

Anyone who cannot look beyond Michael's rotten spelling and see the humor and wit, the responsiveness to his audience (Imagine a seventh-grade rotten reader going to this trouble for a teacher! Michael told me his family thought he was nuts when he said he had an urgent need to go into a vegetable market for Mrs. O.), should not be making decisions about children. Certainly, he should not be responsible for guiding the work of teachers. Children deserve better. It isn't enough for a teacher trainer to be erudite, smart, a facile lecturer; he must also be a model for treating children well.

Funny thing: Over the years I have shown Michael's letter to almost every audience I've ever addressed. And, without exception, these audiences, filled with teachers, respond with delight and admiration to the wonderful letter that it is.

IN HIS FIRST LETTER to me Barry writes, "I *hate* writing letters. My weekend was terrible." Barry ends up in our class several months after school starts. He is sullen, withdrawn, uncommunicative, and so antagonistic about being in the class that I decide to leave him alone. Sometimes there's nothing a teacher can do but step back while a child begins to find his own way. I do insist on the notes, however.

Dear Barry,

My husband would sympathize with you. I have never seen anyone who hates to write letters as much as he does. After being married to him for more than ten years, I have finally given up trying to force him to write his parents. I write to them instead. However, Barry, I am not ready to give up on you. You just need some practice.

What was so terrible about your weekend? I'll tell you what was terrible about mine. I HATE snow! My driveway is so long to shovel, it makes me sore just to look at it.

Your friend,
Mrs. O.

Dear Mrs. O,

I love shoveling snow. Shoveling snow give you strong muszels.

My snowmobile blew a clutch. And I had to buy a new one.

Dear Barry,

Do you go snowmobiling when the weather is this cold? David wrote that he went ice fishing. I think he is crazy. What do you think?

Your friend,
Mrs. O.

Dear Mrs. O,

When you ride a snowmobile you don't get cold because the heat from the motor keeps you warm. But when you go ice fishing you get cold because you are just standing there. Or sitting.

Our letters continue in this fashion. I am careful to sign every letter "your friend"; Barry doesn't even sign his name. I am also careful to ask Barry a question in every letter, and he always answers it. Then one day he asks me a question: "What do you do during the summer when there is no school?" Instead of writing him the answer, I take the chance of speaking to him directly. (Up to this point all our communication has been on paper.) I say, "Wow, Barry, your question really makes me wish for summer." We talk for ten minutes about what we like to do in the summer. Other kids join the conversation, another first. It is the first time Barry has talked to anybody in the class. Soon afterwards, Barry starts doing work in my class and teachers in his other class report a metamorphosis in his behavior and study habits. Standardistos would insist that I have wasted a month with Barry. I say a teacher does what she can. And so does a student. Imagine how I feel the day Barry writes this note, accepting my offer of friendship:

Dear Mrs. O,

I like the country a lot. I was born on a farm. A BIG farm. In the summertime we have a BIG BIG garden. WE have a tractor. In our garden we have corn, tomatoes, strawberries, carrots, potatoes, and other things.

Your friend,
Barry

During open house in the spring, I ask kids if I can share their notes. By then, my exchange with Barry has filled four small spiral-bound notebooks. I hand them to his mother and stepfather. They glance at the notebooks and then pull up chairs, reading aloud to each other. They laugh at his recounting of the day his eight hamsters got loose, and they look pensive at his yearning for the country. It is a wonderful moment to see these parents so engrossed in the words of their son. No, there is no business letter on display or a persuasive essay containing five paragraphs, each with a topic sentence. But the next day Barry comes in and reads all his notes, mumbling something about his parents "talking about them so much."

THE LIBRARIAN INVENTS Question of the Day for Michael. She and I both think it's a disgrace that my students can't read her books. But we're also sympathetic—because the library has been stocked by someone who believes in standards. We have three copies of a biography of Oliver Cromwell, four novels by Faulkner, and two copies of *Crime and Punishment*. My students like to go to the library to look at films or to take the screws out of bookshelves; they don't go there to read.

Even though the Question of the Day is invented for Michael, the librarian and I know better than to approach him directly with this research prompt, because we know that Michael will shut us out—and shut himself down—with, "I don't think I can do that" or "Do I have to?"

So we tell Laurie about the Question of the Day. Laurie is the kind of student every teacher is grateful for. Like Michael, Laurie decodes at a third-grade level, but often she doesn't comprehend 20 percent of what she decodes or what the teacher reads aloud to her. Unlike Michael, who is adept at avoiding work, Laurie is eager to do any work she can find.

My team partner and I give out a monthly prize for "most homework handed in." We have to give two prizes: one to Laurie, who always does three or four times as much homework as anyone else, and one to the leader of the rest of the pack. Laurie is the kind of kid who will demand eight pages of dictionary drill before a holiday weekend. "So I will have something to do," she explains. I have mixed feelings about giving in to such requests because even though Laurie loves looking up long words and copying out mountains of definitions, she can't read any of it. Even when I read her copied-out definitions aloud to her, she doesn't understand them. But Laurie doesn't ask that school work make sense; she just wants to be productive, to keep busy. I try to get her to read books over the holidays, books that she can understand. But she wants to produce things; for Laurie, reading is too passive.

On a Monday morning I announce that the librarian is starting a contest. Few kids pay any attention. *Contest* is not an enticing word for kids who have themselves pegged as losers. And from a mile off, rotten readers can spot a teacher's ploy to get them to read something. Laurie is the only kid who responds, "What kind of contest?" Laurie decodes on the same level as Michael, understands about one-tenth of what he does, but she sees herself as a winner.

"Every day the librarian will ask a question. At the end of the week the person who has answered the most questions will win a prize," I explain.

Laurie is out of her chair and off to the library before I finish the explanation. She hasn't been in the library all year. It is the one thing I haven't been able to persuade her to do. Her favorite position is at my elbow. I suspect that Laurie is afraid I'll hand out extra homework if she ever leaves the room.

Laurie is back in five minutes. "The librarian needs to know what mammal has webbed feet and lays eggs." Laurie takes the *E* encyclopedia off the shelf. "*E* for *eggs*," she explains.

This is why so many rotten readers have so much trouble doing work in their academic classes. Just a week before, Laurie tried to research famous battles for her social studies class by starting with the *F* encyclopedia. "Do you know what a mammal is?" I ask. "Where would you look to find out?" The bell ending the period rings as Laurie is making a list of mammal characteristics from the dictionary definition. I practically have to shove her out of the room to go to her next class. A frequent complaint of poor readers is that just as they get interested in something, the bell rings and they have to go to a different class and start something else. We insist on the college model for everybody, as if growing up and accepting responsibility means changing classes—and teachers—every forty-five minutes.

Kevin has heard about the contest from Laurie and wants to know if I know the answer. I confess that I didn't know that there were any mammals that laid eggs. Michael wants to know what we're talking about, so Kevin explains the Question of the Day. Michael is immediately intrigued. "Dolphins are mammals—no webbed feet though." He looks at me. "How about ducks?" He hopes my face will reveal the answer. Ten years of working with poor readers has taught me how good they are at waiting for the teacher to give the answer, even when she isn't aware she's doing it.

"Where could you find out the general characteristics of mammals?" I ask.

"The dictionary," Michael smiles. He can't resist a little dig. "But I'll never find it, since I can't spell it. There are a lot of *m*'s in here, Mrs. O." I don't give him a phonics lesson; I just spell the word. He and Kevin read the definition together: mammals have a backbone, body hair, are warm-blooded, and nurse their young.

"I think it's a frog," said Michael. Kevin agrees. They get the *F* encyclopedia and find frog. Sure enough, there are the webbed feet and the eggs. All three of us are excited. Then they read, "Frogs are cold-blooded."

Michael points out the futility of wild guessing, adding, "Maybe I'd better get a book on mammals." Here it is, as simple as that, one of those intellectual breakthroughs teachers pray for. I can pray for it, but I've learned not to write it in my plan book, certainly not in one of those "*Michael will. . .*" statements that people with an assembly-line sense of skill delivery speak of so blithely. Michael avoids the library, always complaining that they don't have "any good books down there." What he means, of course, is that they don't have any books he can read.

Michael returns fifteen minutes later with a huge book on birds. I am stunned. I mean, Michael is smart; he has common sense. He's not the sort of kid who goes looking for a book on mammals and comes back with one on birds. What happened? "Why did you choose that particular book?" I ask, keeping my tone as even as possible.

"Well, I looked in the card catalog, the way you showed us, and they had so many 599 books . . ." He sighs. Michael's sighs as indicators of intellectual exhaustion are monumental. He has definitely turned the sigh into an art form.

"Too many mammal books so you chose a bird book instead?" I can't help it. I start laughing. Michael laughs too.

"Not really," he explains. "Birds are mammals, too." He pauses. "Aren't they?"

"Look at your list," I suggest. "Do they nurse their young?"

"Sure. They bring them worms and stuff."

"Nursing means something very specific," I explain. "Do you know what it means when a mother nurses or suckles her baby?"

"Oh." Michael blushes but then he laughs. "Well, I just got a little mixed up. I guess I got the wrong book." But he is still interested. He doesn't become defensive. He doesn't give up. He is even fairly cheerful about going back to the library and facing the monumental shelf of 599 books.

My students are very familiar with the layout of the library. I'd made a lot of laminated cards with tasks to help students learn how to use the library:

find a book about mountain climbing, a recipe using chocolate, three facts about the Taj Mahal. I chose topics I hoped would intrigue kids enough to browse in the books. My notion is that even kids who don't read very well can learn to use a library, to locate specific information when they need to. My hope is that in the process they might even learn to enjoy books a little. I continually exhort very kind library aides, "Don't do it for them; they need to learn to use the card catalog, to distinguish between an atlas and an almanac, to use an encyclopedia."

This time the librarian has "planted" a mammal book written on a third-grade level. When we heard of an elementary school closing down, she and I begged for their picture books and easy readers. People expressed amazement that a junior high library needs *Rumpelstiltskin* and *Madeline*. No one who has taught seventh and eighth grade for longer than twelve minutes would question our need. Even good readers like to relive old pleasures, to pore over old favorites, and children who have never experienced fairy tales or not enough of them, have more than a casual interest. Their need is real and necessary.

Michael finds the mammal book, and it doesn't take him more than ten minutes to discover a picture of a duck-billed platypus, complete with webbed feet. He reads the text and finds that it also lays eggs. Kevin, a much better reader, doesn't participate, but he has kept half an eye and ear on the whole process, so now he knows the answer, too, without lifting a finger.

When Laurie comes back, she finds the answer in pretty much the same way as Michael. Other kids in the room are interested—mostly in making wild guesses. Laurie and Michael are the only ones to write down the answer and turn it in to the librarian.

Tuesday morning, Laurie stops off in the library before school begins, and then she stops off in our room to announce the new Question of the Day before going to her other classes: "What two birds can't fly?" Michael groans. "See? I did need that bird book after all." He tries the encyclopedia in our classroom and finds *ostrich* mainly by luck. Kevin suggests that penguins don't fly, so Michael looks up *penguin* and he has the answer without much work. I ask Kevin why he doesn't enter the contest. He just shrugs and says maybe he'll try next week. That's okay. I've already had my "breakthrough" with Kevin this week. In a note, he tells me that he went to the stockcar races over the weekend. I ask him what he likes about stockcar races, and he writes me a fourteen-page answer.

Meanwhile, all this talk about Question of the Day is beginning to sound interesting to Arnold, so he starts looking up mammals. He finds the answer and moves on to birds. With birds, he throws strategy to the wind and makes wild guesses. "Chickens. I bet it's chickens." He watches my face for clues as he continues with his wild guesses. Finally Arnold looks up *birds* in the encyclopedia, but he doesn't read the text. He looks at the pictures, jabbing his finger at the page and shouting, "These! They don't fly. I don't see any wings." When he doesn't get any reaction from me, he yells "Peacocks! That's what it is, peacocks." "Swans! I bet it's swans." This goes on for half an hour. "Flamingos!" "Parrots!" "Turkeys! That's it—turkeys!" I begin to wish the Question of the Day would self-destruct.

Finally, I suggest to Arnold that he needs some sort of system. I help him set up a chart of the birds he wants to investigate. He decides to add columns of characteristics that have nothing to do with the contest: color of eggs, habitat, and so on. I'm pleased to grab this "teachable moment" and see where it will take us. Arnold is enthusiastic about checking off columns on his chart. I wonder if I can use this scheme to help him bring order to his larger universe. Arnold takes his chart with him and cuts his next two classes to continue his work in the library, the locker room, and wherever else he can hide out.

Interesting to me, Arnold eventually finds the right answer, but he doesn't write it down. Arnold doesn't care at all about the contest; he just found this one question appealing. He then entertains and annoys us with bird trivia for many weeks. He keeps pestering the librarian, asking, "When are you going to ask another bird question?"

Laurie, having found the answer to the bird question in the morning, is afraid she won't have anything to do in the afternoon, so she begs the librarian for another question, which she immediately shares with the class: "What people discovered glass?" Two students immediately go for the *C* encyclopedia. When I point out to Dick that he's looked up *class*, he insists, "I know. I'm just looking in here for what it says. This is interesting. I'll get to the other one later." I am reminded that all his school life people have been telling Dick that he mixes up letters. Now, in seventh grade, he still has a hard time admitting that he can't always make the proper distinctions.

This question is the easiest so far for the kids—except they don't know what to make of the answer. No one can pronounce *Egyptian*. Laurie has an extra problem. Thinking that *people* means family name, she goes down the chronological listing of the development of glass until she comes to a listing of a man's first and last name. I try to explain that *people* can have the general meaning of nationality as well as the specific meaning of, say, Nancy Jones. But this is too abstract a concept for Laurie to grasp.

LAURIE IS NOT ALONE. Once students hit middle school, the standards setters, the textbook writers, curriculum developers, and too many teachers take it for granted that kids are able to categorize and deal with abstractions. Our social studies curriculum is a good example. After much complaint that the text was too difficult, a book written with a fifth-grade readability was purchased. But we soon discover it isn't the "readability" that gives us fits; the concepts are impossible. The new book still expects students to answer questions about the Spanish influence in the New World, checks and balances in government, the westward expansion, the causes of World War I, the differences between communism and democracy. James Joyce posed the question: "Who gave us this numb?" Students in social studies classes across the country have the four-pound answer sitting on their desks.

And now that the politicians and their state ed department flacks have raised the standards, the situation is worse than impossible; now it's absurd. The right-wing Thomas Fordham Foundation, in *The State of State Standards 2000,* declares the California history standards to be the best in the nation, lauding the fact that they are "easily measurable." The report insists, "The only problems left to resolve are how to ensure that these exemplary standards are properly taught—and that student achievement is well assessed." The authors of the report, Chester Finn and company, like the fact that the California standards aren't "watered down." I like the standards for the fact that they provoke a sure laugh: All one has to do is stand up and read them aloud. No comment needed. California is joined by other state lackeys of the Standardistos. How about Arizona, another recipient of a Fordham grade of A in history standards? Arizona's Standard 1 states:

> Students analyze the human experience through time, recognize the relationships of events and people, and interpret significant patterns, themes, ideas, beliefs, and turning points in Arizona, American, and world history. For students in grades six through eight this includes:
>
> • assessing the credibility of primary and secondary sources and drawing sound conclusions from them.
> • examining different points of view on the same historical events and determining the context in which the statements were made, including the questions asked, the sources used, and the author's perspectives.

My oh my, don't we wish that members of the media could do this?

Of course this is just one standard among many. Like California, Arizona Standardistos also insist that seventh graders will:

> Describe the geographic, political, economic, and social characteristics of the ancient civilizations of Egypt, Mesopotamia, and China and their contributions to later civilizations. . . .

> Describe the political and economic events and the social and geographic characteristics of Medieval European life and their enduring impacts on later civilizations. . . .

And on and on. An A from Fordham indicates that the Standardistos have constructed a very high pile of manure. Nobody has yet seen the test for this range of impossibility.

THE ENLARGED CITY SCHOOL DISTRICT
OFFICE OF THE COORDINATOR OF LANGUAGE ARTS
JOHN PARACHINI, ED. D.

11/23

TO: ALL LANGUAGE ARTS FACULTY
RE: STRATEGIES FOR ENHANCING STUDENT-CENTERED
    INSTRUCTION, PART 1

DEFINITION: STUDENT-CENTERED INSTRUCTION INVOLVES STUDENT PARTICIPATION IN CLASSROOM DISCUSSION. THE CLASSROOM CLIMATE SHOULD STIMULATE BOTH THE FREEDOM AND THE OPPORTUNITY TO DISCUSS ISSUES FOR THE PURPOSE OF SEEKING CONVERGENT AND DIVERGENT POINTS OF VIEW. THIS PARTICIPATION DOES NOT PERTAIN ONLY TO TEACHER-STUDENT INTERACTION. IT INCLUDES INTERACTION AMONG STUDENTS.

1. IN ORDER TO CONDUCT A MEANINGFUL DISCUSSION, THE TEACHER SHOULD ESTABLISH GUIDELINES FOR THE DISCUSSION:
   A) PURPOSE FOR THE DISCUSSION
   B) TOPIC
   C) ISSUES TO BE CONSIDERED
   D) DISCUSSION TIME-FRAME

2. TEACHERS SHOULD PREPARE STUDENTS FOR CLASS DISCUSSION THROUGH LECTURES, AUDIOVISUAL AIDS, AND CLASS READINGS.

3. STUDENTS ARE PLACED IN WRITING GROUPS (4–5 STUDENTS IN EACH GROUP). STUDENTS LEARN TO EVALUATE EACH OTHER'S EDITING ATTEMPTS AS WELL AS IMPROVE UPON THEIR OWN.

4. STUDENTS WORK AT THE BLACKBOARD FOR THE PURPOSE OF DIAGRAMMING SENTENCES, WRITING SAMPLE DIALOGUES, ETC. THE STUDENTS EXPLAIN THEIR OWN WORK.

5. SOME STUDENTS IN THE CLASS TUTOR THOSE INDIVIDUALS NEEDING HELP WITH GRAMMAR DRILLS AND WRITING.

6. STUDENTS WRITE DAILY JOURNAL NOTES TO THE TEACHER
   AND VICE VERSA. THE TEACHER CORRECTS THE NOTES AND
   RETURNS THEM TO THE STUDENTS.

7. ESPECIALLY IN REMEDIAL CLASSES, QUESTIONS COULD BE
   SEQUENCED BY DEGREE OF DIFFICULTY. THE EASIER QUES-
   TIONS GIVE IMMEDIATE, "SUCCESSFUL" FEEDBACK TO RELUC-
   TANT STUDENTS. THIS ENHANCES STUDENT PARTICIPATION IN
   REMEDIAL CLASSES.

8. GROUP STORY WRITING. THE CLASS WITH TEACHER GUIDANCE
   CREATES A CHARACTER FOR A STORY. THE STUDENTS ALSO
   CHOOSE A SETTING. THE STUDENTS DIVIDE INTO SMALL
   GROUPS TO WRITE THE PLOT. IN A SKILLS CLASS, ONE PER-
   SON IN EACH GROUP SHOULD DO THE ACTUAL WRITING. ALL
   STUDENTS SHOULD SHARE IN THE PROOFREADING. EACH
   PARTICIPANT IN THE HONORS CLASSES SHOULD HAVE AN
   OPPORTUNITY TO DO THE ACTUAL WRITING.

I read this memo and I want to vomit. Or slit my throat. The communiqué is followed by two more, listing eighteen additional strategies. This is what happens when you put people who have never worked in rough-and-tumble classrooms in charge. I wish the fellows who wrote the California or Arizona or Virginia history standards could hear Arnold's oral report on George Washington. We require oral reports from all students, meaning that a student is expected to get up in front of their peers and talk about information they've found in the library. Such reports usually last from one to five minutes, and students are graded on their listening as well as their oral presentations. Our laminated card collection provides the kick start for many students' first report. The cards contain provocative questions: How much does a newborn elephant weigh? What does it eat? How long does it live? Students are interested in all the animal data. Surprisingly, other favorites are foreign architectural landmarks such as the Leaning Tower of Pisa, the Eiffel Tower, the Taj Mahal. Once students get their feet wet, they use cards with pictures only. They have to think of their own questions. Finally, there are no cards. We call it "independent research" and insist that students choose their own topics.

When we start the oral reports, Arnold is refusing to go to the library, so I suggest that he choose a famous American and read a biography. His social studies teacher agrees to give him credit if he does a report in our class. Arnold chooses George Washington and for about a month he won't do any work except on George. He frequently interrupts other students with "Hey! Guess what!" anecdotes from George's boyhood.

Finally the big day arrives and after much prodding, Arnold stands before his classmates. For a kid who is always pestering everybody, Arnold is suddenly very quiet. He stands in front of eight other kids and grins, blushes, twists his legs. Then he sits down and says he can't do it. The other kids coax, and finally he stands up again and starts talking. "When George was born," he begins, "his father looked at the dollar bill and said, 'I think I'll call him George Washington,' and that's how the baby got his name."

I must have looked startled because Arnold addresses his next remarks to me. "You have seen his picture right there on the dollar bill, haven't you?" He reaches into his pocket, pulls out a dollar, and holds it up. "That's how he got his name. Right off the money."

According to the Standardistos, this boy needs a few lessons in cause-and-effect.

At the end of the report one of the students asks Arnold if he's ever met George Washington. "No," replies Arnold. "But I've seen him on TV lots of times." Nobody disputes this, and it isn't out of politeness that nobody challenges Arnold's claim. Plenty of them have seen George on TV too. I'm not saying that most seventh graders don't have some sort of fuzzy notion about the fact that George Washington is long dead and that those fellows on TV are actors. But plenty of seventh and eighth graders find it perfectly reasonable to suppose that their parents or maybe their grandparents voted George into office. Just because we teachers remember where we were the moment we heard of President Kennedy's shooting and just because we remember Nixon's resignation, doesn't mean that these presidents are any more real to our students than is George. Standardistos are big on distinguishing primary from secondary documents and fact from fiction, slippery slopes for many adults. After all, Sherlock Holmes still gets mail at Baker Street, and some of us never quite remember if Horatio Hornblower is a historical or fictional figure. I asked that very question of my husband recently. He replied, "Don't be silly." So I still don't quite know.

When I try to help students study for their final exams, I'm supposed to explain time lines; kids used to be expected to place in chronological order Columbus, Magellan, Daniel Boone, Woodrow Wilson, FDR, the cotton gin, Hiroshima, and *Sputnik*. Now we throw in events from medieval Asia, Africa, and Europe. And we wonder why so many kids fail.

THE LIBRARY CONTEST is good for me. It provides a very clear reminder about individual learning styles, things I am too apt to forget in the day-to-day pressure of trying to drag kids through the curriculum. First of all, only about one-third of my students participate. Since I don't see my primary function as teacher preparing my students for assembly-line regimentation, this is fine. Maybe plugging them all into the same sequences would be efficient, but it would also be wrong.

The Question of the Day reminds me that sometimes I react too much to Dick's obnoxious attitude, forgetting that he'll go to any length to cover up or avoid admitting a mistake. Michael can shrug off reversed letters with an "oh well." Dick can't. So I've learned a lot from the Question of the Day, and I think Michael has also gained a little insight. I have tried to talk to him about his "defeatist attitudes," but he has such a charming way of shrugging it off and deflecting my serious intent that we've never made much headway. After his great success with the duck-billed platypus—the whole class tries to say it quickly ten times—I again bring up the old issue. "Michael, do you realize you conducted independent research, and not once did I hear an 'I can't' or a 'Do I have to?' And, Michael, *I* learned a lot besides. I didn't know half that stuff you researched. I certainly didn't know a thing about duck-billed platypuses." He grinned. Then he grinned some more. "I know," he said quietly.

Michael doesn't win that first Question of the Day event, but, to my surprise, he perseveres, and he wins the second one. Michael, the boy whose mother reads all his texts aloud because he "can't do it," finds a way to answer the questions. He finds a way to use materials in the library. He finds a way to cope.

Michael's mother reveals a nice spin-off from the contest when she comes in for conferences. "He comes home with the most intriguing information. Every night at dinner he stumps his older brothers with questions like 'I bet you don't know two birds that can't fly.'" She looks at me, "Michael has always been able to remember things he's been told, but he insists that no one is telling him these things. He says he's finding this information in the library, in *books*." I tell her it's true. She cries a little, and so do I.

I have been hinting to Michael's mother that she should stop reading all of his texts to him. So this seems like a good time to push the issue. "Let him do some of the work. It's possible that Michael can cope much better than either of you think he can." I suggest, "Why don't you just leave the house some evening, telling him you expect the homework to be done when you get back?" This is a radical suggestion to make to the devoted mother who has patiently read every science chapter, suffered through every social studies assignment since second grade. "Michael is not going to have you sitting at his side all his life," I insist. "You must help him to become independent."

She does it. The Question of the Day provides the breakthrough, the evidence that Michael can cope. All three of us then have to live with the decision. Michael tells me he'll probably fail science if nobody reads the chapters to him. "Maybe so," I say, "but you'll never know what you can do until you try."

He starts bringing his books to class, starts assuming responsibility for asking for help when he really needs it instead of claiming he can't do any of it by himself. His grade in science drops, but he passes.

I suggest that Michael's mother continue reading to him but that they read together for pleasure. I send home books that they can enjoy together. This plan flops. Reading for the fun of it is impossible for Michael and his mother. Reading has been too deadly serious for too many years. Schools have a lot to answer for.

Michael is one student who comes back to visit once he's in high school. "Do the kids here still read? Do you still get all those newspapers? Do they do library research? Do you read stories to them? Do they read jokes to you?" I keep nodding. Michael adds. "I never liked reading. You made me do it. I should be reading now, but we don't read in my English class. Filling out workbook pages isn't the same thing." Funny that Michael understands what Standardistos don't, that reading must have a purpose, and ultimately, that purpose must be linked to our curiosity, our need for beauty, humor, order. Rotten readers need the same things good readers need: poetry, humor, mystery, and tragedy from words. Words tell us about the world and about ourselves. Even reading an encyclopedia passage to find out if penguins can fly is of infinitely more value than answering irrelevant questions about how many ducks are on the pond. To call drilling for state competency exams a curriculum is worse than a lie; it's a mistake.

When he is in tenth grade Michael asks me if he can come back to my class. The high school is only one block away; he'll come out of study hall and I'll make him read. Michael tries to make the arrangements with the guidance counselor, but things never work out. I don't push it because I don't think one can go home again. His mom assures me that he is actually doing "okay" at the high school, though I'm not sure what that means. What I do know is that the materials we use reveal the values we hold. I am continually amazed and disheartened by the low esteem in which so many educrats hold books—and kids.

And Michael's mother's "okay" reassures me. Michael is fortunate that his parents also see him as more than his test scores. They see him as a fun-loving, gregarious, and popular boy with lots of friends, tight end on the football team, a loving grandson who is helpful to his grandparents.

The week before his graduation from eighth grade, Michael's mother sends me a note. "I was going to phone you," she writes, "but Michael told me to write a letter. He says when you care about someone and you have something important to tell them, you write it in a letter. He learned that from you. He learned a lot. And we are grateful forever."

I share Michael's asparagus letter almost every time I give a talk. I share it to remind teachers of what really counts in education. A teacher who has heard the asparagus story more than once sends me a cloisonné asparagus pin and now I wear it in every public appearance—for Michael. Fifteen years or so after Michael wrote that letter, I give a talk at the State University of New York at Albany. Afterwards, a teacher from my old district comes up to greet me. She was Michael's first-grade teacher and she still lives next door to Michael's parents. Michael is now a big-time chef in a toney restaurant in Connecticut, she tells me.

I wonder if our asparagus connection gives me the right to claim partial credit for Michael's success. I need this because, after all, I can't tell you Michael's score on the Stanford, or the New York State Regents, or any of the other tests that beset him along the way. Maybe my refusal to tailor my curriculum to suit these exams is why my program was ultimately canceled. Asparagus or no, test scores or no, I do know that Michael learned something important from me. Michael learned that he could find out about duck-billed platypuses on his own. He learned that words count, that words can give joy, that carefully chosen words will last. He learned that when you care about someone you send them a letter. I think that these are far finer gifts than the ability to circle *a, b, c,* or *d* on anybody's test.